HUNTING
THE LAND OF THE
MIDNIGHT SUN

HUNTING
THE LAND OF THE
MIDNIGHT SUN

A COLLECTION OF HUNTING ADVENTURES
FROM THE ALASKAN PROFESSIONAL
HUNTERS ASSOCIATION

Safari Press Inc.

The trademark Safari Press ® is registered with the U.S. Patent and Trademark Office and in other countries.

Alaska Professional Hunters Association

Safari Press Inc.
Long Beach, California

Second edition 2003

ISBN 1-57157-212-0

Library of Congress Catalog Card Number: 00-104814

10 9 8 7 6 5 4 3 2 1

Readers wishing to receive the Safari Press catalog, featuring many fine books on big-game hunting, wingshooting, and sporting firearms, should write to Safari Press Inc., P.O. Box 3095, Long Beach, CA 90803, USA. Tel: (714) 894-9080 or visit our Web site at www.safaripress.com.

TABLE OF CONTENTS

ACKNOWLEDGMENTS

Safari Press would like to thank the following guides and outfitters for their contributions to this volume.

Pete Buist
Clearwater Guides and
    Outfitters, Inc.
P.O. Box 71561
Fairbanks, Alaska 99707
Phone: (907) 457-7189

Fred Cook Jr.
7329 Arctic Boulevard
Anchorage, Alaska 99518
Phone and fax: (907) 344-5501
Messages: (907) 349-5878

Bob Hannon
P.O. Box 22
Koyuk, Alaska 99733
Phone: (907) 963-3221

Robert P. Hardy
Bucking Horse Ranch
P.O. Box 876485
Wasilla, Alaska 99687
Phone: (907) 376-8986

Jim Harrower
13830 Jarvi Drive
Anchorage, Alaska 99515
Phone: (907) 345-2891
Fax: (907) 345-4676

Joe Hendricks
Fair Chase Hunts
P.O. Box 102104
Anchorage, Alaska 99510
(907) 274-2996

Rob Holt
P.O. Box 489
Talkeetna, Alaska 99676
Phone: (907) 733-2723
Fax: (907) 733-2724

Rob Jones
R&R Guide Services
3705 Arctic Boulevard
Anchorage, Alaska 99503
Phone: (907) 272-6739

Gary "Butch" King Jr.
2024 Stonegate Circle
Anchorage, Alaska 99515
Phone: (907) 522-1164
Fax: (907) 522-6235

Gus Lamoureux
Ugashik Lake and Kodiak
Bear Camps
P.O. Box 90444
Anchorage, Alaska 99509
Phone: (907) 248-3230
Fax: (907) 245-7338

Gary LaRose
LaRose Guide Service
5025 Whispering Spruce
Anchorage, Alaska 99516
Phone: (907) 345-6321
Fax: (907) 345-4218

Ray McNutt
Wrangell R Ranch
P.O. Box 222475
Anchorage, Alaska 99522
Phone: (907) 349-8159
Fax: (907) 349-1868

Roger D. Morris
AAA Alaskan Outfitters
10621 Republic Circle
Anchorage, Alaska 99515
Phone: (907) 349-9112
Fax: (907) 349-7764

Littlejohn Navarro
P.O. Box 16022
Two Rivers, Alaska 99716
Phone: (907) 488-4929

Larry Rivers
P.O. Box 107a
Talkeetna, Alaska 99676
Phone: (800) 393-2471
Fax: (907) 733-1070

John Runkle
Alaskan Outdoor Adventures
P.O. Box 9127
Nikolai, Alaska 99691
Phone: (907) 293-2329

Wendell Runyon
Grizzly Creek Adventures
1389 Headens Bridge Road
Bedford, Virginia 24523
Phone: (540) 297-0373

Rod Schuh
1000 Stroganov Drive
Anchorage, Alaska 99516
Phone: (907) 346-3983

George Siavelis
P.O. Box 74
Aniak, Alaska 99557
Phone: (907) 675-4510

Tom Stick
Kodiak Discoveries
P.O. Box 8972
Kodiak, Alaska 99615
Phone: (907) 486-8972

John Swiss
Swiss Alaska Trophy Hunts
129 F Street
Anchorage, Alaska 99501
Phone: (907) 272-1725
Fax: (907) 277-5030

A special thanks goes to *The Alaska Professional Hunter* and its editor, Rene Limeres, for allowing Safari Press to use many of the previously published stories.

INTRODUCTION

The boom of cannon reverberated through the Sitka spruce as the Stars and Stripes ascended the ninety-foot flagpole. The double eagle of czarist Russia had already been taken down, and now both Russian and American cannon saluted America's acquisition of a frigid, virtually unknown land. American optimism was running high on that misty day of 18 October 1867. Sticks were being driven into the Panhandle soil to mark homestead boundaries, and a restaurant, two tenpin alleys, and several saloons were under construction. The main thoroughfare of Sitka was named Lincoln (the Russians had never named it), and the two cross streets, Russia and America. Eight months later, Sitka celebrated its first Fourth of July. Civilians, soldiers, and children paraded down Lincoln, laughing and dancing. Even dogs were part of the procession. At the end of the parade, a wagon rolled bumpily down the dirt street, brimming with young ladies dressed in white, one for each state of the Union.

America had not yet paid for the territory; that would not occur until 27 July 1868, twenty-three days after Sitka's first Fourth of July. Indeed, most congressmen were not at all excited about the purchase, which was instigated by Secretary of State William H. Seward.

The price was $7.2 million, and America could have gotten it for less. In 1866, Czar Alexander II had instructed the Russian ambassador Edouard de Stoeckl to try to sell Russian America (as the Russians called Alaska) to the Americans for at least $5 million. No other country, including Britain, was interested in the territory, and Russia needed money badly, having depleted its national treasury by fighting numerous wars over the previous several decades. Moreover, the empire was overextended and would not have been able to defend Russian America had a foreign power pressed the issue. But the overzealous Seward kept upping his initial offer of $5 million without waiting for a counteroffer from de Stoeckl, who at that point knew he had a live one. After paying the $7.2 million, Congressman Hiram Price expressed the general feeling of Washington over the purchase: "Now that we have got it and cannot give it away or lose it, I hope we will keep it under military rule and get along with as little expense as possible."

At the time of the purchase, about nine hundred Americans lived in Alaska, mostly in the Panhandle. These hearty men and women received almost no help from Washington in the way of money or exploration of the land. Indeed, most of Alaska had never been visited by a white man. The Russians had come for sea otter pelts, and remained primarily in southwestern Alaska. Only a handful of Russians had ever ventured to the interior.

In the first decade after the purchase, the United States government made one lackluster exploration of interior Alaska. In 1869, it sent the U.S. Army in Sitka to the Canadians' Fort Yukon to determine if the fort was in Alaskan territory. The army's engineers set up their transit instrument and telescope and determined that the fort was 121 miles across the border. When the army informed the Canadian fur traders at Fort Yukon of the measurement, the traders calmly packed up their gear and left that day, apparently to avoid an international incident.

The first organized explorers of Alaska were from the private sector. The Western Union Telegraph Company wanted to string a telegraph wire across Canada, Alaska, and the 56-mile Bering Strait, where it would link up in Siberia with a wire from Europe. Along with the surveyors and wire-stringing crews was a corps of scientists, one of whom was the naturalist John Dall. Western Union gave up the project in 1866, when Cyrus Field succeeded in laying a transatlantic cable. Nevertheless, the expedition had produced the first map of the 2,000-mile Yukon and, thanks to Dall, the first cataloging of big game in Alaska. In the next decade, other explorers such as Henry Trueman Allen, discoverer of the Suslota Pass in the Alaska Range (through which the Alaska pipeline would pass, over a century later), and scientists such as the geologist Alfred Huse Brooks supplied the new Alaskans with invaluable information on the territory's game and topography.

In 1877, through the efforts of a five-foot-tall frontier preacher named Sheldon Jackson, the Organic Law was passed, placing the territory under the laws of Oregon. Jackson also helped establish sixteen schools in the territory, and he was responsible for bringing the Siberian reindeer to the land. The preacher had learned that the Inuit along the Alaskan west coast were starving because their primary game—walrus and bowhead whale—had been greatly reduced by seafaring white hunters. Displaying Alaskan ingenuity, Jackson imported domesticated reindeer from Russia's far east, and the animals thrived on Seward Peninsula. Siberian reindeer became the Longhorn of Alaska, thanks to the preacher's efforts.

Two decades after the Alaska Purchase, there were still only a couple of dozen white men living in the interior, but the discovery of gold on the Alaskan side of the Yukon basin changed this. Thousands of prospectors poured into the interior, many of whom had no idea what they were getting into. Among them were eighteen New Yorkers, led by YMCA director Arthur Dietz, who chose to cross the Malaspina Glacier as a route to the goldfields. Soon after starting out, the doctor of the expedition fell into a crevice, taking with him his sled, dogs, and medicines. One year later four men returned, two permanently blinded from the sun's reflection off the ice and snow. They had found no gold.

But others had found it—if not in the Yukon basin, then in other areas such as Juneau and Nome. With the influx of prospectors, the white population of Alaska jumped to 30,000 by 1900. In 1912, Congress declared the region an official territory of the United States, and on 3 January 1959, the territory became the forty-ninth state of the Union.

From 1882 to 1917 the Alaska Treadwell Gold Mining Company, located in the Panhandle, produced ten times the purchase price of Alaska. During the twentieth century, platinum and silver were discovered, and in 1973 oil was found beneath Prudhoe Bay, leading to the construction of the Trans-Alaska Pipeline, which extends 789 miles from the North Slope to Prince William Sound. Among the states, Alaska is second only to Texas in production of crude oil. Commercial fishing in the state contributes 25 percent of the country's annual catch, including all canned salmon produced in the United States. Tourism is a $1.8 billion industry, employing a work force as large as that of the oil industry. And it is a hunter's paradise, with 40,000 brown bear and grizzly; 20,000 black bear; 70,000 Dall sheep; 155,000 moose; 1,000,000 caribou; 375,000 Sitka black-tailed deer; 14,000 mountain goat; 2,100 muskox; 1,500 elk; and 50,000 wolves and wolverines. Indeed, Seward's folly was a brilliant purchase, in some ways comparable to Jefferson's Louisiana Purchase in 1803.

* * * * * *

Alaska is sometimes called the Land of the Midnight Sun. In Arctic Alaska at Point Barrow, the state's northernmost point, the sun never sets between May and August. Indeed, the oxymoron midnight sun aptly suggests the climate in the southern part of the state, where it can be sunny almost every day in April and rainy almost every day in summer. The term Alaskan heat wave is another oxymoron. People in the interior can expect 90-degree temperatures during summer, and Fort Yukon holds the state record, where a temperature of 100 degrees was recorded in 1915. And yet the temperature in the interior can be minus 60 degrees during winter.

A second characteristic of the state is that almost everything there is big: big mountains (Denali, at 20,320 feet, is the highest point in North America), big glaciers (one is larger than Switzerland), big vegetables (70-pound cabbages, 30-pound turnips), big marine life (king crabs that measure three feet from claw to claw), big winds (clocked at over 100 miles per hour on the Aleutian Islands), and big game.

Kodiak Island is world-famous for its brown bear, which can weigh up to 1,500 pounds. Gorging itself on the high-protein salmon that run the streams on the island from mid-July to mid-September, the Kodiak brown is the largest land carnivore in the world.

Grizzlies live inland and are smaller than the coastal browns because they have no salmon runs to raid, but they are also quicker and more easily provoked. When going after grizzly, the hunter glasses from a vantage point, and when he spots a legal bruin, he begins a long stalk over difficult terrain. To bag one using a rifle is difficult, but it is even more so with a bow.

According to the Alaska Department of Fish and Game, bow hunters have taken only eleven grizzlies since 1959, when records began to be kept.

Another big-game animal in Alaska is the Alaska-Yukon moose, the largest species of moose and historically the most important game animal in the state. In the interior, the Athabascans hunted moose for thousands of years, and professional hunters hunted them to feed mining camps and scientific expeditions. And then there is the caribou. Following a rhythm as old as their trails, caribou migrate hundreds of miles to calving grounds, rutting areas, and winter feeding grounds. The migration in late August of the western arctic herd (about 300,000 strong) from the North Slope to the northern interior is an awesome spectacle, symbolizing the boundless and primeval qualities that define the Alaskan experience.

Perhaps the most difficult animal to hunt in Alaska is the Dall sheep, which can be found in the Talkeetnas, the Wrangell and Chugach Mountains, and the Alaska and Brooks Ranges. Dall sheep climb narrow ledges and scree slopes with ease. To get to them the hunter must climb. And climb. And climb.

Just as sheep hunters must navigate jagged cliffs and ridges, brown bear hunters must put up with cold, rain, and extremely strong winds. Moose, caribou, and grizzly hunters spend days glassing from hillsides, often in cold and rainy weather.

Throughout these stories, there is a common thread: Not in spite of but because of the Alaskan hunter's herculean efforts, exposure to rude elements, and close encounters with big game, nature's light shines in him. The aspens, the tundra and taiga, the animals, the rain and snow, the midnight sun—these are not mere tinsel. Nature breathes through the Alaskan hunter to a degree that the comfortable tourist can never know.

PART ONE

HUNTING
SOUTHWEST ALASKA

IF AT FIRST YOU DON'T SUCCEED

BY
LEONARD WASS

In May 1996, I traveled to Kodiak Island to hunt the great Alaska brown bear. My guide was Tom Stick, who runs Port Vita Lodge on Raspberry Island, twenty minutes by floatplane from Kodiak Airport. Raspberry and the nearby Afognak Islands are the only places in the Kodiak chain where one can hunt Roosevelt elk in addition to brown bear and Sitka black-tailed deer. (All three can be hunted in the fall; spring hunting season is only for bear.) Port Vita's location also offers outstanding sport fishing for Pacific salmon, halibut, steelhead, and Dolly Varden.

Tom is an interesting guy. In 1964 he graduated from the U.S. Naval Academy, and, after receiving an M.S. in nuclear engineering from Stanford, he spent a number of years in the U.S. nuclear submarine force. Tom also finished dental school and owned and operated a successful dentistry practice in California. He then gave it all up for the life of an Alaskan hunting and fishing guide. Always the adventurer, Tom manages to fill his off-season with unique activities. A few years back, for instance, he was the 18,000-foot base camp manager for spring climbs of

F/V Nakchamik *Captain Lee Robbins and assistant guide Cam Rader stocking the trawler with provisions for the hunt.*

Mount Everest. Clever and energetic, Tom also works his butt off to show his clients a great time.

Port Vita Lodge is a comfortable and pleasant base camp. Built originally as a herring oil refinery in the 1930s, it came into Tom's hands several years back, and he has been remodeling and enhancing it ever since. With running water, hot showers, electricity, two steam baths, and superb chefs, the Port Vita facility offers an experience that could hardly be called "roughing it."

We spent a good part of my hunting time on a 44-foot commercial fishing trawler, which Tom charters from his neighbor Lee Robbins. This gave us access to a number of bays where bears are plentiful and hunters are few and far between. Hunting from the trawler also enabled us to glass hillsides from early morning until dark, substantially increasing the acreage covered.

Kodiak hillsides are a mix of alder thickets, berry and wildflower patches, and tall wild grass. Bears love the dense alder, where they can lie hidden and keep cool in the shade. But to the hunter, the tangle of down-curved limbs is pure anathema. The limbs severely hamper visibility, make it almost impossible to track animals without causing a racket, and they frustrate the hunter by always being in the way.

We saw twenty-six bears during our hunt, and I learned quite a bit about their behavior and how to spot them. Both brown and grizzly bears are classified as the same species, but brown can grow to twice the size of grizzlies (to 1,300 pounds and 10-foot-square hide dimensions). This is possible because brown bears enjoy a high-protein diet, feeding on the abundant runs of salmon along the coast. Kodiak brown bears also possess physical features distinct from coastal browns, such as proportionally larger heads. A big Kodiak bear is a treasured and sought-after trophy, and we were out to get one!

Tom and I had talked a great deal about the factors that make a hunt successful. On Kodiak, the weather is always a consideration, since the wet, windy, and cold days there can make it almost impossible to hunt. The weather also affects when the bears leave hibernation and their subsequent behavior patterns. For example, an early hot spring may encourage the bears to rub their hides or pursue mating interests earlier than normal.

The hunter's physical condition is another important factor. Because of difficult terrain, I knew I would be limited in my ability to approach some of the bears we might spot. But my long experience as a hunter and my shooting ability with a heavy-bore rifle were definitely in my favor. Tom and I acknowledged that plain old-fashioned luck plays a major part in the success of any hunt. We prayed that ours would be good.

We flew out to Tom's camp, where I got squared away and sighted in my rifle. On my first day of hunting, we hiked into a nearby valley to glass, and that gave me a chance to try out my new gear on the Kodiak terrain. I was not in optimum condition, but I still could get through the tangles and up the hills. We saw no bear, but did spot dozens of Roosevelt elk, several deer, and numerous foxes and eagles.

The next day we glassed from the boat and sighted bears, but none were worthy of a stalk. Late in the day, however, when we were anchoring up, we spotted a medium-size boar moving slowly across a hill. We hastily set off after it. There was only about an hour of light remaining, and our stalk was hampered by steep slopes, dense alder, and shifting winds. But we persevered and finally made it to within range. Tom warned me to get ready. I was huffing and puffing like a steam engine, and for the first time during the hunt, I felt the electrifying excitement of being close to a large animal.

The shifting wind and the noise of our approach alerted the bear, for it suddenly broke from the brush above us, running straight uphill. Anything but an offhand shot was impossible, and soon the animal vanished in the dense growth. We began the dangerous descent to the boat. It was only the second day of the hunt and we were already experiencing the difficulties we had predicted. Nevertheless, I was encouraged by how I was handling the terrain, and was ever confident in my ability to hit the mark next time.

In the days that ensued, we spotted that elusive beach bear more than once, but our timing just wasn't right to bag the animal. In general, we found the bears near the beach to be unusually wary of the motorized sound of our boat, so we began to concentrate our efforts on the bears on the hillsides. One afternoon, I used my rapidly developing hiking skills and newly found stamina to climb for three and a half hours to get to a large boar. We somehow lost its tracks on the steep, slippery slope. I was resigned to head back down before darkness set in, but then Tom and his assistant suggested that we extend our stay on the mountain a bit longer. Tom and the assistant sidehilled to the next ravine to look for the boar; they were hoping the boar had scented a lone sow, which we had seen resting on a distant ridge upwind. I chose to remain behind on a comfortable rock.

Within minutes, the assistant guide appeared and motioned for me to come quickly. But I was too late. A rifle shot cracked the silence, followed by two more. Tom had been charged by the big boar and had been forced to kill it in self-defense. Consequently, the enormous bear hide—10 feet square—and the 27⅞-inch skull (just shy of the B&C record) would have to be given to Fish and Game authorities. Damn the luck!

Tom came within twenty feet of certain death from the jaws and claws of that enraged boar. Since a large Kodiak can take twenty-foot strides and snap three-inch-thick alders like toothpicks, Tom was flat lucky to be alive. He felt very bad about being forced to shoot the animal. Under the same circumstance, many guides and hunters would be tempted to use the hunter's tag for such a magnificent beast. But not Tom. He would not compromise himself ethically and violate state game law. This reaffirmed my belief that he is the very best of guides.

The weather warmed up and we continued to see many bears. On the thirteenth day of the hunt, we spotted from the boat two immense specimens, a boar and a sow, several miles away. They quickly vanished in the dense alder-covered hillside, so we left to glass elsewhere. By 11 A.M. we had spotted no other bears, so we returned to the valley, hoping to locate the boar and sow again.

The afternoon wore on with no sign of our bear couple, and I found it hard to stay awake in the sweltering spring sun. When it seemed obvious the boar and sow were off in another valley, the two suddenly appeared a half mile away on the opposite side of the valley. Backlit by the bright afternoon sun, they looked quite magnificent. We immediately set off after them, noting that the boar would make a great trophy. But there would be no

The author enjoying the view of Raspberry Strait and Afognak Island. (Photo by guide Tom Stick)

easy way to stalk it if we crossed the stream and tried to locate it in the dense alders on the other side. This was especially true with two bears in proximity.

We worked our way to what appeared to be the optimum position on our side of the valley, hoping the bears' erratic movements would take them closer to the stream, where we would have an excellent shot at the big boar. At times we had difficulty tracking them because the setting sun blinded us, but eventually we saw the sow wandering off uphill about 250 yards distant. It was still within range for the .375 H&H.

Tom instructed me to shoot as soon as the boar appeared in a clearing large enough to enable me to get more than one shot off. When the giant bruin finally emerged into an adequately open area, it seemed much more than 250 yards away (we later determined the range to be more like 350 yards). My first shot was low, but I managed to get two more shots off before the boar vanished back into the brush. I apparently did not compensate enough for the range, and, since it was too late to track the bear, I missed my chance to bag it that day.

We returned the next day but were unable to locate the boar or its spoor. At that point we terminated the hunt and returned to the comfort of the lodge. I promised myself that the next time I had a long shot, I would have with me one of those fancy range finders and a ballistics chart. I vowed to return another day.

* * * * * *

I returned to Alaska in April 1997, and Tom was again my guide. The 1997 hunt would pose special challenges. First, the area I'd be hunting would be different. The Alaska Department of Fish and Game prohibits a hunter from hunting the same area two years in a row. The reason for the regulation is probably that the hunter who becomes overly familiar with the area and the habits of particular animals has an unfair advantage. Second, my hunt would take place two weeks earlier than the one last spring, meaning the habits of the bears would be different due to differences in snowmelt and foliage development. Third, early hunts mean fewer bears, because some of the animals are still in hibernation. But on the plus side, those available would be bigger, I hoped and would have no rubs. (A late hunt, by contrast, means more bears, but also the chance of more rubs as well as interference in hunting the animals due to mating behavior.)

Despite these challenges, I was very confident. During the off-season, I bought and outfitted a new rifle for Kodiak brown bear. With the help of Tom's camp director and master chef, "Big Lou," I purchased a Winchester Model 70 in .338 Winchester Mag. This caliber is similar to the .338 Winchester except that the Mag's bullet trajectory is flatter. Big Lou recommended the Winchester because of its reliable Mauser-type action and claw ejectors, which don't jam easily, a real plus if a bear, for whatever reason, starts to chase you. Big Lou cut the Model 70's barrel so that I could get through the thick alder patches on Kodiak more easily. The few inches he cut from the barrel resulted in very little loss in muzzle velocity. Big Lou also fitted the rifle with iron sights and a detachable scope. As he explained, if you chase a wounded (and angry) bear into an alder thicket, a scope is a liability. The range of vision of a scope is very restricted, and the odds are that you'll find the bear a few feet away and have to shoot quickly and accurately, which is easier to do when using iron sights.

During the off-season, I practiced shooting at various distances and in various firing positions, while using a scope and while using iron sights. The Federal Ammunition Company faxed me the entire ballistics printout for their Safari Grade, 275-grain Nosler Partition ammo, the ammo I had chosen to use, and I prepared a table that showed the energy (foot-pounds), velocity (fps), and drop (inches) of the bullet at various distances to 275 yards.

I called Mack's Sport Shop on Kodiak Island to have them mail me the official U.S. government topographic charts of my hunting area, and I purchased from Mack's the new 10X42 Swarovski binoculars. In 1996, I had learned how important quality binoculars are during a bear hunt. Finally, Santa (my wife) heard my request for a Bushnell laser range finder, and (ho, ho, ho) I found one under the Christmas tree.

The author with a packer after shooting a Kodiak brown bear. The bear measured 8 feet, 3 inches square and had a 23-inch skull.

I arrived at Kodiak Airport and met Tom. We stayed in Kodiak that night and awoke early the next morning to meet the rest of the crew that Tom had assembled for my hunt. What a pleasant surprise this crew was! Besides the charter-boat skipper, Lee Robbins, Tom had brought another registered guide named Darrel Lindgren, an assistant guide, and two packers. I had two full crews to support me on my hunt! Tom explained that the extra personnel were for a hunt that was to begin in two weeks, but since the personnel were available, they were going to help us in our hunt. Grinning, I told Tom, "Now we're really loaded for bear."

After a great Alaskan breakfast of reindeer sausage and eggs, we sighted in my rifle and proceeded to the 44-foot fishing trawler that would be our home for the next several days. The weather was beautiful—warm and sunny—very unlike typical weather on Kodiak. During the boat trip to our hunting area, we glassed a number of bears. The ones I remember most were a sow and its three cubs near the snow line. As the sow lay relaxed but attentive nearby, the cubs slid on their rear ends down a natural snowslide and into a small depression about one hundred yards long. As soon as a cub reached the end of the depression, it would pick itself up and run back up the hill for another slide down. It was as if we were watching a rerun of *Laurel and Hardy*, *The Three Stooges*, or *Our Gang*. My sobering thought, though, was that these lovable and seemingly harmless creatures would soon grow into the largest and most ferocious carnivore on earth!

Since brown bears are omnivorous, Kodiak Island, which is essentially an island rain forest, is a perfect environment for them. There they can feed on lush vegetation, and by early summer, the island is so green that some call it the Emerald Island. By midsummer, the bears gorge themselves on salmonberries and a variety of highly nutritious vegetation. The crescendo of their eating occurs when the salmon run begins.

On the first two days of our hunt, we saw many bear, including fifteen on day two. But most of those animals weren't worth stalking, and the ones that were we couldn't get close to. On day three, we awoke to a storm. Our captain had anchored us securely in a well-sheltered cove the night before, so we had not felt the brunt of the storm during the night. But when the captain moved the vessel to open water, which is where we would be glassing from, we found ourselves in a maelstrom. The rain was dropping at a 45-degree angle. The wind was blowing between fifteen and thirty knots; the disparity in speed was due to occasional lulls in the storm, where it seemed that Mother Nature was taking a break to regroup for her next onslaught. Luckily, the wind came from one direction, which might be helpful in the event of a stalk.

After abandoning thoughts of stalking two bears we had seen that morning, our prize came into view in the early afternoon: a large brown bear with no rubs and a very nice-looking hide. The bear settled for a snooze in some alders halfway up the hill. As was customary, Tom assembled his crew in order to strategize. Darrell had guided me the day before, but because he couldn't convince yesterday's bear to amble into my sights, he wanted to guide me today to make amends. Rod Simmons asked to accompany the stalk team as our packer.

Darrell guides bear hunts with Tom on Kodiak, as well as hunts on the Alaskan mainland for goat, sheep, caribou, and moose. Now in his forties, Darrel has many successful hunts under his belt. Rod, a twenty-five-year-old, grew up on Parker Ranch in Hawaii, where hunting is a way of life. Having once lived in Hawaii, I can attest the island's similarity to Kodiak. Kodiak is a natural extension of the love of the outdoors Rod developed in Hawaii.

The only hitch in our stalk was my bright-yellow, Cape Cod-like rain gear. Darrell wanted to eliminate anything that might sabotage our stalk, but I assured him I would stalk extra stealthily to compensate. The wind fluctuated between twenty and thirty knots, and it was raining like the dickens. The wind was good because it would carry our scent far away from Brownie, and it would also mask any noise we might make during our stalk.

In about an hour, we were positioned, according to my laser range finder, 310 yards above Brownie. During the stalk, Darrell told me to be alert for other bears in the area. (In fact, before

Returning with our trophy bear to Port Vita Lodge on Raspberry Island, our main camp.

and after the stalk, we sighted three other bears near the hill's peak.) When we got to our position, we were unable to see Brownie, but we knew it was still bedded down in the alder thicket. Tom had arranged for some people on the boat to wave flags to signal when and in which direction the bear had moved. We spent about three hours in the miserable wind and rain, waiting for the bear to move.

Finally it moved, and was now about 175 yards away. It was sitting on its rear end like a dog, looking downhill and sniffing constantly (the sniffer being a bear's first line of defense). We discussed the possibility of shooting it through the alders, but my experience has been that such a shot is usually deflected. I had learned that the hard way, while hunting deer, and I wasn't about to relearn it on bear. The problem was, once again, a seemingly endless alder thicket. If the bear moved toward us, it would first have to go into a large opening 145 yards distant. If the bear went the opposite way, it would enter the alder patch and be gone forever.

A very small clearing ten yards square was between the bear and the alder patch. My laser range finder told me the middle of the clearing was 196 yards distant, and my ballistics chart showed that I would have virtually no bullet drop at that range. I also knew that if the bear went the opposite way, I would have only a second or two to set up and shoot.

With the wind and rain in my face, I had to regularly clean and dry my scope sights (and my eyeglasses). This routine was interrupted when the bear got up and started walking. Which direction was it walking? Away from me and toward the endless thicket. I quickly shed my hat and scope covers, took careful aim at the moving animal, and squeezed off a round just as it was about to exit the small clearing. The bear had been solidly hit and began rolling downhill. Complying with prudent bear-hunting principles, I continued shooting, putting several more rounds into the rolling animal. Hallelujah! My second hunt was a success, thanks to my off-season preparation and the wonderful assistance and support of Tom Stick and his competent staff.

After claiming the animal, we received congratulations from the boat below when the captain blew the ship's horn. In a way, though, I was melancholy, knowing that I would soon have to leave this beautiful place to return to the rigors of work and suburban life. We all went back to the Port Vita Lodge for a few days before I had to leave for home. During those days, I took the opportunity to extol the virtues of Cape Cod bright-yellow rain gear as the ultimate in bear camo.

We had seen twenty-eight bear, stalked two, and killed one. Not too shabby for less than three days' work! The hide of my bear was plush, unrubbed, and beautiful. It measured 8 feet, 3 inches. I later learned from the Alaska Department of Fish and Game that a tooth analysis showed that my bear was eight years, three months old.

THE MIGHTY BRUIN

BY
BILL KATEN

It was overcast and drizzling lightly when my guide, Billy, and I went up the mountainside to our lookout point. The wind had dropped off to a light breeze, a welcome relief from the pounding we had taken from it over the last two days. So far we had seen three bears, but I wasn't after just any bear on this hunt.

Billy moved ahead, picking his trail carefully. We wanted to come out on a grassy hillside overlooking the valley floor, and then move to a small rock outcropping that gave us a protected view of the whole valley. I was just coming out of the alders and into the high wet grass when Bill motioned for me to ready my rifle. Sitting in the alders fifty yards away was a bear, its head up and alert. It must have heard us because the next thing I knew it swung around to look. In a moment it was on its feet and coming straight at us, its flesh rippling with stored-up fat. It came through the thick alders as if they were grass.

I grabbed my rifle, threw off the safety, and was ready to fire. The bruin stopped, only yards away from Billy and me. It

The Super Cub on the beach.

stood shaking its head and snorting. I held my fire, hoping I wouldn't have to shoot. I remember thinking how long I had waited to make this hunt and how I didn't want to end it by shooting an animal out of necessity. Then, just as suddenly, the bear turned and ran away, and Billy and I watched it until it left the valley. Billy estimated the bear to be eight or nine feet in length.

* * * * * *

The bear charge took place during a hunting trip I had booked with Larry Rivers Outfitters. I had been to Alaska on several previous hunts with the famous bush pilot and guide Don Sheldon in the Talkeetna area in southcentral Alaska. Unfortunately, Don had passed away in 1975, and his air taxi license had been sold. I made a call to his wife, Roberta, to ask if she could recommend an outfitter. She suggested Larry Rivers. I contacted him immediately and was able to book a hunt on the Alaska Peninsula for the following October.

In October 1979, I flew to Alaska and was greeted by Larry. I transferred my baggage into a trailer located a few hundred yards from the airport, and after a quick lunch and a change of clothes, we packed the Super Cub and departed for spike camp. Thus began my long-awaited bear hunt. Thirty minutes into the flight, Larry pointed out a camp pitched at the edge of a partially dry lake. As Larry maneuvered the Super Cub into position for landing, he pointed out the landmarks I would need to be familiar with. Larry touched the plane's tires to the sand and taxied to a stop.

"Bill, I would like you to meet Billy," Larry said as I climbed out of the plane. "He will be your guide on the hunt." Billy was twenty-six years old, 5 feet, 7 inches, and a solid 155 pounds. He had grown up in Boston but had lived the last several years in Alaska, mainly in small tents and cabins he used on his trapline.

"Come on, let's get this gear into the tent so that Larry can get back into the air," Billy said. We soon had my gear unloaded, and as Larry and Billy discussed the last-minute details, I had a chance to look around.

Spike camp was near a small, partially dry lake located on the floor of a large valley. The lake was perhaps one hundred yards across and two feet deep. There was a strip of semi-dry ground between the water and the lake's four-foot-high bank, which marked the lake's circumference. The strip was about three hundred feet long and twenty feet wide, with small knots of tundra growing across it in some areas. Climbing on the lake's bank, I could see several miles up the valley to a point where it turned sharply to the right and out of sight. (Later I learned that this pass led to the Pacific Ocean.)

As I stood by the lake, I noticed that the valley was about one and a half miles wide and a thousand feet deep, and it was full of rows of eighteen-inch-high, dark-green tussocks and some grassy muskeg. Numerous small lakes dotted the landscape and drained into one large stream, which eventually emptied into the Pacific. The only brush and alder in the valley was on the western wall two miles away. The day was overcast, and the northern breeze carried the fresh smell of ocean, grass, and rain. I was excited and pleased to be in such a beautiful location.

"Bill," called Larry, bringing my attention back to camp, "Billy seems to have everything under control. We are expecting some bad weather, so I'll be back in three days to check on you. Good luck!"

Larry's saying that the weather would be bad was an understatement! On the first day out the wind and rain were terrible, but we still took an excellent bull caribou at a range of about two hundred yards. The second morning, we spotted twenty or thirty caribou and two wolves far out on the valley floor. About 11 A.M. I spotted a bear feeding in the valley. My heart beat loudly. I had come for a bear and was now looking at a large one.

Since the wind was right, we were able to work to within thirty yards of the animal as it fed in a small creek. I stood up and saw the top of its back but could not get a shot. It would have been foolish to move closer, so we waited for the bear to move onto the bank. The next twenty minutes seemed like hours as we sat and waited. Finally, we could stand it no longer and we stood up to look. It was gone! After a quick and careful search, we saw it about 150 yards away in thick brush, and then it vanished into the grass. We were never able to locate it again.

On the third day the wind really began to howl, blowing, it seemed, a hundred miles per hour, and it rained fiercely. I managed to take a white wolf a few miles from camp, but the trip back to camp is what I remember most. Billy and I were leaning into a strong wind to such a degree that when the wind momentarily quit we fell to the ground. Several hours later we arrived at camp exhausted. The fourth morning we dried our gear, had a good breakfast, and headed back into the field. We had been on the hill only a few minutes when Billy pointed to a large brown shape moving at the edge of the alders a mile and a half away. Billy picked up the spotting scope to have a better look. I continued to watch through my binoculars, awaiting his decision. "Looks to me like the best bear we've seen," he finally whispered. "Probably would go well over nine and a half feet." That was what I wanted to hear.

While Billy watched the bear, I packed my gear into my backpack. It would be a difficult stalk, for we would have to use the low areas and creek beds for cover. Four hours later we were still several hundred yards off, and we watched the bear feeding along the base of the mountain on the western side of the valley. Since it was now midafternoon, we expected it to lie down at anytime, which would give us the chance to move in for a shot. The wind was blowing favorably at about fifteen knots, so we were not concerned about the animal scenting us, and the wind's howling would drown out any sounds we made during our final stalk.

But as we prepared for the stalk, I heard something in the distance, and it occurred to me that this was the day that Larry had planned to return to spike camp. The sound I heard was the drone of his Super Cub. I looked up and saw the small aircraft headed up the valley.

Billy tugged my sleeve and pointed to the bear, now standing and looking in the direction of the aircraft. Out of the corner of my eye, I saw that Larry was turning the aircraft away, his engine cut to an idle. Apparently he had seen the bear and was trying to leave as quickly and quietly as possible. I had no time to think. The big bear had dropped to the ground and was walking up the mountain toward the alders, from which it had emerged earlier that day. It was obvious where it was going and that it was set on getting there as quickly as possible.

It would be a long shot for my .375 H&H, but it was now or never. I would have to take the best shot possible and hope that my many hours of practice would make up the difference. Billy was right beside me as I threw myself on the ground, lined up on the bear's shoulder, and fired.

"You hit him!" Billy exclaimed. "Bust him again!"

I quickly followed up with two more shots. I was sure that they had connected, but the bear disappeared into the grass.

When we saw it again, the bear was moving at a steady pace up the face of the mountain. There was blood on its leg and it was walking with a limp, but it was still moving quite fast. The bear was approaching the mountaintop, and we were moving after it as fast as we could. The remainder of the day was spent

Author with his brown bear.

looking for its trail, but tracking was impossible on the rocky mountainside. Reaching the mountaintop, we could see into the next valley, which was about two miles long with no brush. But the bear was nowhere to be seen. I was greatly disappointed. Its tracks indicated it was a bear well over ten feet. Larry came in the next morning and, after hearing our story, decided to move us to another valley. Meanwhile, Larry would continue to try to locate the bruin by air.

A short time later, we landed on the beach, the surf breaking only a few feet away. We set about anchoring the camp near a dune. We hunted this area for two days, seeing sows and cubs and small adult bears, but since the winds were again picking up, it was difficult to hunt. On the third evening, Larry flew over at high tide and dropped a note. The weather pattern that year had been unusually bad, and another strong system was moving in. The note said that the weather was supposed to get worse and that he wanted to get us out of there. We would have to walk one and a half miles to a flat behind the sand dunes where he would pick us up with two planes. We took only what we needed and headed out.

We worked our way through the alders, full of fresh bear trails. The weather was getting so bad we couldn't see twenty feet. Billy was confident that we would soon reach the stream that separated us from the airplanes, but when we did we discovered that the stream had turned into a raging river. We tried twice to cross but could not. Larry was on the opposite bank, and we motioned to him that we couldn't cross. He indicated that he would pick us up on our side.

We were standing on a sand strip about ten feet wide and one hundred feet long. The strip was encircled by water except for one

The author's bear measured 11 feet, 3 inches.

side, which was grass. Larry flew his Super Cub very low over us, making four passes to gauge the turbulence. On the last pass he opened the door and yelled, "When I touch down, grab the wings!"

He came in almost like a helicopter, and we grabbed the plane's struts. It seemed like the plane would pick us up, even with the engine at idle. Larry opened the door and told me to get in. I did so quickly and we took off from the position where he had stopped. It didn't seem like five feet. He flew to where the other plane was parked behind a large sand dune, let me out, and then returned for Billy. It was really incredible.

A short time later, after I had returned to New York with an unfilled tag, Larry told me that he had seen from his plane the bear I had wounded. He also told me that his next client, Johnnie Lowe, of Houston, Texas, took an 11-foot, 5-inch brown bear in the same area I had hunted. While skinning it out, they found a fresh bullet cut on the brisket and a single .375 H&H bullet lodged in its right foot. When officially measured, the skull went 29 inches and is listed No. 87 in Boone and Crockett. I was disappointed, but not beat. Before I left, I booked another hunt with Larry for fall 1981.

* * * * * *

For the 1981 hunt I prepared for the worst. All the gear I brought had been waterproofed, and I also brought extra-long aluminum stakes to better anchor my tent in case of strong winds. I had a full sixteen days to look for the bear of my choice.

On the first day, we glassed from the observation point. We saw nothing that morning, but around 3 P.M. we located a small bear coming toward us, nervously looking over its shoulder. A short time later it was followed by a large bear. We knew it was time to travel. As quickly as we could, we moved through the valley on a course plotted to intercept the big bear at the river. It got there ahead of us, and we moved into position just in time to see it come out of a creek dripping wet on our side of the bank.

The bear was moving steadily, looking for salmon and feeding on the vegetation along the stream. Upon reaching the bank, it started to move away from us at a speed that would be hard for us to keep up with. I estimated the range to be two hundred yards, within the capability of the .338 Winchester I was carrying that year. For a rest, I laid my rifle across my jacket and told Billy that I would fire the next time it came out of the creek. Shortly thereafter it stepped up on the gravel bank. I fired at its shoulder and heard a sharp *splaaat*, the bullet having hit the animal's wet hide.

Outfitter Larry Rivers holding up a paw of my bear.

Instantly, it started to run for the mountain Billy and I had just come off. I hit it two more times before it reached the slope, upon which it turned and headed straight at us. "This is my last shot!" I yelled to Billy as I took aim. The bullet hit the creature squarely in the chest. The bear spun around in its tracks but never went down. It headed back to the mountain and took refuge in an alder patch.

With heart pounding and Billy standing cover, I quickly reloaded. Billy led the way around and above the patch in an attempt to catch sight of the wounded bear. All was silent and still except for the occasionally moving brush. After fifteen minutes and no sight of our quarry, we decided to throw in a stone or two, hoping for a response. The first rock thudded into the soft earth, and the bear stood up less than twenty yards away. "Bust him!" Billy whispered. I placed the cross hairs on its neck and dropped it in its tracks. The impact rolled it down the hill, where it came to rest in a swamp. I thought for sure the shot had killed it, but as we moved toward it, we heard it moving around.

We inched into the swamp. Only a small knoll separated us from the bear, less than fifteen yards away. We moved into position, but it saw us and took off at a run for the mountain. Twice I knocked it down as it splashed through the swamp. I had to fire one last shot into its neck to finally kill it.

It was the biggest bear I had ever seen. Needless to say, Bill and I danced around the swamp for quite some time. It took everything we had to skin the bear, and we had to spend a second day fleshing it before it was light enough to pack out to the beach. The biggest thrill came when we squared the hide. It measured 11 feet, 3 inches, only 2 inches less than the bear I didn't get two years earlier. It was one of the greatest hunting experiences I have ever had.

GIFT BEAR

BY
DR. DAVE GANDEE

There is a giant, fully furred Alaska brown bear headed for my hometown of Buckhannon, West Virginia, and I'm not sure I fully understand why. I'm the one who slugged it out with nature for twenty-one days of gloom and pouring rain to find it. And I'm the one who squeezed the trigger and brought the giant creature crashing to the earth. Yet if I consider this kill anything less than a gift from the Almighty, I am fooling myself.

I am no novice to big-game hunting. I've been at it since 1976. I know what it takes to get a trophy. At the risk of sounding brash, I will tell you this: I seldom get excited and lose my composure. Just ask the guides who have hunted with me. But on this particular hunt, I did.

I arrived in Cold Bay, Alaska, on 7 May 1994, three days before the start of spring bear season. Roger and his crew had been weathered in for several days, unable to completely set up spike camp. We took Zodiacs across the bay to base camp, where we enjoyed sunshine for a few hours. Had we known the kind of weather that awaited us, I'm sure we would have valued the sunshine more.

The next morning we rushed out to finish setting up spike camp. The sun had disappeared and would hardly appear again for the duration of the hunt. One of the worst springs in Alaska history had begun, and, unknown to me, fate was moving me in an unforgettable direction.

For the next two days until the season began, we watched for bear. We saw a few sows, but with the early spring their coats were badly rubbed. I learned years ago not to let discouragement ruin a hunt. As in life, so in hunting: A goal must not be abandoned because of disappointment. My chance for a ten-foot-plus bear was good. I would not let rain wash away my dream.

We trudged sixteen days through miserably cold spring rain, hunting until at least ten o'clock every evening. We arose early each morning, and the first order of the day was always to go outside the tents and glass for bear. On the second and third day, Dan and I both had fleeting glimpses of a big bear on a mountain peak, bolstering my hope. But nothing really happened until the fifth day. John and Roger were up first on that day and glassing. Then Dan got up and spotted a gargantuan dark-brown

AAA's spike camp.

bear only five hundred yards from camp. John, Roger, and Dan were stunned that this immense bear was so close to us. It looked to me like a world record!

The other hunter with us, Pete, was as avid a trophy hunter as I. Both of us had always hunted one-on-one, and we had agreed that there would be no flipping coins or drawing straws. The bear belonged to the hunter who spotted it first. I stepped aside as Dan and Pete threw their gear together to pursue the giant bruin. I admit feeling a pang or two of envy, but I wished them well. Meanwhile, I retired to my tent to check my gear, battling some discouragement—almost impossible to avoid, given the situation. In my heart I knew I could still bag a big bear, perhaps even a record one. My resolve was strengthened minutes later when John stuck his head in my tent. "Dave! Two bears, big ones, have come down! Let's go!"

I rushed outside and glassed them two miles up the valley. One was standing up, and it looked fifteen feet tall! A boar and a sow, and the sow was about nine feet. John and Roger manned the spotting scope, trying to determine how big the boar was. They quickly decided it was our man. We were off!

We headed up the valley, across the creek, and through the thick alders, coming out at a lookout point, where we met Dan and Pete. The giant bear they were after had winded them. It had rushed into the alders, never to be seen again for the rest of the season.

We sat on the lookout for twelve rainy hours, watching the two bears move about the valley. The following days were a nightmare of solid rain, with only brief glimpses of the sun. We hunted hard but with no success, and we began to feel the pressure of time.

We did not see the boar and sow again until 9:30 P.M.—the second to last day of bear season. There they were, exactly where we had seen them days before. Realizing we had nothing to lose, Roger, John, and I peeled almost everything off but our essentials—gun, shells, camera—and covered about two miles in less than forty-five minutes. I'm a forty-seven-year-old smoker, but I was with these guides all the way. When we got to the

A good Cold Bay day.

base of the mountain, the bears, instead of coming down, as we had hoped, had been climbing.

Now it made sense. The sow was apparently not quite in heat, but enough to tempt the boar into trailing it all over the valley. They both had stopped feeding and were sleeping all day and moving back up the mountain at dusk. I was ready to climb after them, but Roger reminded me that there was not enough daylight left to reach them as long as they were still climbing. So it was back to camp. I had one day left.

All the other hunters had left camp. I had Dan, Bob Wambach (another guide), John (who was still packing the camcorder), and Roger all to myself. Four guides and a hunter went up the valley on the last morning of bear season with all the determination of General George Washington in his pursuit of Cornwallis. This time we went to the other side of the creek, which was a half mile from where the bears had been bedding down. From there we glassed for more than two hours, but saw absolutely nothing until after lunch, when John spotted the sow getting up in an area Roger had pinpointed.

We knew where the bears were, but what would they do next? We discussed several options, and it didn't take long for

Roger and Dan to devise a plan: Roger, John, and I would go up the creek about a mile and a half and then glass from there. We made it in good time, but the wind turned straight against our backs, so we hightailed it again, going another mile or so downstream. We started up a long, steep ravine, walking for what seemed forever. At the end of the ravine, Roger and I climbed a snowbank. When we were near the top, Roger reached out and stopped me. "There's the bear, Dave," he whispered. "It's right there. Don't move!"

Now I was excited—and remember, I don't usually get excited. Roger led me to an area he felt was a good place to shoot from. We had no idea what the bears would do. I glanced at my watch—3:30. We quietly set up and began the wait.

"We'll give them until four," Roger said. But by four, the elusive bruins still hadn't moved. We waited until five. Then six. The spring hunting season was fast ticking away—and I'd been at it sixteen days in the cold rain and wind.

At 6:15 I said to Roger, "Those bears are going to do exactly the same thing today that they have been doing every day. They'll stay until dark and then head back up the mountain. We've put things off long enough."

Roger agreed. He signaled to Dan and Bob to go upwind and try to drive the bears toward us. As they began the drive, we got into position. Roger showed me an area where he reckoned the bears would come out. Hearing the drivers, the sow broke down the hill. It went through a thick alder patch so fast it was just a streak. Bears can travel up to forty miles an hour on flat ground. Given the angle of the hill, the sow must have been doing sixty.

"If the boar comes out that fast, I don't have a prayer," I whispered to Roger.

We could hear the drivers getting closer. They were talking loudly and often changing direction. We thought we saw movement, but the boar didn't break. It just roared. It didn't want to come out of the thicket, but it finally had no choice. The boar broke cover and came in the direction we had wanted. My shooting zone was about 150 yards wide. I was using a .340

Weatherby Custom Magnum zeroed for 3½ inches at 100 yards, which, with a 250-grain Nosler Partition, has about the same ballistics as a .270 shooting a 130-grain bullet.

I've dropped running game at longer distances than this, so I had complete confidence in my shooting ability. But before I could shoot, the boar vanished behind a small knoll and then ducked into a ravine. When it finally emerged, it was more than two hundred yards to my right and running uphill. I swung over and fired. No hit. The big boar turned and went down into another ravine. When it started up the other side, I fired again. This time it seemed to slow, running not much faster than a walk, which gave me time to set up for another shot. I put the cross hairs on the tip of its nose. When the gun cracked, the giant bear dropped. It was over. The "gift" bear was mine!

The author with his 10-foot, 3-inch brownie.

The author with his dream trophy.

As we approached the fallen giant, I could tell it was truly immense. But after nineteen days in the cold rain, it didn't matter how big it was. It didn't matter if it was a record. As we walked up the hill, all I could feel was gratitude. There lay a ten-foot-plus bear with the most magnificent pelt I had ever seen. What a gift! The bear was killed only four hours before the close of the season. *How strange,* I thought, as we prepared to skin the beast, *that success could come so unexpectedly from such drudgery!*

My guides told me, as we trudged down the mountain taking turns carrying the monstrous 110-pound hide, that I was the first hunter who had ever helped pack a bear skin back to camp. I could have gone farther. I felt light. A load had been lifted.

The gift was far from over. My bear has taken on a new life far beyond the Alaskan wilds. The bear was mounted by Mike Boyce, world-renowned taxidermist, and it made its debut at the 1995 Safari Club International Annual Convention in Las Vegas. I approved Mike's plans for the mount, but the final results were more breathtaking than I had imagined. Throughout the United States, excerpts from the video of my hunt have been released by AAA. Thousands have been witnesses to the bear's magnificence.

Even if I were inclined to take the glory, one nagging detail keeps me grounded. After the hunt, I questioned whether or not I had properly zeroed in my brand-new Burris Posi-Lock scope. As we say in West Virginia, "You figure that one out!"

GOAT'S HEART SOUP

BY
ROB HOLT

I've never actually cared much for heart as something to eat. Sheep, moose, deer, caribou, you name it—I just never gave it much consideration. Just another piece of the gut pile left for the ravens.

In the past few years, though, my native hunting partner has been packing out (or bringing in, depending on where you are from) hearts. They are mostly from caribou or moose kills. A moose heart is large enough that, if it's left in the field, you feel like you're wasting meat. My other partner, not a native of any sort, decided last season to collect deer hearts (and tongues). He was amassing quite a pile of hearts. I think he had nine hanging nicely in the alder just outside the cook tent, along with a few mallards. I've never seen a retriever put its lips on a duck once back in camp, but the deer hearts must have seemed just too tempting, and sometime during a clear November night, they disappeared.

So this practice of salvaging hearts from a kill along with all the real meat has been slowly creeping into my way of doing things—conceptually, anyway.

I had cleaned out the goat heart, soaked it a few days in some salt water, and split it open, wondering just what to do with it. After all, I did have some tenderloins, so it would have to wait until I had consumed them.

Spending a few days in the village this time of year usually nets quite a few dinner invitations. Everybody is out enjoying the wild harvest, and all want to share. Deer, duck, crab, and fish are all hard to turn down, especially when someone else is cooking. I started boiling the goat heart on the galley stove, figuring if anyone came by to ask me up for dinner, I could treat it as an experiment and leave it for tomorrow. After all, if I boiled it enough with a few spices, how could it go wrong. Fine salt, pepper, and curry powder were all I could find in the boat's galley, so they all got dumped in.

* * * * * *

The weight of the heart wasn't a factor, although the pack did seem a bit heavy for the terrain and conditions—loose rocks from baseball to Volkswagen size, and snow four inches deep and falling hard. Each piece I put in the pack—rib meat, backstrap, loins, neck, and the complete hide—was light by itself, but all lumped together it was heavy. When I looked back at the stripped backbone lying on the moss-and-rock hillside, I saw the heart among the other internal parts. It was unpierced and undamaged by the traumatic death the goat had met. I saw it, and it was as big a piece of good meat as others I had thrown in the pack. So I took it.

Something about walking around in Kodiak's high alpine sinks into the bone the very first time. If I don't go there for a long time I don't realize I'm missing it, but when back there again, breaking away from the highest brush, leaving "lower earth" behind, it fills me again. I feel the magic of the first time and wonder why I wait so long between trips to this world.

The shot broke the spine and delivered enough shock to end the goat's life. It hadn't been around all that long, a mature breeding male. I was in awe of the toughness of the animal; I had seen quite a few brown bears take a lot of lead to finish up, but was surprised at this goat. From the first shot to the fifth was a very short time, probably fifteen to twenty seconds, but it played out slowly.

It had been grazing on a ledge when we first saw it. Then, as if it had only stepped out of the cracks in the mountain to let us know it was there, just as quickly it moved back out of sight, allowing us to cover most of the valley floor undetected.

Back at the boat the skipper was piling weapons into the skiff for a cruise around the bay, like preparing for an assault. A 12-gauge for ducks, a .17 mag for deer, and a .22 for seal, and don't forget the spinning rod for rockfish and bass.

One more chute to climb up through, and the goat that would eventually lend its heart to my soup would be in view. I was anticipating a long shot.

I suppose 11:30 is as good a time as any for a goat nap, and that was how we found it, napping in fairly negotiable terrain, with just its back in view, long white hair standing straight up and just a puff of wind from it to us.

"That soup looks a little thin. Why don't you throw in a can of tomato sauce?" Not a bad idea, though I'm thinking tomato sauce will have my soup looking like it belongs on spaghetti. By now I've got quite an investment in BTUs and tinkering time. If I put in the tomato sauce, I can't take it out. . . . This is a pivotal point in the whole project.

I'd closed the distance down to about forty-five yards, and I still couldn't tell which end was which. Just white hair and its back line sticking up above the smooth rock between us. Not being fond of gadgets but still falling victim to their seduction from time to time means constantly being presented with options. Do I use the gadget or not? This time it was the quick detachable scope mount on my rifle. I was thinking to myself I should get closer, remove the scope, and shoot with iron sights. Why not? Around forty yards I slipped the scope off and stuffed it down the front of my shirt. Pressing on, I was walking on one of those granite rock faces that is horizontal, and I felt like a lizard walking on a basketball, exposed but quiet. Around twenty-five yards, just as I was thinking I could get a little closer, it sensed me. I thought about noise but was sure I didn't make any.

As quickly as it awoke, the goat jumped to its feet and spun around to face me in one fluid motion. I raised my rifle to shoot. *What the hell? Oh, yeah, I took the scope off, use the sights!* One shot to the center of the chest and it bolted off the rock we were sharing. Running down and to my left, the goat took two more shots into the shoulder as fast as I could get them off. It piled up in the boulders; two more rounds into the spine and it was over.

As my partner and I admired this beautiful animal and the surreal landscape around us, the first specks of snow started to fall. We were pushing the envelope for hunting in the goat rocks; it was 18 October, and the high shoulders of the Big Island were due for a good covering of snow. Three hours up and nine hours down meant all the daylight had been gone a while when we stumbled out of the cottonwoods onto the beach. A cool skiff ride, some warm clothes, and coffee on the *Candida Dawn C.* separated the evening from the long day. A day like this, spent with good friends, carries the weight of a month's worth of normal life.

* * * * * *

Having worked on this soup for four days, you would think at least one evening I'd get to have a bowl of it. Finally, with spike camp in place, I've moved off the boat and into the camp I'll use during the bear hunt. I'm relieved. Settling into camp, I'm reminded how much I like this spot. The mountains that form the spine of Kodiak staring down at me, mallards laughing along the shore, and the valley ahead hiding the bears we will be after in a few days.

The soup is almost hot, a pilot board with butter and a few jalapeños, I'm finally having some goat heart soup. . . . It's good.

IT PAYS TO WAIT

BY
ROGER MORRIS

I wrote this story sixteen years ago. It's about the first hunt I ever guided. My guiding operation has since guided over six hundred clients, and it is still true that it pays to wait. A true trophy hunter passes on many animals, for he is willing to wait for that perfect trophy. This story, as well as Dr. Dave Gandee's "Gift Bear" (chapter 3 in this volume), is a reminder that patience is among the attributes a hunter must possess.

As Brente Jones and I stood in the air terminal at Cold Bay waiting for the Reeve Bird to touch down, I thought back to the last three months of planning, equipment shipping, and camp setup. Our first brown bear season as partners of AAA Alaskan Outfitters was about to begin.

We had worked hard getting everything we needed, but I kept wondering if we had forgotten or overlooked something. It was too late now, though, for the plane had landed and our very first clients, George Caswell, of Enid, Oklahoma, and Tim Orton, of Walker, Minnesota, were standing in front of us. The excitement of taking a big brown bear was evident on their faces. After quick introductions, we grabbed the luggage and were on our way.

Each outfitter that operates in the Izembek Wildlife Refuge on the Alaska Peninsula is limited to two bear hunters per season. George and Tim's names had been given to the refuge manager as the two bear hunters for our outfit.

Because inflatable boats are portable and handle well in rough water, we chose them as our mode of transportation. The trip across the bay was typical, and we ate a little salt water from the overspray as our boat crashed into the one- to two-foot swells. After reaching the shore, we pulled the boats above the tide line to avoid damage from the surf.

Base camp was two four-man Eureka drawtight tents dug into a fifty-foot bank two hundred yards from shore. It was well protected from the wind, which is of prime importance in the Cold Bay area. Several weeks before our arrival, the winds were clocked at over a hundred miles per hour and had blown down a weather tower and the Flying Tiger refrigeration building. We didn't need any problems like that.

Typical brown bear country on the Alaska Peninsula.

As supper was being cooked, we talked of previous experiences and the plans for this hunt. George was looking around at the numerous boxes of food and asked if he could have more. We all laughed. I told him to eat hearty because we wouldn't have much at spike camp, which was three miles inland. However, Brent and I had made numerous trips to the spike camp, so we knew its food supply was about the same. We wouldn't go hungry, that was for sure! Supper consisted of spaghetti, fresh garden salad, rolls, and cheesecake. It was delicious.

After supper we finalized our plans. George would hunt with Brent; Tim, with me. Brent and I had already decided we would first hunt the shoreline for a day or so, since during our many trips inland we hadn't spotted a bear. The local reports said that most of the bears were still hibernating.

The first morning, we were up and at 'em early, but the long, hard day produced nothing. On day two we moved inland, but another day went by without spotting a single bear. The third day we hiked about two miles to a good spotting hill, where Brent sighted a wolf crossing the flats. We watched it until it came within a couple of hundred yards. What a great shot it would have been, had wolves been in season.

Brent finally spotted one. Excitement at last! Both spotting scopes were set on 60X so that we could study the animal carefully. The bear we spotted was at the end of the valley in the snow, a good three miles away. We estimated it was an eight-footer. We watched it until it disappeared into a draw on the side of the mountain. Things were looking good.

Brent and I spotted from the same hill. It was the highest hill on the open valley floor, and we could glass 75 percent of the inland area from the hill. Brent had been successful here the previous fall, spotting a nine-footer one day and a ten-footer-plus a couple of days later, and both bears were successfully taken. But it was spring now and things were different.

On day four, we went into the mouth of the valley where we had spotted the bear. We climbed a little higher to see the whole valley, but we sighted only a lot of old tracks. We spent the morning glassing together, and as afternoon approached,

Brent and George decided to check out a couple of other valleys. Tim and I chose to stay put. Around 4 P.M. I spotted a seven- to eight-footer. Tim and I watched it look for food in the snow. There were windblown areas around the animal that were frozen solid, and this seemed to aggravate the hungry bear in its desperate search for early spring dinner.

We continued to glass, and at 6 P.M. we suddenly saw a big one high up on a snow-covered mountain. "He'd go nine feet plus," I told Tim. Tim was ready to go. He had taken an eight-foot grizzly a few years before and was hoping to get a ten-footer this year.

The wind had been blowing out of the valley and in our faces all day, so it was in our favor. It was fairly open across the valley floor, but the terrain was uneven, and there were a few creeks flowing down and out. The bear was about a mile away, still angling down the mountain. I told Tim we'd cut across to an intersect point and meet the bear there. We crossed the valley to that point when, all of a sudden, the wind switched, hitting us from behind—the absolute worst thing that could have happened. The bear was still coming down the mountain and was now moving faster. Suddenly it stopped, sniffed, looked around, and bolted back up the mountain. It was moving so fast we couldn't gain on it. The higher it went, the more slowly we pursued it, since the snow was getting deeper and deeper. Here was our big bear, and it was getting away! As we watched it run over the ridge, I wondered with sickened heart if we'd ever see it again.

Day five rolled around, and we were at it early again. We didn't spot any bears that morning. However, that afternoon we spotted two other bears high in the snow; one was too small and the other disappeared across the mountain.

The weather had been great, but on the sixth day it started blowing and raining a bit. That afternoon, Brent and George went back to base camp to hunt the shoreline, and Tim and I decided to move spike camp to the hill we had used for spotting, which would save us about two hours of hunting time.

We packed a light camp and were on our way early. It stopped raining, and it looked like we were in for another nice day. As we crossed the second creek in the middle of the open flats, I turned to check the area behind us. "There's a wolf," I said. Tim turned and expected to see the wolf a long way off, but there it was on the bear trail thirty yards away. When we stopped, it stopped. I eased a shell into the chamber of my .357 H&H, not knowing what to expect. It started to circle us, getting closer and closer. Every five steps or so it would stop and turn its head, as if to say, "What is this?" I asked Tim to take my camera out of my pack. I continued to keep Tim covered, still not knowing what to expect. Did the wolf have rabies? Was it brave? Or was it just dumbfounded at seeing humans?

The wolf eased its way to within fifteen to twenty yards. I took a few pictures and got Tim's camera out so he could take a few too. Meanwhile, the wolf moved back and forth in front of us. What a great experience! We had never been this close to a wolf in the wild.

Our pet wolf on the Alaska Peninsula.

It was getting late, so I told Tim we needed to move on. I figured the wolf would run off as soon as we started walking, but I was wrong. It followed right behind us like a dog. I suggested to Tim that he try not to limp because the wolf was checking us out to decide which one it was going to dine on. Tim got a big chuckle out of that. We had about three-quarters of a mile to go before reaching the hill from which we planned to glass. The wolf stayed right with us. When we reached the hill, we sat down and so did the wolf. How ridiculous. A pet wolf!

While we rested, we glassed the hillside. I spotted a bear moving along the base of a hill, but it disappeared into the alder. I didn't get a very good look at it. With the wolf still hanging around, I didn't relish leaving behind the gear for the spike camp. We made our way to a small knoll that was four hundred yards from where we had last seen the bear. No bear. We sat and glassed for five hours. Still no bear. I figured it had lain down. Then, out of the corner of my eye, I caught some movement. "There he is," I exclaimed. The bear had crossed a draw and had lain down about four hundred yards from where we had last spotted it. It was nice, a little over eight feet. Though an extremely pretty bear, with lots of blond highlights, Tim debated and then decided to pass it up.

Time was running short; we had only three more days. On our way back to camp, we discussed our choices and decided to stay inland one more day, and then head for the shoreline.

We had a late supper and finally went to bed around midnight. "What's that noise?" Tim asked. We listened intently as paper rustled and cans clanged, disrupting the silent night. Since we had eaten supper so late, I had left our dinner trash right outside the small two-man tent. I got my gun ready and started to unzip the tent door. As I peeked out, I turned on the flashlight, only to have two eyes meet mine. Three feet away was a fox. Its nose was in one of the cans. I shouted, hoping to run it off, but it just stared and continued to eat. Then it carried a peach can and lay down with it five feet away. I clapped my hands and shouted, and it finally took off.

As I crawled back into the tent, mumbling something like "There, now we can sleep," the night's silence was broken by familiar sounds. This time Mr. Fox had brought a friend. As I unzipped the tent's door, I found them so close I could almost touch them. I shouted, but it didn't even faze them. Each one had an empty can, and since I'd left only two cans and some candy wrappers in the garbage that day, I decided that they couldn't do too much damage. We left them alone and snuggled back into our sleeping bags, and we finally got some sleep.

The next morning was beautiful. As soon as we started cooking, the aroma of breakfast sausage filled the air. And lo and behold, what appeared? You guessed it—the previous night's guests. They showed up dressed in their early fall dinner jackets, ready to eat. We took pictures of them and made sure all the garbage was cleaned up and put away. Then off we went in pursuit of the elusive bear we had so diligently been hunting.

Camp fox.

Guides Brent Jones and Roger Morris with 10-foot, 10-inch and 10-foot, 2-inch

brown bears. Bears taken by George Caswell and Tim Orton in May, 1984.

After a half day of glassing and no bear, we decided to use the afternoon to travel to the coast. Even though we had seen several bears, I figured Brent had to be doing better than we were. There just weren't that many bears out. We stopped by the other camp to pick up Tim's gear, and then we were on our way. When we arrived at base camp, it was bursting with excitement, and rightfully so. George had taken a beautiful 10-foot, 10-inch bear a few miles down the coast the night before. The skull was later officially measured at 29⁵/₁₆ inches, placing it No. 58 in the Boone and Crockett record book. Out of the 224 bears taken on the Alaska Peninsula, George's was the largest.

Even though it was late, we still had a couple of hours of light left, so Tim and I loaded some gear into the boat and were off. Less than half a mile from base camp, I spotted a nice bear on a hillside five hundred yards from shore. We docked the boat and made our way up the mountain to get above the bear in order to study its size. Another eight-and-a-half-footer. Tim was tempted again, but decided he'd hold out.

It was getting dark, so we headed back to base camp to work on some strategy details and, of course, to hear George and Brent's successful bear story. After all, nothing's better than a good bear story late at night in bear country. Brent told me that he hadn't spotted a bear until he'd spotted George's. They were making plans to move inland to where we were when they spotted "Ol' Granddaddy."

It was the morning of the ninth day when Tim and I left early for the area of the valley where George had taken his bear. They had spotted two others while stalking George's bear, one being at least nine feet. But no luck. The thought that one more day and it would be all over for Tim kept nagging at me. Tim talked about the ones he had passed up and his reasons for doing so. The pressure was really on. We had to connect—we just had to.

It was the last day, and we examined our plan and options and decided we'd spend the day in the same valley. We spotted a sow with cubs but no lone bears. Dismayed, tired, and a bit quiet, but not totally defeated, we left the valley around 8 P.M.

Glassing the shoreline on the trip back would produce success—or would it?

"There's one, Tim!" I shouted. A real dark one, and did it look big! I checked the wind before we went to shore. We motored past it in our boat. The bear was only two hundred yards up the mountain and in the open surrounded by alders. It was eating the early spring grasses. This was Tim's last chance. I knew Tim would shoot it if it was over eight feet, and it was at least nine. We moved slowly up the bluff and through the alders, staying near a small babbling creek to cover up our sound. As we came into the open, we couldn't see the bear. We nodded excitedly to each other about the hill having different levels, so we continued to climb higher. And there it was, moving slowly—very slowly—away. All we could see was its backside as it started down into a streambed, stopped, stood up, and rubbed its back on a tree. What a sight! But still not a good shot.

We were within seventy-five yards when it disappeared into the creek ravine. I put Tim in front and instructed him to take the bear when it came up on the other side. I knew now it was a good nine and a half feet, maybe more. Waiting seemed like a lifetime, but I'm sure only a minute or so passed before the bear ambled up the other side and turned broadside for the perfect shot. Tim readied in his position and squeezed off a well-placed round and the bear was down. Tim's .338 did the job. It was 11:05 P.M. on the last day.

After congratulations and the rush of excitement subsided, we hustled over to check the animal out. What a bear! It was close to ten feet, a dark chocolate with no rubs. Tim was ecstatic. The darkness of night was coming upon us, so we hurried to take pictures. We marked the area, left some of our gear, and went back to camp for a lantern. Brent had lit a lantern and set it out so that we could find the camp. He had supper waiting, but we didn't stop and went back to skin the bear. Tim had to catch his plane early the next afternoon, and we had a lot of work to do in the meantime. That was the first bear I ever skinned by lantern. We arrived back at camp at 3 A.M. and celebrated with a prime rib dinner. What a treat! Tim and I were exhausted, but very happy.

We were up at 6 A.M., packing, fleshing, and measuring. The bear measured 10 feet, 2 inches, the fourth-largest taken on the Alaska Peninsula. It had a 28⁵/₁₆-inch skull, officially measured for Boone and Crockett. It really did pay to wait. Two Boone and Crockett ten-footers! All in all, a great start for AAA Alaskan Outfitters.

TOO CLOSE FOR COMFORT

BY
GARY "BUTCH" KING JR.

Francisco "Poncho" Salazar of Hermosillo, Mexico, was on his very first Alaskan big-game hunt. The weather was cold for the Mexican hunter, but for the guides and me the fall weather had been better than average, with temperatures holding in the low twenties with little snow. There are plenty of bears on the Alaska Peninsula, though, so it was merely a matter of finding Poncho the right bear, in the right place, at the right time.

Poncho had stalked two average brown bears during the first few days of his hunt, but both stalks were foiled by changing winds. As the days counted by, time was getting short and there was pressure on both the hunters and the guides to get the last bear of the season. It was on the evening before the final day of the hunt when assistant guides Dennis Gearhart and Mike Mackay located an exceptionally large brown bear lying in heavy brush. The bear was a long way off, and it was too late in the evening to attempt a stalk. The hunter and guides reluctantly returned to their spike camp just before dark with only one more day of hunting left.

Pilots and guides at the Cider River Lodge airfield.

Dennis and Mike had no doubt that that was the largest bear they had seen in their many years of hunting the Alaska Peninsula. From the looks of the worn trail between the bear's hole and the river, the animal had been fishing for some time in a very productive spot. Dennis and Mike agreed that with luck the bear would be fishing the same stretch of river in the morning.

The next morning, Dennis, Mike, and Poncho glassed from a ridge and located the bear lying in a deep hole it had dug near the river. They had plenty of time to plan a stalk. Mike watched the bear from the ridge as Poncho and Dennis dropped off into the thick alders. It took less than fifteen minutes for their plan to go amiss. The bear, for no apparent reason, just up and left its hole.

From his vantage point on the ridge, Mike watched Poncho's dream bear amble off through the brush. It crossed a ravine and finally dropped into another deep bear hole, a full two hundred yards from where Dennis and Poncho had expected to find it. To make matters worse, the monster brown bear had nearly disappeared from view; only the top of its broad umber head poked above the tall amber grass that blanketed the hillside.

Dennis, unaware the bear had relocated, crossed thirty feet in front of the animal. Mike, unable to signal Dennis and Poncho about the danger they were in, decided to leave his vantage point on the ridge and catch up to them before the bear did.

Mike slowly circled the location where he had last seen the bear, creeping like an Indian through the tall grass and thick brush. He then got a terrible feeling that he had entered a forbidden zone, for he distinctly felt the brown bear's presence. Mike's nostrils flared and blood began to pound in his temples. Where was it? He remained frozen but knew the bear wouldn't wait long. Seconds seemed like hours as he tried to clear his mind and keep his composure.

Mike heard heavy breathing. Twelve paces to his left he saw two ears. He froze and watched the silver-tipped ears lower into the tall grass. He waited, wondering what to do next, afraid that if he moved the bear would charge. Where was Poncho? Where was Dennis? Several long minutes passed before the bear's heavy breathing settled to a slow slumber. He had to find Dennis! Placing his wool hat over his gun barrel, Mike quietly waved his makeshift signal above the alders. He wasn't sure if Poncho and Dennis could see the brown hat above the thick brush, but it was worth a try.

Mike remained steady, forty feet from the monster bear. Minutes passed like hours, and his hope was diminishing. He had to try something else. Till now, Mike had been leery of bolting a round in the chamber of his trusty .375 H&H Magnum, knowing that the bear would react to any metallic sound. However, the time had come to attempt an escape— or do battle with the bear. Watching in the direction of the now-sleeping bear, Mike carefully removed a 300-grain cartridge from his breast pocket and quietly eased the bolt back. Holding his breath, he pinched the magazine with the fingers of his left hand and with his right slid the single cartridge ahead of the bolt. Without taking his eyes off of the tall grass, Mike inched the bolt ahead and quietly locked the load in place. Habit brought his thumb up to return the Model 70's safety lever to the aft position. *Click!* Mike's heart raced.

The author, a master guide (left), and Poncho, with trophy 11-foot, 4-inch Alaska Peninsula brown bear.

The click was all it took to bring the monster bear out of its hole. As the mountain of dark brown hair emerged from the grass, Mike brought the rifle to his shoulder. Mike's and the bear's eyes met for an instant before the deathly silence ended with the roar of a rifle.

It was Poncho's! From sixteen paces, Poncho's first shot struck the monster bear in the rear between the shoulder blades. Though its spine was now severed, the bellowing brownie started toward Mike. Mike's open sights settled on a spot between the bear's beady eyes. He touched the trigger, as did Dennis, who was with Poncho. Two shots rang as one. The mighty brown bear collapsed instantly. Dennis had placed a 300-grain softpoint at the base of the bear's broad neck, and Mike's bullet impacted high between the eyes, following the ridge across the top of the bear's skull and lodging in the neck only inches from the point of entry of Dennis's bullet.

As often happens to Alaskan guides, Mike Mackay had been in a tough spot and had to shoot it out at close quarters. An experienced guide knows when to fire and when to hold his ground. Fortunately, help arrived in time.

Poncho's 11-foot, 4-inch bear was the largest of eleven taken at the Cider River Lodge during the last fall season. This is possibly the largest-bodied brown bear that I can remember in over twenty years of guiding on the Alaska Peninsula.

The natural aggression and awesome power of the Alaska brown bear is not to be taken lightly. Though there have been surprisingly few injuries and fatalities to Alaskan bear hunters, the potential always exists. Caution and common sense are the name of the game when you are in heavy brush at close quarters with these animals. Brown bear hunting in Alaska is serious business—and the ultimate Alaskan experience.

RAIN, WIND, WOMAN, AND BEAR

BY

RHONDA OVERMAN

I couldn't believe wind could blow so strongly and steadily. For nearly a week it had not dropped below forty miles per hour, and the sheets of rain carried by the wind hit my face like BBs. My outfitter, Larry Rivers, had been telling me for a couple of years that weather on Alaska Peninsula hunts is usually horrible. Still, I didn't imagine it would be this bad. Somehow, though, it didn't seem to matter. The country was so beautiful and primitive that the wind and rain seemed to be in order.

It was now 8:15 P.M., and my guide, Bob Meals, and I were intent on glassing the mountainside for a very large bear we had spotted the night before. The bear had chased a sow and two cubs up a valley wall, a chase that had ended with a fifteen-minute battle on the skyline. The wind had been blowing rain and snow, often obscuring our view, and the darkness descended so rapidly that there wasn't any time to pursue the beast. We went back to our tents, got a few hours' sleep, and climbed back to our lookout early in the morning.

For a change the weather was exceptionally nice. Since the wind and snow flurries had stopped, we spent the entire day basking in the sun under blue sky. But in spite of the beautiful day, we saw nothing. With evening coming on, we normally would have been back in camp by now, but we remained at our glassing point, hoping the bear would return.

I was scanning the beach and the mountainside for the two-hundredth time when Bob touched my arm. "Rhonda, the big boar is coming down the mountain and headed straight at us! You have got to move quick!" I crawled the few remaining feet to the top of the knob, and as I parted the salt grass at the top, I saw the bear just two hundred yards away, walking slowly toward us. It was unbelievable; the bear was so big, and its color appeared almost red. I was sure this wasn't the bear we had seen the previous night, as that one, I thought, was dark. But this wasn't the time to be wondering. I pushed my .375 into position and rested it across my pack. The bear was already broadside, angling away from my position. It was all happening so fast that there was hardly time to get excited. I placed the cross hairs just ahead of its shoulder and prepared to fire. . . .

I had arrived in camp nine days earlier, the conclusion of over two years' planning that had included delaying the hunt for one year due to unexpected knee surgery.

Now the time for the hunt had arrived, and on 9 May, I had been picked up by Larry and flown to main camp. There I sorted out my gear, and on the following morning I was flown into spike camp. Bob was busy "digging in," placing the tents in protected holes cut in the mountainside. We had been told to expect high winds of sixty to eighty knots in the next few hours, and he had a lot to do to prepare the camp.

We finally got to bed around 10:30 P.M., and I had a fitful first night. The next two days were extremely windy and cold, and though we glassed all day, we saw only a few caribou. The valley we were in was still locked in winter; the snow reached from the valley floor to the rimrock on the skyline. So far the bears were all in their dens, and not even a set of tracks could be found on the mountainside.

The author with the brown bear.

Larry had told us to watch the upper mountainside for freshly opened dens, but no matter how hard we looked, we saw no bear.

On the third day we awoke to snow and more wind, but we still maintained our vigil at the edge of the valley. We were rewarded with the sight of a seven- to eight-foot blond bear chasing caribou and wandering the valley. At one point it came to within three hundred yards of us, and we were a little concerned that it would come into camp. The following two days were uneventful, with the exception of more wind, rain, and cold. The westerly winds, known as the Siberian Express, were blowing off the ice pack, bringing with it unseasonably bad weather. I was sure my toes would never warm up again.

We had been out only a short while on the sixth day when a large white wolf appeared about three hundred yards away. It didn't see us, since it was intent on stalking caribou. At one point the wolf walked to within twenty-five yards of us. It was extremely interesting to watch. The lone wolf worked to within thirty-five yards of the herd, and then made a quick dash. The caribou bolted and quickly outran it, but the wolf stayed behind them until all the caribou had left the valley.

Larry stopped in to check on us on the seventh day, having been kept out of camp until now by the strong winds. He came to us with word that it appeared a bear had been working another valley and wondered if we were interested in moving camp. By now I was ready for a change of scenery, so we packed up camp and moved about twenty miles south to another coastal valley.

We set up camp in a protected hollow behind several large sand dunes and prepared to hunt the following day. The eighth day started the same as the previous days—strong winds, rain, and snow. At 8 A.M. I saw two cubs run right through camp within twenty feet of my tent. They were obviously concerned with something besides us, as they kept looking back over their shoulder. Bob hurried to a vantage point, hoping that a large boar might be chasing them. But it was to no avail, so we settled in for another day of glassing. That evening we again spotted the sow and cubs, and this time they were indeed being followed by a large boar.

Now the large boar was in my sights and I was squeezing the trigger. My shot hit it in the back of the chest cavity. I hadn't led it quite enough, not realizing how fast it was moving. The shot had almost no effect other than to cause the bear to stumble and change direction and speed.

"Keep shooting!" Bob yelled, as the boar broke into a run.

I fired three more rounds from my .375, each of which turned the boar a little but did not stop it. By now it was about 250 yards away. I had one shot remaining in my rifle, but I really did not have time to think about it. I placed the cross hairs just ahead of its shoulder and squeezed. The last shot crashed through its chest. The bear folded

The bear in a full-body mount.

in its tracks, coming to a stop piled in a small mudhole.

I couldn't believe how big the bear actually was! It was so large and blond that it looked like a big mound of tundra. Its head and legs were buried in the mud, and only after extensive pulling and prying were we able to extract it from the mud. And then we took pictures. It was a great conclusion to the hunt, especially considering the weather and the uncertainty involved in any bear hunt. But that is not the end of the story.

The next morning, Larry stopped back in camp and said to Bob, "Did you get the big one that walked by camp?"

"Yes, got him yesterday afternoon and just got him packed back into camp."

"How big was he?" Larry asked.

After we told him and showed him the hide hanging out of Bob's pack, Larry looked up, smiled, and said, "A bigger one just walked down the beach this morning. I crossed his tracks as I walked up from the plane. It looks like he probably just went through a few minutes ago."

We couldn't believe it and hurried down to the beach. Sure enough, there was a set of tracks just a little bigger than my bear's walking down the sand just thirty yards from camp!

"Well, Rhonda," Larry said, "there isn't any reason for you to stay out here. Let's grab your gear and head back to main camp while Bob packs the rest of the gear to the beach. We will make a turn down the way, and perhaps we will be able to catch a glimpse of the fellow that just went past camp."

It took only a couple of minutes for me to grab my pack, sleeping bag, and pad. We bundled the bear hide into the back of the plane, and in a few minutes we were headed down the peninsula. Sure enough, in about two miles we caught up with the bear, an extremely large old boar digging up the mountainside.

We never knew just how big my bear squared, since I had had it skinned out with a dorsal cut for a life-size mount. But the skull measured $28^{3/16}$ inches green, and Larry assured me the hide would've squared well over ten feet. Dinges Taxidermy Studio in Omaha, Nebraska, later confirmed this, for they had to enlarge the largest life-size form they had in order to mount it. Their final estimate of the bear was 10 feet, 8 inches.

It was a great hunt, and, believe it or not, the weather was part of what made it great. I guess my realization that I could enjoy a hunt in such horrible weather made the hunt that much better.

I SURVIVED
A BEAR ATTACK

BY

GARY LAROSE

On 23 October 1996, I was preparing for a brown bear hunt on Kodiak Island with client Quincy Hines. He had hunted with me the previous spring on the Alaska Peninsula, but we had failed to locate his trophy. To utilize his license and tag, we opted for the fall hunt on Kodiak. The weather was clear and cold at night with temperatures warming to forty during the day. I feared a long, cold hunt, as daylight was down to ten hours. I packed in my backpack extra fuel and a small Coleman lantern to help heat the three-man tent. I also threw in a couple of books for those long nights.

We left my father's warm, comfortable lodge by boat for the short run up the bay. We set up a larger tent at the head of the bay to be used as a fallback position in case Kodiak's infamous weather blew us out of the upper drainage. After stashing some of our food and fuel, we were on our way. Four hours later we were setting up camp, and as light faded, we crawled into the tent, knowing daylight wouldn't return for fourteen hours.

After thawing out the water from a fifteen-degree overnight temperature, I served up an oatmeal breakfast that gave us the energy to hike the mountainside to a more advantageous glassing area. It was cold there, so I took a walk around the top of the ridge. I spotted a black-tailed deer in search of a doe or two. As I completed my walk, I noticed Quincy was on his feet coming toward me. I knew right away he had located a bear, and my first thought was that it was too early in the hunt for it to be the right one. After a half hour, the bear reappeared, and I got a good look at it with the spotting scope. Though it looked small, it was very dark, almost black. It had to be an older bear, given its color. The bear certainly deserved a closer look.

Two hours later, Quincy and I were moving through thick alders and salmonberry brush, and we changed direction many times. I figured we had three hundred yards to go when I looked to my left and down to see a bear feeding two hundred yards away. I estimated its size at over eight and a half feet. Quincy said he would take the bear. We watched it feed in the clearing and turn broadside. Quincy made his shots count, and after many pictures and three hours of skinning, we headed back to camp in a full-blown snowstorm.

With the cloud cover and snow, darkness was coming fast, and we pressed on toward camp as decreasing visibility played tricks with my mind. For a while I thought we had passed the tent, and then the ridge the tent was near came into focus and we crossed the small stream from which I had dipped water that morning. We found a white mound in place of the tent, but after some brushing, the tent appeared. We crawled back into the tent for another fourteen hours, knowing the trophy was in the backpack and we would be spending the next night in the warm lodge.

Eight inches of fresh snow greeted us the next morning, but a big brown had come up the trail to within forty feet of the tent and, in the process, had broken a trail for us all the way to the beach. At 7 P.M. we were back at the lodge eating a fine meal, cooked by my father, to celebrate our successful short hunt. The next few days were spent fleshing the hide and cleaning the skull. The hide measured 9 feet, 2 inches, and the skull was nearly 27 inches. Not bad for a one-day hunt.

Four stormy days later, I was ready to get out for some exercise and maybe bag a large Sitka blacktail. My freezer was already full, so my need for meat was minimal; it would have to be a high-scoring buck for me to pull the trigger. With a backpack, an extra coat, and my .300 Winchester Magnum, I headed up the mountain to a notch that acted as a natural pass. My brother-in-law had hunted there over the past few days and had killed several bucks. That area, I felt, would be a good place to start.

As I neared the notch, the wind hit me directly, and chilled me. I stopped to put on my extra coat, for I knew it would only get cooler as I topped out on the mountain. I passed through the notch and turned left, following a trail cut into the hillside. I could see fresh deer tracks, but no other animals had left their signature in the soft dirt. The trail split, one going straight up the ridge and the other cutting to my right. Between the trails at one hundred yards, I saw a group of magpies in the alders, an indication of a possible deer kill. The wind was blowing through the area, and if there was a bear working the site, it would certainly catch my scent and be gone. With two hundred yards through a series of alder patches to the next open area, I knew that a few standard precautions were in order. I took the .300 off my shoulder and chambered a round. With safety on, I carried the rifle so that it would be more readily available.

I proceeded through the first alder patch to one that was denser, which I tried to go around. Denied my preferred route by the infamous Kodiak salmonberry brush, I continued through the alder patch reluctantly. As I neared the far side, I heard at thirty yards the breaking brush. A medium-size bear was bounding through the tall grass at an angle, at which it appeared to be passing me at ten yards. I fired a warning shot when it was at twenty yards, and over the next few seconds I couldn't see it. When I did, I realized my first assumption about the bear passing by me was dead wrong. It had turned sixty degrees and was coming straight at me at a full run. Not really thinking, I fired the .300 magnum and worked the bolt for the next shot, but the bear was on me before I had the round chambered.

It hit me at full speed, spinning me and knocking me back ten feet. When I came to, I was lying on my side with the bear three to four feet in front of me. My jaw had been shattered, and the skin on my left cheek and right jaw was ripped open. My first thought was utter disbelief. *How the hell could this be happening to me?*

The bear growled and woofed as it bounded back and forth like a boxer waiting for the next opening. As it came toward me, I backhanded it in defiance and my arm went in its mouth. The bear bit my tricep off at the elbow and backed away. One thing was very clear—this bear could take me apart at will. It had bitten me only twice, but the results were devastating. If it continued at this rate, there wouldn't be enough of me left to put back together, let alone get off this mountain. Playing dead was the only option. *Do it now, or be it later,* was a very clear thought.

I rolled facedown, my backpack protecting me somewhat. The bear immediately went for my sides and shoulders, biting me four times. I didn't try to fight. The pain wasn't severe, and I knew the bear wasn't hurting me too bad. I felt it pulling and tearing at my backpack and heard the aluminum break as my waist belt was torn loose. My back protection was gone. The bruin bit me in the center of my back, somehow getting all four canine teeth through three layers of clothing. Then it was gone, leaving in the same direction it had come.

As I lay facedown, I feared it was waiting to charge if I dared to move. I tried to slow my breathing to appear more dead, but this was too painful. After two minutes of waiting, it was time to move. My rifle lay under me, pointing toward the bear's departure direction. I closed the bolt, pushing the last round into the chamber. I hesitated briefly, waiting for the worst. Nothing happened. I raised myself up on my left elbow and then onto my knees. I grabbed the rifle and turned to meet the charging bear. But there was nothing. It had gone as quickly as it had appeared.

But it might come back, and I certainly didn't want to be there if it did. The area was littered with the shreds of the two coats and the shirt I had worn. In the middle of the mess was my LaRose Guide Service hat. I picked it up and quickly left the area.

Moving in the opposite direction of the bear and away from my father's lodge, I headed toward the salt water, where an outfitter was based. My legs were performing well, although a little shaky. I knew if I kept moving and stayed focused, I could cover the mile to the beach in an hour. As I picked my way down the hillside and through the drainage guts that mar the Kodiak terrain, I soon learned that short deliberate steps kept my broken jaw from shaking, though a couple of times, when I took long steps, my jaw actually rattled. The bleeding from my face had slowed. Indeed, I never was concerned with bleeding to death, though one of my doctors said it was a wonder I hadn't.

As I approached the Hidden Basin Outfitters Lodge, I saw a man on the dock. One of my worst fears had been that no one would be there, and relief swept over me. He asked me several questions as I closed the last feet to the dock, but I couldn't respond because of my jaw. He finally saw the blood and figured out what had torn me up. He got on the radio and contacted a friend across the bay who had a more powerful radio, and soon the Coast Guard was on its way. My rescuer took me upstairs to be near a stove. I was warm from my hike, but I soon was chilled to the bone, and my rescuer wrapped me in a blanket. I warmed up, but the pain was starting to hit hard, making it very difficult to find any comfort.

After one hour, I heard the beat of rotors as a helicopter passed over the ridge and bay, and within thirty minutes I was headed for Kodiak Hospital. While there, they cleaned up my back wounds and arm, but left my face for an Anchorage specialist. At 11 P.M. I was aboard a Medivac flight to Anchorage. Gary and Kathy King met me as I was rolled into the emergency room. Later, Gary painted a haunting picture of the way I looked. Ten hours of surgery in three separate operations put me back to a close resemblance of my old self. It took the bear less than eighty seconds to do the damage—a grim reminder of its sheer power.

* * * * * *

I wish I had all the answers, but I don't. When it comes to bears, or any big game, no one knows everything, and nobody does it right every time. I certainly made some major mistakes that day, which I have difficulty accepting.

Like all Alaskan fishing and hunting guides, I have spent a lot of time around bears. Many times while fishing, I have seen bears, but the encounters were brief. At most, a shot fired in the air and they were gone, off to a more private fishing hole with no human presence. At this time of year there is no competition for food, which makes it easy for man to prevail. Bears are used to social interaction while on salmon streams, and, whether it be other bears or humans, there is a level of tolerance. Sows with cubs, however, are a dangerous combination at any time. I generally stay away from fishing areas when they are present. And since the availability of salmon diminishes as summer gives way to fall, the competition for food becomes greater in fall and bears' tolerance for man decreases.

Most guides would hesitate to kill a bear while in defense of life or property, hoping for a simpler way out of a bad situation. The more you are around bears, the less you tend to take them seriously. When fishing clients asked me what to do if a bear approached, I usually told them to ignore it and it would probably go away. That would not be my answer today. On 1 November 1996, I received new insight into bear conduct. I'm not going to be so sure of my predictions and take the chance of being wrong. The bear that attacked me had my scent from the moment I saw it. It knew what it was going to do if given the opportunity. My passive judgment gave it that opportunity.

I love to guide, but when the client goes home, it is time for me to go hunting on my own. I enjoy these hunts, if only for the lack of pressure and responsibility. I enjoy just being out there and coming home with nothing. It was in that state of mind that I left the lodge on 1 November. My attitude was a little too casual.

I was traveling in the "white zone"—a state that prepares you for nothing, so when you need to make split-second decisions, you are not able to. The "yellow zone" is when you are totally aware of your surroundings. You are prepared for danger, and you judge and react to the danger in a timely manner. There is also the "red zone," when you are running on adrenaline and reacting without much thought. I went from the white zone to the red zone. In the future when in bear country, I will travel in the yellow zone.

I hope no innocent bear dies because of my experience with that one juvenile. I know that given the chance I will give bears a little more room. There is one statement about bears that always holds true: They are unpredictable and they are incomprehensibly fast. If you have a bear running in your general direction, shoot while it is still far enough away so that you can plan your shots properly. If you wait until you fear for your life, it is already too late.

In closing, I would like to thank my clients and friends from all over the world who sent cards and called with wishes for my speedy recovery. APHA members outdid themselves as they auctioned my bear-torn shirt at our annual convention and then passed the hat for contributions toward my insurance deductible. A humble thanks for your gracious giving.

BEAR HUNT WITH LITTLE RED AND ROBIN HOOD

BY
GUS LAMOUREUX

"You've got one of those?" area biologist Roger Smith remarked when I mentioned I had an archery client coming to Alaska for Kodiak brown bear. After completing the necessary paperwork, Smith bade me good-bye, and then added emphatically, "Good luck!"

Spring had arrived early in Anchorage, with unseasonably warm temperatures. As the snow disappeared, I rushed to finish collecting the necessary supplies to begin my spring hunting season on Kodiak Island. I was especially eager to begin this season because I was faced with a new challenge. One of my clients, a doctor from Montana, wanted to take a Kodiak bear with a compound bow. I had met Dr. Lloyd Garrels and his wife Joyce in Reno, Nevada, during the Safari Club International Convention, where we discussed the many challenges of such a proposition. Being a bow hunter myself, I was well aware of the difficulties inherent in taking a Kodiak bear with a bow.

On 27 April, my wife and I boarded a jet for Kodiak Island. It was raining when we arrived, just as it has every spring season for the last fifteen years in that area. We quickly collected our gear, rented a car for our chores in town, and checked in with our air taxi. Later, we drove into Kodiak to pick up our clients' brown bear permits from the Department of Fish and Game. Delayed by bad weather and late freight, we didn't arrive at the camp on Kaiugnak Bay, located on the south end of the island, until late afternoon. The lagoon where we landed was about five hundred yards from our cabin site.

After two days of packing gear and making repairs to the cabin, we were ready for the arrival of our spring clients. The wind was blowing strongly up the bay, and it wasn't until 7:30 P.M. that my wife and I heard the drone of a plane. The wind and waves had quit a couple hours earlier, and PenAir was able to bring in one guide and a pile of gear. The rest of the folks and gear followed in another plane. After supper we took care of all the necessary paperwork, checked out our weapons, chatted, and then slipped off to bed.

After morning breakfast, Lloyd, Joyce, and I were on our way across the bay in our 18-foot Bayrunner to scout from one of our lookout points. I quickly spotted our first bear directly across the valley, but it was much too small. Joyce later

Lloyd holding up two sporting halibut, weighing in the neighborhood of forty pounds each.

spotted one far up a snowy valley, but again it was not worth bothering with. Toward evening, she spotted still another one that also proved to be too small. By that time, I understood why Lloyd had brought his wife along—since she always had her binoculars up and ready, she was damn good at spotting game!

When we got back to camp that evening, I was met by my assistant guide Gary Keen, who reported that they had taken a nice 9½-foot bear on the beach a couple of hours into their hunt. A short celebration ensued that evening after supper.

The following morning, everyone was up and eager to get on with hunting, spurred on by the quick success of Keen's group. Joyce came out looking her usual self: red muffler and makeup (Lloyd had to carry her makeup kit in the field every day). Everyone in camp began calling her "Little Red."

After breakfast, we went across to Seal Bay and glassed from our usual spot, and then we hiked to the back of the valley where a large lake is located. Many big bear cross this area, but after trekking for an hour, we reached the top without seeing any. On the trip back to camp that evening, we stopped and caught two forty-pound halibut.

It looked like rain on the third day of our hunt, and everyone was reluctant to go out. Lloyd, Joyce, and I were willing to brave it, however, and I picked a spot to glass from just across the bay. It took only minutes to get there, which was good in case the weather turned serious and forced us back to camp. We had no sooner got there when I spotted a bear, a small one, directly across from us. Joyce then spotted another bruin that we determined to be in the nine-foot category. I suggested we take a closer look. Five hundred feet lower and across the valley floor we spotted the bear entering a large patch of brush. Since it was spring, the barren bushes made it fairly easy to follow the bear.

We discussed strategy. The bear was heading to our left, so the bottom of a talus appeared the most likely spot for an ambush. While we strategized, the bear bedded down and we lost its exact whereabouts. We knew it was still in the brush, so, leaving Joyce at the bottom of the hill as a spotter, Lloyd and I picked our way up the rocks. It started to rain heavily, and, to make matters worse, Lloyd and I could find no sign of the bear.

Archery hunter Lloyd Garrels of Anaconda, Montana. Garrels made a beautiful lung shot from twelve yards. The Kodiak brown measured 9½ square feet.

By 6:35 I decided enough was enough, and we headed down the hill to pick up our gear and head in for the day. When we had reached Joyce and exchanged chuckles about Little Red looking pretty wet, I looked up the hill one more time and spotted a bear, but it was the small one we had seen in the early morning. Seconds later, we were surprised to see the bear we'd been searching for all day pop out of the bushes.

Time for quick action! Lloyd weighed the possibility of taking the beast with a rifle, but at my urging he got hold of himself and joined me in a mad scramble up the rocks to intercept the quarry. There was now bounce in our steps. Once in position, a glance at Joyce confirmed that the beast was heading our way; her hand signals were coming so fast it made her look like a Dallas Cowgirl cheerleader. The bulky bruin passed directly beneath us, a scant eight yards away. Lloyd's bow looked pitiful next to the huge animal. Seconds later, the hair on my neck stood up when the bear turned and came straight at us!

Lloyd and Joyce sharing a happy moment together with Lloyd's bear.

Lloyd drew back his Hoyt overdraw compound and let fly a small composite arrow with a 100-grain, cam-lock Wasp broadhead. The bear spotted us just as the arrow flew. Fortunately, the arrow hit home and the big brownie roared, quickly retreating into the brush. Some fifty yards into the brush, it lay down and died.

We photographed and skinned the bear and assessed the broadhead's damage. It had gone through the back of the front leg, passed through both lungs, and lodged against the bone of the other front leg. We wasted little time getting our packs loaded and headed quickly toward the warmth and dryness of the cabin. Our Gore-Tex gear had long since soaked through, and the rain was unrelenting on the walk home. At one point, I slipped on a log and landed on my ribs, cracking two.

With darkness fast approaching, Joyce and I got into a small tiff over the location of the gametrail out of the valley.

"This is the trail," Joyce claimed.

"No, that is not the trail," I replied.

"The one we came down on is more to the right."

Joyce, being a feisty lady, stood on her toes to put her face close to mine and shrieked, "Do ya wanna fight about it?"

I laughed but was too tired to argue and started up her trail. We returned shortly thereafter to proceed on *my* trail!

Due to the weather and the fact that it was nearing midnight, assistant guides Gary and Dan had begun to worry and had gone out searching for us. We bumped into them at the bottom of the valley, and they were kind enough to relieve me of the bear hide and pack it up the hill. The following days were spent in hide care, getting plenty of rest, and doing a little seafood gathering, but that's another story. Lloyd's bear measured 9½ feet square, and he later told me that it scored No. 8 in Pope and Young. That was one hunt neither of us will ever forget.

SERGEANT ROCK

BY
GARTH LARSEN

I know I'm in trouble when at daylight (3:45 A.M. in May) my client—a 6-foot, 3-inch, 160-pound former marine—springs up in his bed and says, "Gee, it's great to be alive and in the corps!" *Oh God,* I groan, as rain spatters the tent. I try to return to my dream. Sailing in the Bahamas, cold Heineken in hand with mermaids splashing around my boat . . . *zzzzz* . . .

"Hey, big guide, which mountain are we gonna assault today?"

"Uh? Hey man, you don't holler at the guide! And this isn't a safari; you don't walk around while bear hunting," and then I mumble, "you sit and look."

This usually lines out most overly zealous hunters, but not "Sergeant Rock." He takes it as a challenge and launches into a dissertation on how he ran his drill sergeant into the ground on a thirty-mile march. Meanwhile, he cooks us one cup of tea and one package of instant oats, packing his share in the four-by-eight-inch vest pocket of his ten-pound wool Mackinaw rain gear and sleeping bag combo. *What the heck, this guy wants to kill something,* I think.

I am mulling this over and working on my third cup of coffee when Rock passes by the opening of my tent. He is on his third lap up and down our mile or so of beach. Outside the tent, as I stuff thermos, scope, and my six-pound lunch in my pack, I notice the unique assortment of glass balls, rope, and five-gallon cans scavenged from the beach and piled around our tent. The rain hisses as it hits Rock's combat boots, hot from his six miles of beachcombing.

We wander our way up the valley to a good point on a low ridge. There we gaze at the grassy bear trails, the blue ocean on both sides of the peninsula, and the peaks dusted with snow, and listen to the squawk of gulls and seabirds. A beautiful spring day in the Aleutians, and Rock, I think, senses the uniqueness of the spot.

After eight and half minutes of glassing, Rock is ready to roll. "Hey, what's behind that hill?" he asks. "Is that the ocean over there? What's on top of that mountain?" Afflicted with a touch of spring fever myself, and having a difficult time doing what the big guns taught me—*sit and look, and don't walk around and stink up the place*—we throw caution to the wind, take the bit in our teeth, and boogie (as Terry Overly would say) down the trail.

Over the first five days (never mind the weather), we walk twice from the Bering to the Pacific, and we investigate the old village of Morshovi, where we watch a friend of mine repair his gear for the coming red salmon season on the Ikatan Peninsula. We see False Pass from five different peaks, walk no less than ten miles a day, and commonly do 5,000-foot verticals in a day. We leave the valley smokin' with our tracks. By the time our outfitter, Larry Rivers ("Sky Chief"), drops in to check on us, I am ready to cut my hair, enlist in the marines, and go to Nicaragua, or wherever it is happening. (This dude is infectious.) Instead, I get scowled at, lectured to, and flown out of our playground to the base of a big peak, where Rock and I immediately bemoan the fact that we have no axes, ropes, or crampons—not to mention skis!

Rock's home is at the base of Mount Saint Helens, and before the mountain blew, he climbed it three times a week. Now he just runs, eats health food, does yoga, drives his Mercedes fast, and sells plywood to anyone who'll buy it.

Rock and I cook indoors for two days because of the seventy-knot windstorm. During that time we play war games, trench our tent, eat too much, and get tired of each other's lies and idiosyncrasies. Rock babbles in his sleep about companies and assaults, and wakes me each day with, "Gee, it's great to be alive and in the corps!" And me . . . moaning about various women who took the money and ran. To appease our broken lives, we are ready for some mindless fun and hunting.

Finally, the weather gets better and we go out to hunt, and we soon see a bear at the head of a fork in the valley. Off with the rain gear and on with the charge! Crazed by our inactivity, we do a twenty-miler in ten hours, with a 3,500-foot vertical thrown in to check out a six-and-a-half-foot three-year-old. The next day we do a repeat performance on the other side of the valley in less than ten hours. This is like training for the Iditarod and living on jerky and seal meat. The next day my Christian sense of duty catches up with me. Guilt-ridden about stinking up another valley and invoking the wrath of my employer, we hide behind a rock, out of the wind and with a good view of the entire valley.

Peering through our "sport views," we try to see bears among the various tussocks and rocks until our eyes twitch and water. We then begin eating snack packs, pudding, and tuna out of boredom. We fall asleep in the afternoon sun and are wracked by nightmares of being overweight in an old folks' home in Pensacola.

That evening back at Camp Foxtail, as the alpenglow lights the upper ice falls of our peak, we discuss whether or not we should burn all the camp gear and food, save the pilot bread and Hefty garbage bags, and sleep on a mountaintop—or, as ol' Ray McNutt would say, as he searched the black spruce bogs for his horses, "Get lean in the belly and hungry in the eye." Then, what do we see but Ol' Billy Bear kickin' the snow from his hole some one thousand feet up the south flank of our adversary, the mountain. Throwing our gear together, we are on the offense by 7:30 P.M., reasoning that the day's inactivity was part of a master plan to save us for our night mission.

Two hours later, we are positioned two hundred yards away on the same lateral plane as the bear. But Mr. Bear is nowhere to be seen, and we are soon discussing what the enemy will do if fired upon near his encampment. I contend he will run for cover, seeking the security of his den. But Mr. Commando views bears with the discerning eye of an urban guerrilla and contends that when those little pig eyes see us, he'll come directly at us!

I'm trying to convince Rock of his insanity, instructing him not to shoot until I can judge the bear and he is at least fifty to seventy-five yards from his engagement. Meanwhile, Rock is setting up on his rest and peering through the semifogged, two-power Weaver scope on his J. C. Penney 7mm mag loaded with "Herter's Deluxe" ammo. Then, who should appear but Mr. Bear, groggily wandering about his hole, sniffing the air for signs of spring, fish, or a new love. I'm eyeballing the bear through the spotting scope, and I tell Rock that the bear's not rubbed and looks to be about nine feet. Then all of a sudden *crack . . . wwwzzz . . . thwack!*

Rock lets off a round! Mr. Bear swaps ends and is gone before Rock can work the bolt. I'm speechless for a hundredth of a second, and then I give him my rendition of a drill instructor's welcoming and storm off toward ground zero. One hundred fifty yards from the bear's den I jack in a shell and tell "Trigger-Happy" to do the same. We then advance on the enemy, getting all the excitement I can take at $100 a day.

As we approach ground zero, the law of karma dictates. I place Rock on the low side of the hole. We holler and jive around, and I fire a couple of rounds into the hole, trying to entice an eight-hundred-pound bear to take on "macho man." Fortunately, he doesn't take us up on it and I regain my senses, realizing 2,000 feet up a 30-degree snowfield near a bear pumped with adrenaline is no place for us to be. With the calm assurance of a seasoned big-game guide, I say, "We'll let him sleep on it and come back tomorrow."

The walk back to Camp Foxtail is a quiet one, followed by a quiet dinner and an introspective short night. The next morning, we begin our assault with a ten-foot alder and, Marlin Grasser's favorite weapon, a short-handled spade. Back at the scene of the crime, all is quiet. As we ponder our next move, the Super Cub lands at camp. Sky Chief dismounts, stretches his back over a tire, and walks to camp. I relish the next few minutes as I watch him ponder the note written with a bullet on a paper plate: "Gone to dig a bear out of his hole on south flank of mountain." I'm sure Sky Chief thought he had a couple of live ones and was contemplating insurance premiums and next of kin. He flies off in his Super Cub to look for us. But you can never find anything from the air when you want to. That's Murphy's Law 100.

Shining my flashlight down the hole does not illuminate the situation, so we decide to poke a ten-foot alder through the snow and into the den. I watch the alder penetrate the den's entrance, and Rock moves the alder slowly down the hole. Bingo! We hit something soft. We punch it a couple of times and it doesn't move.

I don my rain gear and a .357 and assume the fetal position for entry into the war zone. About halfway down the hole, I realize it would probably break my eardrums to shoot the .357 in there. Then I lose my footing and . . . *ziiipp!* Mr. Ruger and I go streaking down the hole and come to an abrupt stop against the brown bear. Oddly, I have no sensation of fear. My days of downhill racing, my belief that God protects the innocent, and my acceptance of Murphy's Law 101—"If you're gonna be dumb, you gotta be tough"—give me a peace that passes understanding.

Being an amateur naturalist, I am intrigued by my surroundings. It is not a small, dingy hole but a small, cathedral-like snow dome, with one side bare mountainside and the rest all snow. Ten big bears could fit in this den. I holler for Rock, and soon we both are left staring at the power of the 7mm magnum and wondering why we are so fortunate.

Skinning a bear in its own home is a bit unnerving, and because of the cool temperature and our claustrophobic feeling, we do it quickly. I take a break to look around and then crawl up the tunnel, which is about three and a half feet in diameter, fifteen feet long, and angled at 30 degrees. Unknown to me at the time, on a far ridge a guide and client watch snow come out of the bear hole. The guide, ol' Don, perks up and says to his hunter, "We got bear, Duane."

I pop out. A bear in rain gear? Don's ego is damaged beyond recovery. His relationship with his client has been strained already due to his food preparation—breakfasts of dry oatmeal cereal with a package of dry Dream Whip, instant coffee, sandwiches for lunch, and maybe cold Spam or some other mystery meat for dinner. Don tells his clients, "I'm here to hunt, not cook."

Meanwhile, I'm back down the hole skinning away, but on my next trip up I see a three-year-old bear chuggin' up the slope eight hundred yards below! I practice some disco moves and talk in tongues to convince Junior to change his route. Junior finally moves off to a position about six hundred yards above us. Then and there, I decide to post Rock as a sentry around the war zone while I finish removing Mr. Bear's jacket. Rock and I then drag the hide up the hole for the last time, and I stuff what I can of the bear in my pack and head for camp.

By now, Rock has regained his old stature and is visibly puffed up over his one-shot kill. He double-times it to camp to prove his physical superiority. All I can do is watch him as I stumble along, burdened with ninety pounds of bear hide on my back. The remaining two miles from the mountain to Camp Foxtail is a series of rotten snow gullies and rocky ridges. My weight, plus the weight of the bear hide, causes me to break right through our old tracks. I am up to my armpits in snow and rocks, anchored by my "hideous burden," as Edgar Allen Poe would say. For twenty minutes I ponder my situation and wonder what Rock is up to, when finally he appears like some demigod on the ridge above me. He at last has me where he wants me. He glows as he helps dislodge me, and I have to admit that they don't make men like him anymore.

It was a wonderful hunt. Rock had a 9-foot, 6-inch brownie, and I had a plane ticket to Anchorage to see a chiropractor.

A DEER HUNTER'S EDEN

BY
LONNIE L. RITCHEY

We waited five days, listening for the drone of engines. Every day had been a problem of being either too cold or too windy or both. Not the type of conditions to fly in. For the last three days, the temperature had been holding steady at 8 degrees below zero. We were trying to fly out of a small bay on the southwest corner of Kodiak Island. My father and I had been hunting Kodiak's famous Sitka black-tailed deer. We had to fly out on Saturday, but bad weather had kept us cooped up inside the small cabin we had called home for the past two weeks. It was late November, and the cold front that had hit was the worst in many decades. In fact, it was the coldest winter on record throughout most of Alaska, but that did not affect the deer hunting.

I had heard tales about Kodiak's Sitka black-tailed deer, but I thought they were just hunting stories. I was told when I booked the hunt with my good friend and outfitter Gus Lamoureux that collecting a trophy deer would be no problem.

Until recently, Kodiak Island has been associated mainly with monster brown bears, but now people are beginning to know it for the record-book deer taken there each year. In fact, many quality deer there are "beach" deer, stalked as they feed on seaweed that washes up along the shore. And with a five-deer-per-person limit, one can take a nice buck and be picky later. Success is virtually guaranteed.

We had arrived in Kodiak on Sunday, hoping to fly into camp via Peninsula Air that same day. Unfortunately, because of our flight's late arrival, we were short on daylight and had to spend the evening in the town of Kodiak. We were at the airport early Monday morning, waiting for our charter to fly us in. To me, the flight into camp is one of the high points of any hunt, for it gives you the chance to look over new country for the first time, your face plastered to the glass like a kid in a candy store.

After we touched down and unloaded our gear, we quickly made plans for the hunt. My father's legs were not in the best of shape after two knee surgeries, so I wanted him to take the first two good bucks we saw. We had bought two tags each, hoping we could better our first deer with our second.

The next morning, I awoke early and waited for dawn, which in late November on Kodiak is not until about 9 A.M. To get to Kodiak Island requires transportation by boat, and most outfitters use aluminum skiffs by Zodiac. After sunup, we went out in a 16-foot Zodiac, hoping to get a beach buck. Gus pulled us into a small cove that he has always had luck in, and it did not take long for us to locate deer. After a short climb of a few hundred yards, we had gotten to within thirty yards of three Sitka blacktails—one doe, one spike, and a nice four-by-five. Two quick shots and my dad had his first blacktail. I have hunted many places with my father, but I have never seen him so happy after making a kill.

The second day was a repeat of the first. After we went up the shoreline to another cove, we saw a buck feeding along the beach. It was a cold morning, with ice forming along the edges of the bay. As we made our way to shore—the ice breaking across the bow of the skiff—the deer slowly walked up the hillside. We hustled out of the skiff and my dad settled down for the shot. The .270 cracked, and my dad had his second four-by-four in as many days.

After looking over the deer my dad had taken, I was concerned that I would not get one quite as big. Sitka blacktails are not big-horned or big-bodied; they are stocky, weighing in at 130 to 150 pounds. Their racks are similar to a mule deer's but smaller. On Kodiak, a good deer is a four-by-four (I am counting brow tines) with a sixteen-inch spread. A five-by-five is a super deer but not very common. The most common figuration is a three-by-three with little or no brow tines. In fact, many of the deer do not have brow tines, just short little bumps too small to count as a point. Kodiak Island is loaded with deer, but you must look over a lot of them to locate one with a four-by-four rack.

The author with a trophy Sitka blacktail on a beautiful day on Kodiak Island. 13 November 1988.

One very important piece of equipment to bring along is a quality spotting scope. The blacktail's antlers are not as tall as a mule deer's, and with a lot of open range, it is easier to choose a good vantage point and look the deer over instead of running up and down the hillsides. I have also noticed that the color of their horns blends with the vegetation. Without a good scope, it is easy to miss a point or two.

While the morning was still young, we left my dad on a small knoll overlooking a large meadow as Gus and I went searching for my deer. That day we spotted at least thirty deer, but we were not able to find a keeper we could approach. We did spot a buck that was high- and heavy-horned, but it somehow eluded us. When we returned to get my father, we discovered that he had shot a big hybrid fox with red and gray highlights, another bonus of hunting Kodiak.

At breakfast the following morning, it was decided that Gus and I would go back to the same valley where we had seen the large buck the day before. There were deer everywhere, on every hillside and in every ravine. Near the hill from which we had spotted the day before, we located two bucks that deserved a better look. One stood out from the others considerably. Its coat had a reddish tint, and its antlers were heavy. Even with the spotting scope, we were not close enough to count the points, but just by size alone we could tell it was a quality deer.

The deer was feeding its way away from us to a plateau near the snow line. We quickly sidehilled the mountain in an attempt to reach the top before it did. As usual, Gus, with his long gait, beat me to the top. The last fifty feet proved the steepest, and I needed to use my hands as well as my feet. When I crested the plateau, there was a nice four-by-four fifty yards away. I raised my .270 and was still trying to catch my breath when an even bigger deer stepped into view. I did not even count the points. It was just one of those deer you know is a keeper at first glance. When the rifle cracked the deer ran from view, but it did not go far. Gus reached it first, a solid five-by-five with heavy bases and a dark-red coat. This was the big boy we had spotted earlier, the biggest Sitka deer I have ever seen!

As we took pictures, I had time to enjoy the scenery in one of the most beautiful places I have ever visited. Above us were snow-covered peaks, rugged and steep; below us were yellow sloping hills reaching to the ocean. Even as we cleaned the deer we could see other bucks within rifle range. The four-by-four Gus and I had hunted stood unafraid, feeding within two hundred yards of its fallen companion.

Gus and I quartered the deer in order to pack it out, but since it was only noon, we decided to eat lunch before we made our long trip back down to the skiff. As we munched, we watched deer crisscross the hill above us. There must have been at least three or four bucks within a few hundred yards. It seemed like a fantasy. To see so many deer so near was difficult to believe.

After we had eaten, I wanted to take more pictures, so we walked closer to the deer, leaving our packs behind. Kodiak has a large population of bears, so you always want to take your rifle with you. I am glad I did. One of the bucks I saw was bigger than I had first thought. We observed it for five minutes before I decided to fill my second tag.

The buck was following a doe in heat and traversing the hillside above us. The first shot hit square in the shoulder, and the buck headed down the hill. It took a second shot to put it down for keeps. This deer was a duplicate of my first without brow tines, which were too short to count. Nevertheless, it was a good four-by-four Sitka blacktail.

We quartered the deer and loaded our pack frames with one buck each. It was an exhausting descent to the boat, but the thrill of seeing so many deer in such a short period of time made me forget about my fatigue until we finally reached the boat, where I collapsed in a heap.

My dad and I spent the next two days hunting ducks and fishing for some of Alaska's legendary halibut. We did not have any luck fishing, but the duck hunting was fantastic—the best I have experienced anywhere. A hunter could easily go through four or five boxes of ammo a day.

Saturday arrived and it was time to leave. But Mother Nature had other ideas. The weather turned sour, with winds gusting up to sixty miles per hour, making it unsafe to fly. We stayed five days longer than planned, waiting for the plane to pick us up. But somehow it didn't matter how long we waited. We spent our time relaxing, enjoying fresh crab caught daily or clams that we dug up along the beach. My father and I actually gained weight, which is rare on a hunt.

In just two hours I had filled both my tags on good bucks and could have legally taken three more. My dad took the two beach bucks by not traveling more than half a mile from the boat. It just goes to show you the quality of deer hunting on Kodiak.

If you have been looking for the perfect deer hunt—one that is affordable, has some of the most beautiful scenery in the world, has a 100-percent-guaranteed success rate and the opportunity for a "book" deer—Kodiak is the place to be. It is a deer hunter's Garden of Eden; the only difference is that rather than being cast out of the garden you can return to it every year. But don't tell anyone. Let's keep it our little secret!

SPORT AND ADVENTURE ON UNIMAK ISLAND

BY
JIM SHOCKEY

"Honey? Are you still there? Listen, Pumpkin, I'm afraid I have to run. And I do mean run. Remember that pretty volcano called Pavlof, the one I told you about yesterday when I phoned? Well, it's erupting. Uh-huh, yep, I'm sure boiling to death in lava would hurt. Wish you were here. Love ya. Gotta go."

I was calling home from Cold Bay, Alaska, located on the very tip of the Alaska Peninsula. And the volcano really was erupting. When I ran outside after hanging up the phone, the first person I bumped into was my brown bear guide, Rod Schuh, co-owner of R&R Guide Service. "Blows up all the time," said Rod casually. "Don't worry about Pavlof; it's Shishaldin you have to watch. Pavlof smokes all the time, but we still camp right beside it."

Beside a volcano? Rod had mentioned something about volcanoes when I met him at a hunting show a year earlier, but I didn't think he meant real volcanoes. Not that I would have changed anything. I wanted to hunt giant brown bears with my Knight muzzleloader, and if that meant camping on the smoking rim of Dante's inferno, so be it.

Cold Bay might qualify as a town, but I'd call it more a gathering of people who don't like to live around a lot of other folks. Rod and his partner, Rob Jones, run one of only two outfits authorized to conduct guided brown bear hunts from Cold Bay to Unimak Island. Unimak sits squarely on what is referred to as the Ring of Fire—a circle of active volcanoes that rims the Pacific Ocean—and the island is within the boundaries of the Izembeck National Wildlife Refuge.

Unimak deserves more recognition. It arguably contains one of the densest populations of coastal brown bears in the whole state of Alaska. I was lucky enough to experience that large population

The author stands on Unimak Island with Pavlof Volcano in the background.

firsthand during fall 1996. I was one of fifteen hunters drawn for the annual limited-entry brown bear hunt on Unimak. Every year, eight hunters are chosen for the fall hunt (and seven are chosen for the spring hunt). I was chosen because I happened to hook up with the boys from R&R. If I had not met them, I would not have applied for the hunt in the first place. Rod and Rob walked me through the permit application and drawing process.

I instantly liked Rod and Rob when I met them at their show booth at a convention. In the R&R brochure I picked up, it said, "Where hunting and adventure are one and the same." After hunting with Rod and Rob, I'll say amen to that.

My adventure began in mid-October with a flight to Cold Bay from Anchorage on Reeve Aleutian Airlines. When the jet landed, I was met by Rod and Rob, along with Beaufort force 8 winds that kept us from flying to Unimak for two days. Good thing, too, since I got to see Pavlof erupt, an adventure in itself.

When the weather cleared, we flew to Unimak in one of R&R's Super Cubs. That's when I saw my first Alaska brown bear. It stood on its hind legs as we passed high overhead, and it looked impressive. Rod, piloting the Super Cub, told me it wasn't much over eight feet, way too small to bother hunting, even though I was shooting a muzzleloader. Before Rod put the plane down on the black silica sand beach, I'd counted three more bears.

"There isn't a single tree on the Unimak! There's hardly any alder brush either," I said in amazement, as Rod and I screwed in the sand anchors that would hold the airplane in place while we hunted. "You can see for miles!"

"Exactly," said Rod. "That's one of the reasons it's such a great place to hunt."

"What's the other reason?"

Rod nodded his head toward the ocean. "Check out the beach."

I did and, quite frankly, got a little scared. There were bear tracks everywhere—big ones, little ones, old ones, and new ones. Some were gigantic. Unimak was obviously a place where you needed to spend a lot of time looking over your shoulder.

"The bears roam the beaches searching for washed-up whale carcasses," Rod explained later. "But we're not staying by the beach; we're going to backpack a few miles inland, set up camp, and glass the grass flats and salmon streams."

And that's exactly what we did for the next fifteen days, and each day we saw at least five brown bears. Most days we saw nine to ten bears, and there were three days when we counted thirteen of them. Bears were everywhere, including right in our camp.

Wooofff!

"Hey Jim? Did you hear that?" Rod whispered.

Woooooooooffffff!

"Dang!" said Rod, grabbing his rifle and head lamp.

Snooorrt!

"Don't move, Jim, he's right beside the tent."

Wooofff!

"Hey, get out of here!" Rod yelled, slapping the tent wall. Silence.

"Jim, he's gone. Jim?" Rod jabbed me with his finger.

"Huh?" I sat up and rubbed the sleep from my eyes. "What's up?"

"There was a bear right outside the tent!"

"Huh? What was that about the right way to make cement?"

I had slept through the adventure, but not because I have nerves of steel. Rod snored, so every night I shoved big balls of wet toilet paper in my ears. I also pulled the earflaps on my hat down and tied my long underwear around the whole affair. I looked like I had a toothache, but I slept like a baby.

Besides bears in camp and volcanoes, there were weather adventures. Like the night and day we were blasted by the williwahs. Rob and the R&R video cameraman, John, joined Rod and me halfway through my hunt to resupply us and take some video footage. We were all stuffed into the small tent that Rod and I had been sharing when Rob cocked his head. "Hang on to your hats," he warned as he crouched in the cramped tent. "Beware the williwah!" A roaring from the nearby volcano grew louder and louder, and then . . . *Wham!* The tent nearly turned inside out. With us in it!

A williwah, I very quickly learned, is a meteorological mutation, an airborne aberration, a one-hundred-yard-wide landslide of cold air that comes roaring down a mountaintop at

Rod Schuh, the author's guide and outfitter, glasses the flats for giant brown bear.

speeds up to one hundred miles an hour. It's a wild thing to hear and even wilder to experience. All that night I cowered in my sleeping bag, listening to williwahs roaring down the side of Isanotski, the closest snowcapped volcano. Most missed us, thank God, but when they hit broadside, even though our tent was hunkered down deep in an alder patch, it was like getting hit by a giant sledgehammer. The instant change in pressure literally took our breath away.

At least we could hunt in the williwahs, since they came and went quickly, flattening everything in their way for only a few minutes on their way to the ocean. Not so when we were hit, for three days straight, by Beaufort force 11 winds. We're talking sustained winds of seventy miles an hour and forty-foot waves that make the ocean look like a white frothing maelstrom. I'd say the wind drift on my muzzleloader bullet would have been nearly four feet at 100 yards—assuming I could have held the gun steady, which I couldn't have. Unimak, like most of the Alaska Peninsula, experiences violent extremes of weather as air pressure from the icy Bering Sea and the warmer northern Pacific collide over the island's barren expanse.

Experiencing the weather on Unimak was an adventure, to say the least, but hunting the giant Alaska brown bear with a muzzleloader goes beyond the very definition of the word. We stalked and passed on numerous bears that would have squared close to nine feet, a fine trophy most everywhere else, but not on Unimak. On Unimak Island, you have every right to expect to shoot a bear that will square over nine feet and perhaps, if you're lucky, over the magic ten-foot mark. Rod and Rob have taken bears on the island that squared over ten and a half feet!

On one stalk, Rod and I sneaked to within forty-six yards of a sleeping nine-foot-plus boar. We then lay in a patch of grass and waited for three hours for the bear to stand up so that I would have a clear shot. Unfortunately, when it finally did stand up, it took off like a rocket and disappeared over a hill without giving me a chance to shoot. We were disappointed, but things could have been worse. Much worse! John was videotaping the whole time from a nearby hill, and we learned from him later that while we were lying there waiting for the first bear to stand, another bruin had approached to within thirty yards of us. Also, a pure-white wolf had crept to within one hundred yards of where we were lying.

As all good things must end, my safari on Unimak Island with R&R was drawing to a close. It was high time to take a good bear. We knew where one big boar's favorite fishing hole was, so we set up on a high point and waited for it to emerge from the brush. It blundered out of the alders in midafternoon, right where we had expected. Rob and John stayed high on the nearest hill to videotape the hunt, while Rod and I went after the fishing bruin.

The author with his 9-foot, 7-inch boar. Taken with R&R Outfitting.

Adventure is addictive. Once hooked, you need bigger adventures and more of them to remain satisfied. That said, I can honestly tell you that stalking that big brown bear on Unimak was for me the ultimate in hunting adventure. At one point, we were only thirty yards from it, but I couldn't get a clear shot. The bear towered over us, giving me a new appreciation for the meaning of insignificant.

When the bear finally turned and offered a shot, I fired my Knight muzzleloader with a loud *kaboom!* (Later I discovered that this shot—a perfectly mushroomed Barnes X-Bullet—had lodged in the bear's heart.) The huge bruin heaved into the alders and I reloaded. The instant I finished ramming another big bullet down the barrel, it charged out of the alders with a mixture of rage and curiosity etched on its giant face. *Kaboom!* The second bullet penetrated its lungs and nearly exited out the other side of the beast, which, upon taking the shot spun back into the alders.

If you're one of the few folks inclined to believe that the great Alaska brown bear might not be as tough as it's cracked up to be in story and legend, let me give you some firsthand observations to the contrary. Five minutes and four hundred yards from where I had first shattered its heart and lungs with my giant muzzleloads, I squeezed the trigger again to administer the last rites to this 9-foot, 6-inch lord of the tundra.

THE BROWN BEAR BOWHUNT

BY
SHIRLEY GRENOBLE

The giant Alaska brown bear reared up on its hind legs and roared. Three men froze, afraid to breathe. They had stalked to within twenty-two yards of the beast, and now their hard work, dreams—and lives—hung in the balance. The enraged animal scanned the area for whatever—or whomever—had caused the pain in its side. With the wind in their favor, the three men had been able to get remarkably close to a creature known for its keen sense of smell. But eventually the bear had caught their scent and turned away, presenting a perfect rear-quartering shot. The arrow had been true to its mark, penetrating deep into the bear's lungs. The panicky bear spun around and tried to bite the protruding arrow. Unable to free itself, it disappeared into the thick alders along the stream. A deadly silence descended as the three men came out of hiding to assess the situation.

The guide, Demetrios "Dee" Deoudes, told the two hunters to follow him quietly to the center of a gravel bar beside the stream. From there they could command an unobstructed view and wait the bear out. Following a wounded bear into the thick brush is risky business and can be fatal.

The bear weighed 900 pounds and measured 9 feet.

Randy Waddell of Altoona, Iowa, and Bud Claar of Hollidaysburg, Pennsylvania, are not strangers to this kind of adventure. Both are expert bow hunters and tournament shooters and are wise to woodland ways. Together they've traveled many miles hunting game, and this time they had made the journey to remote southwest Alaska for a chance at a trophy caribou for Bud and a big brown bear for Randy. They had contacted AAA Alaskan Outfitters, Inc., an organization that has guided many well-known hunters, including the world-famous bow hunter and outdoor writer Chuck Adams.

On 4 October they flew from Pittsburgh to Anchorage, taking a small plane the next morning to the southwestern Alaska town of King Salmon. From there, a bush plane transported them and their gear to Pilot Point, a remote outpost on the windswept tundra of the Alaska Peninsula. The weather stranded them at Pilot Point for a night, but next morning, Roger Morris, co-founder of AAA, picked them up and flew them about a hundred miles down the coast to AAA's main camp, called the Dog Salmon Camp. They then went to a beach on the Alaska Peninsula across from Kodiak Island. For the next week, they awoke before daybreak; washed in the icy creek; wore wool clothes, hip boots, and raincoats; and trekked a couple of miles each day to a high point to survey the surrounding hills and valleys for bear and caribou.

For the first five days, Randy and Dee glassed miles of rolling tundra and brushy river bottoms. They saw and videotaped many bears, stalking four within range before deciding to wait for something bigger. On the sixth day, Dee nudged Randy and pointed to a gargantuan brownish form over a mile away. "Hey, here's the one we've been waiting for!" said Dee. After carefully checking it out with their scopes, the men began a long, tedious stalk, crouching, slashing, and crawling through thick brush and damp undergrowth. When they were almost there, however, the wind shifted, and the bear caught their scent and vanished.

The next day the giant brown was back. With the height of the salmon migrations washing waves of fish into these rivers with each tide, it was too much temptation for a hungry bruin to ignore. Randy, Bud, and Dee got to within range once again, but, as had happened the day before, the bear vanished before they could position themselves for a shot. Dee figured the brown hadn't been spooked but had just finished feeding and had gone back into the alders to bed down. They wisely decided not to go in after it.

Day eight came and, sure enough, the brownie had returned. The three eager men took off in cautious pursuit of their quarry. After a slow and painful stalk—Randy swore his back would never be straight again—they got to within fifty yards. The bear was so busy digging salmon spawn out of the streambed, it never noticed them. But Randy wasn't able to shoot from his position, and it wasn't possible to get closer. The men had to backtrack and climb a steep, muddy slope, and then negotiate a slow crouch-and-crawl through thick alders to put them within range and above the quarry.

After this long and exhausting stalk, Randy peered cautiously over the edge and spied the monstrous bear twenty-two yards away. The hours spent shooting hundreds of practice arrows with his Blue Mountain bow now had a chance to pay off. He drew back and released the most important shot of his life. The giant bear snapped upright with a roar so ominous it made the hair on the back of each man's neck straighten. It then disappeared into the thick alders.

The men waited two and a half hours on the gravel bar. Then, in single file—Dee leading with rifle ready, Randy right behind with bow drawn, and Bud at the end filming it all—the men cautiously proceeded into the alders to find the brownie. Few feats can equal the tension of bushwhacking through tangled alders and willows in pursuit of the most dangerous animal in North America!

The three intrepid heroes pressed on, their senses alert to the slightest sound. Then Dee spotted a blood trail. Had the bear been mortally wounded? Yes! Yards farther the three hunters found the bear crumpled in a thicket. All three let out a huge sigh.

FROM CAIRO TO ALASKA

BY
CHARLES KARP

This story is dedicated to my son, Brian, and my good friend Bob Wyman.

In 1976, I shot my first deer in Cairo, New York. With me at the time was my best friend and hunting partner, Chris Kenny. From that hunt sprang the dream that would eventually be realized in a hunt for the brown bear of Alaska.

I didn't begin any serious research for the Alaska bear hunt until February 1994, when I attended the Sportsmen's Show in Harrisburg, Pennsylvania. During the next thirteen months, I contacted outfitters, biologists, and Alaska Department of Fish and Game personnel. I also spoke with taxidermists, hunters, owners of sporting goods stores, and anyone else who I thought might know something about brown bear hunting. It was quite an education.

In July 1994, my wife and I took a wonderful backpacking vacation in Alaska, which gave me the opportunity to meet prospective guides. I was very impressed with the guide Gus

Lamoureux for his down-to-earth, no-nonsense attitude and for his honesty. Everyone I talked to who knew Gus had nothing but good to say about him and his dad, "Frenchy." That winter at the Safari Club Show in Las Vegas, Chris had the opportunity to meet Gus, and he agreed that Lamoureux was our man.

12 May 1996. The day (finally!) we began our great Alaska hunting adventure. The flight from Salt Lake City, Utah, to Anchorage passed quickly, and for the first time since I have known him, Chris showed some emotion upon seeing the awesome Alaska Range.

We overnighted in Anchorage, and then flew to King Salmon in a thick fog. There we met our guide, Brad Waitman, a thirty-three-year-old former marine, lean and tough, and a nice guy, too. Branch River Air flew us to Lamoureux's Ugashik Lake Lodge, a clean camp with great food, fine bed linen, and hot showers. What a way to hunt!

We repacked our gear for spike camp, and shortly thereafter Brad and I climbed into Gus's small plane and flew to a pothole-like lake to begin our backpack hunt to Deer Creek. With pack slung on my back, hip waders on, and a .300 Weatherby in hand, I began my dream hunt.

It was tough fighting willow and alders, slogging

Bear tracks on the beach in front of one of the tent camps. The tracks stopped fifteen feet from the tent. The bear woke the inhabitants.

99

through wet tundra, and navigating Deer Creek, and I was glad I had done some physical training over the last few months. We set up camp after several grueling hours and had dinner. How good it tasted after the workout! After dinner, Brad told me of a hunt he had guided on Kodiak a week earlier. His client had bagged a ten-foot brownie on the first day, so I began calling him "One-a-day Waitman." Could I be so lucky? To be honest, an eight-and-a-half-foot brownie would do.

The next day, after a hearty breakfast, we slid into our packs and continued the trek up Deer Creek. A full day of searching and glassing turned up nothing but hundreds of caribou. We pitched our tent in some willow flats near the creek and turned in, hoping for better luck tomorrow.

After an early breakfast, we climbed a high vantage point nearby and glassed the surrounding hills and valleys, reveling in the sun-dappled beauty of Alaska's awesome country. Around a quarter to ten, Brad shouted, "I see a bear!" and pointed to a side hill of black shale a mile and a half away.

"How big is he, Brad?" I asked.

"Hard to tell. Maybe nine feet," he whispered.

The boar scaled the slope and traversed a long, thin snow field, moving in the direction of a canyon not too far away. We jumped into action, moving quickly but cautiously onto the valley floor in the direction of our quarry. Forty-five minutes later we were very close, and caribou bolted nervously around us. Barely two hundred yards away, I saw the big bruin emerge onto a ridge top, and then plunge down into the thick willow below, moving diagonally to our left.

"Put a round in your chamber!" Brad exhorted. I slammed a bullet in and showed my mentor I was ready. The race was on! The behemoth brown was ambling through thick brush to our left, and we rushed to intercept it, fighting willows, tussocks, and a meandering stream, hoping for a shot before it slipped out of range. Through thick alders and up a steep hill we clambered, my heart pounding so loudly it seemed ready to burst from my chest. I knelt exhausted and caught a look from Brad that said, "You can't stop now, man!" After another twenty or thirty yards, gasping for breath, I said to myself, *Come on, Charlie, you can't quit!* I knew I was almost out of gas.

Upward we went, and the bear veered toward us, crashing through willows and alders. I lined the cross hairs on its shoulder and tried to calm my wildly beating heart. Seventy-five yards away this mountain of brown bear stopped, raised its head, and looked straight at us. Its nostrils quivered as it tried to wind its strange pursuers. But the breeze was blowing in our faces; luck was on our side. The bear moved ever closer, and Brad leaned over and whispered, "Be calm and get a good shot."

Fifty yards away, the gigantic bear stopped and raised its head, looking me right in the eye and desperately trying to

The author with his beautiful Alaska Peninsula brownie.

The author holding the skull from his Alaska Peninsula brown bear taken on the first day. Guided by Brad Waitman of Gus Lamoureux's guide service. 1996.

wind us. Its huge chocolate shoulder was now centered in my cross hairs. I don't really remember the sound of the gun or the feel of the recoil as my bullet exploded from the barrel, but Brad said he definitely heard the *whomp,* as the 180-grain Nosler Partition did its job. The gargantuan brown fell instantly, and Brad ordered me to keep shooting. I fired two more shots, but the bear was down. We approached cautiously. What an incredible sight! Such size and beauty!

The skinning took several hours, and then we had lunch and packed the hide and skull back to camp. From there, it was a tough six-hour hike back to spike camp. The hide measured 10 feet, 8 inches, and the skull, $25^{10}/_{16}$ inches.

Two brown bears over ten feet in two days. Quite a feat for my guide, One-a-day Waitman, and quite an adventure for me!

PART TWO

HUNTING
ARCTIC ALASKA

WHITE SHEEP ON DARK MOUNTAIN

BY
SHANE MCCARTHY

I awoke to sun shining through the yellow and blue nylon of the tent. The warmth felt good. The first hunt with my client had been cold and wet, and we shivered ourselves silly looking for sheep. But now it looked like we would be blessed with some beautiful weather. And when the weather is good in August in the Brooks Range, there isn't any place on earth more beautiful.

Things had started off with the usual sorting, cleaning, and packing of food and equipment—preparations that are half the fun of being a guide. Then the clients arrive and the excitement begins. Clients always bring with them a certain optimism, conveyed by their smiling faces, warm and enthusiastic handshakes, and expectant looks toward the stark-gray Brooks Range, which lines the wide valley of the Chandalar River. The mountains are home to the white sheep, which we would be hunting over the next ten days.

We waited at base camp for Larry Rivers—the outfitter by whom I am employed—to return from scouting in his Super

Larry Rivers (left) and Stan Neitling.

Cub. Meanwhile, I wondered which client Larry would assign me. We were working on some last-minute details near the airstrip when Larry circled and banked his blue-and-white Super Cub into its final maneuver over the bright-yellow willows at the end of the gravel runway. Larry landed the plane with a soft bounce on the uneven gravel and hopped out just as we came up the trail from base camp. Larry asked Stan Neitling

Stan Neitling with his Dall sheep.

Stan with his caribou.

and me if we would mind hunting together, and he explained that we could hunt a side valley a few miles downstream from the Chandalar. We agreed and began a hike that lasted all morning. Though we carried minimal gear, stomping over endless miles of tundra and gravel bars was still exhausting.

Early the next morning we moved up to the mountain and that very first day we got up on a band of eight rams . . . just in time to see them go over the ridge, and well before we had time to judge them or get off a shot. We saw no sheep the rest of the day. On the long climb down, Stan and I threaded our way in the dark around the many channels of the river.

Finally we arrived at camp. How great that sleeping bag felt that night!

The next day Larry flew us to Long Creek, where we hunted for three days. On the first day, we passed on a thirty-five-inch ram. After our long walk through the dark spruce, poplar, and willow, which were all alive with fall colors, we took a break. I eased the pack off my shoulders to stretch and then started glassing the valley. I soon spotted a white-as-snow ram on a mountain that looked like a fortress. The ram was about halfway up the mountain but below the real steep stuff. Stan and I watched the ram for a while, realizing it was a real good one. The only problem was that it had worked its way up the mountain and had lain down on top of a pinnacle. There was no way to get within shooting distance. For two hours we discussed the ruggedness of the terrain and the size of the white ram. Little did we know how well we would get to know that jagged mountain.

Over the next three days we played hide-and-seek with the ram. It seemed every time we spotted it and began our stalk, it would disappear. Finally, on the fourth day, we spotted the ram below the steep stuff, but there was little cover between it and us. With a little creative climbing, though, we managed to get in position for Stan to make a real nice thirty-yard running shot just as the ram jumped out of its bed. After the excitement of the stalk had worn off, we realized what a really great ram it was. It taped out at 40¾ inches. Stan and I slept great that night.

Larry picked us up the next morning, and we spent a day at base camp. Then Stan and I went out to hunt caribou. Stan's luck came through again; on the second day he scored on a really nice caribou. Stan, thanks for the great hunts. Let's do it again. Real soon!

STALKING SHEEP AND CARIBOU

BY
J. P. OWEN JR.

It was March 1982, and my good friend J. O. Richard and I were catching up on each other's news in the den of my home in Lafayette, Louisiana. When I mentioned that I was interested in making a hunt for Dall sheep, he told me that his Alaska outfitter Larry Rivers and his brother Rick were in Lafayette and that he would arrange for us to meet if I wished. I expressed a desire to do so, and arrangements were made to meet the following morning.

The next day my wife and I met Larry and Rick. Over coffee, we discussed hunting and looked at pictures from Larry's different areas. We liked what we heard, and after listening to J. O.'s story of his hunt the year before, we wrote Larry a check to confirm our hunt for the coming August.

My wife Lessleen and I have been avid hunting partners for the past thirty-seven years. We have hunted together in Africa, South America, Spain, Portugal, and Honduras. We have hunted many times in Mexico, as well as across the United States. Having been in every state except Alaska, we eagerly planned this trip and decided to tour the state about ten days before the hunt. Our tour would carry us across the south-central coastal part of the state, then up toward Fairbanks. We started with a stopover in Denali National Park, where we saw abundant wildlife and beautiful scenery, including Mount McKinley.

Arriving in Fairbanks, we picked up our hunting luggage, which we had sent in advance. Then we checked into our hotel, where we met John Turnbull and Bob Priest, of Oregon, who would be on the same hunt. The following morning we took a flight out of Fairbanks on an Arctic Circle Air Service flight to Fort Yukon. About an hour later we caught our first look at the fort, located on the northern bank of the Yukon River, at its northernmost point, about eight miles above the Arctic Circle. Here we changed planes, transferring our gear to a Cessna 207 for the last leg across the Yukon Flats and into the Brooks Range, about 320 miles north of Fairbanks.

Larry Rivers and his family met us in Fort Yukon. They had picked up additional supplies in Fairbanks and were returning in Larry's Cessna 206. Bears had broken into their cache of supplies, so nearly everything had had to be replaced. Departing Fort Yukon together, we flew north for another hour before setting up for landing at Larry's main camp strip on the Chandalar River. This "strip" is a 1,100-foot stretch of gravel bar located on the riverbank beside camp. Mike McCrary and Hawk Greenway, who were to guide and assist us throughout the hunt, met us in camp. Larry's wife Naomi was soon at work in the cook tent and prepared a delicious dinner. After supper, over a hot cup of camp coffee, we discussed the coming hunt. During the course of the conversation it developed that Hawk and I were second cousins. You can imagine my surprise at being introduced to a cousin fifty miles south of the Arctic Ocean in a remote hunting camp! It was certainly exciting.

The following morning Larry set about moving out our spike camps by air, while Lessleen went fishing with Larry's son Shane and his friend Robert Sheldon. They caught a nice string of grayling.

I was soon removing my gear from the Super Cub in preparation for the first part of my hunt. When I arrived in

The author with his second cousin Hawk Greenway, with the horns of three of the Dall sheep the author took on his 1983 hunt.

spike camp, about fifteen miles out from main camp, Mike had already set up camp and had spotted a band of sheep on the mountain to the west of camp. Larry was off to move additional camps, and we were left to discuss our plan of attack. Alaska regulations do not allow you to shoot game until after 3 A.M. following any day in which you have been airborne. However, there was nothing to prevent us from using up some of the distance between us and the sheep during that period, so we lightened our packs for the climb and set off around 8 P.M. Since this was early August, it did not get completely dark at night, and we were able to set a comfortable pace.

We climbed until 11 P.M., stopping on a ridge below our sheep and about a quarter of a mile away. Not wanting to take a chance in getting closer, we sat down, hoping to catch a little sleep. I did not rest well at first, as I was damp from the effort of climbing and got chilled. However, after Mike wrapped a space blanket around me, I was able to catch some sleep, while he monitored the sheep through his binoculars. At 2:30 A.M. we decided to get under way and began the climb necessary to get above the sheep. The going was rocky and tiring, but the sheep ahead made the impossible possible. While climbing, we saw four excellent bull caribou grazing on the tundra below us, but they were secondary to the sheep at that point, and we passed them up.

Around 5 A.M. we were closing in on the sheep and spent another thirty minutes getting into a favorable position for a shot. As we glassed the sheep, from around three hundred yards, we were able to pick out five or six legal rams. Mike identified the ram with the best curl—thirty-nine inches, in his estimation. As I tried to locate a good rest, the sheep sensed we were there and became nervous. I no longer had time to look for a rest and had to settle for a shot from sitting position. I was exhausted from the climb and breathing hard. That ram was all over the scope. Needless to say, I missed the shot and the two that followed. It made me sick to see that ram run out of sight and to think of all that climbing for nothing. We had climbed from 2,500 feet to 5,500 or 6,000 feet and now had nothing to do but set off for another mountain in search of other sheep.

The descent from the mountain was uneventful until we were two hundred feet above the stream level. There we stopped to rest, looking across the stream at the black shale-covered cliff. In contrast to our slope, which was covered in vegetation, the opposite slope did not have a blade of grass on it. As I gazed at the mountain, a dirty spot of white caught my eye. I pointed it out to Mike, and he quickly identified it as another ram. At this point I did not want to shoot, as I was so tired I was afraid I would not be able to hit it. Mike directed me to sit and rest while he moved across the slope for a better look and possible improvement in position.

I sat and watched him move carefully across the hill. In a few minutes he motioned for me to follow, which I carefully did. He told me that the ram had a nice curl and would indeed make a nice trophy. After looking at the ram, I decided that I would go ahead and try for it, as there was a boulder thirty yards closer that I could use for a rest. I moved very slowly into position, where I could rest my rifle on the rock. Estimating the distance again to be over three hundred yards, I held my aim high on its shoulder and squeezed off a shot. Even at that range I could hear the impact. The ram turned slowly and then fell one hundred feet down the cliff, nearly into the creek, and was out of sight.

My heart was pounding. We moved quickly down the hill until we could see the sheep. It was dead, lying against a shrub of bush near the bottom of the canyon. Mike waded across the stream and recovered my trophy. We took pictures and caped it out. Leaving the meat to cool, we packed the head and cape the

The author with his Dall ram.

half mile downstream to our camp. It was now around 8:30 A.M. and we were exhausted. We lay down for a rest, after which Mike returned and packed in the sheep. We were so tired that we did not eat that night. I slept for thirteen hours.

We spent the next day in and around camp. We glassed a lot and saw wolf, caribou, sheep, and eagles. The temperature in the day was from the forties to the sixties, and it dropped to around thirty degrees at night. That evening Larry flew in to check on our progress, and, deciding we could do better for caribou in another area, we packed up and flew back to main camp. The following morning we had sheep backstrap and French toast for breakfast. It was excellent, as were all the meals Naomi prepared in main camp. Later that afternoon, Mike and Larry flew out and set up a camp high on a mountain ridge, overlooking three or four miles of valley containing grazing caribou.

Larry flew me out a short time later. Mike and I arranged camp and turned in. Around 4 A.M. the following morning, we broke camp and moved our equipment down to a flat spot where Larry was to pick us up when he returned. He had not landed us there originally, as the caribou were actually on the strip at the time we flew in. In this high valley we traveled down and parallel to the stream. The walking was much easier here, and we were able to move much more quickly.

We had walked about two miles when we spotted several caribou coming over a ridge toward us. They were 1,500 feet away and were intent on grazing. We crept down a draw and climbed a rocky outcrop, where we waited an hour. Finally, sixteen bulls came into view, feeding in our direction. Eventually they moved into range, and, selecting the one I liked best, I fired. The 165-grain Nosler, fired from a 7mm Ruger No. 1 Sporter, hit it solidly in the shoulder and dropped it. The range was around 110 yards. We took a lot of pictures, and Mike performed the customary surgery. I took part of the load, and he packed the head, cape, and meat the two miles back to spike camp. This fine caribou had a double shovel and thirty points. It was indeed a respectable trophy. While Mike was working on the cape, two more bulls, with even larger racks, walked within easy shooting range of us. Mike had previously told me that this could happen.

Knowing the number of caribou in the area, Larry decided to check on us that evening, thinking—correctly—that we would probably be done. The weather at this altitude—6,000 feet—was rapidly deteriorating, and we were happy to fly back into main camp. Back in camp we met John Turnbull and Bob Priest, who had returned from their hunt farther up the valley. Both of them had been successful on sheep. John had taken a fine 39-inch Dall, and Bob had a heavy-based 38-inch ram. Bob had also taken a nice caribou bull. John had taken a caribou here a couple of years previously and had elected not to shoot another. With everyone successful, we all decided not to push our luck any further, so Larry loaded up his 206 and flew us back to Fort Yukon. There, we caught a flight back to Fairbanks—with each of us full of the memories of a great hunt with wonderful companions.

A FAIR-CHASE RAM HUNT

BY
JOE HENDRICKS

Joe Hendricks* had once guided me on a fair-chase bear hunt on Kodiak. I took the Kodiak brown, which measured a little less than ten feet, and had it mounted in a full-body pose. It is presently on display at my home in Rock Springs, Wyoming. Knowing Joe has a sheep-hunting area that he has harvested from and managed for close to thirty years, I was naturally quite eager to book a Dall ram hunt with him as soon as possible. I hoped to bring my wife, Sue, but shortly before the hunt she declined. That was unfortunate, as I know Joe specializes in husband/wife and father/daughter/son hunts.

As I discovered during my bear hunt with Joe, there is much more to hunting than just bringing home an animal. Although his success rate is among the best, his hunts are known just as much for their challenging wilderness adventure, since he adheres to strict ethical standards of fair chase. This would

---

*Note from editor: Joe Hendricks chose to write this story in the third person.

not be a hunt for spoiled neophytes—of that I was certain. There would be extensive hiking, some climbing, and, of course, the Alaskan weather to contend with.

In order to carefully manage the harvest, each year Joe guides hunts to different parts of his hunting area. Fortunately, his hunting area is quite large, so there are always places that have not been hunted for several years.

The day after I arrived in the Franklin Mountains of the beautiful Brooks Range, we started out for a long valley with sufficient supplies for several days. This was an area that had not been hunted for a while. Late in the day, we hiked way back and found a good spot for our tarp and sleeping bags. We saw sheep but no big rams during the long hike up the valley. The next day, we continued up the long valley to where it made a bend. Joe thought a few good rams might be just around the corner. There were six of them, and two were exceptional. Even though they were almost right where he had expected, we were still amazed by our good fortune.

The author with his magnificent Brooks Range Dall ram.

Though we had been cautious and clung to the hillsides, we were spotted by one of the more curious animals. Concerned but not really spooked, it moved away from us up the talus on the opposite side of the valley. The other rams followed it. I wanted to back off and try again the next day, but Joe said, "No way! They will be four canyons away and extra cautious by morning. We have to move now!"

Since the rams had already spotted us, there was no reason to hide. We raced in the open across the gravel wash to try for a better position. We found a good rest on a rocky bench, where I tried to catch my breath and calm my heart. Joe, looking through his favorite 10X Swarovski, picked out the two largest rams. I missed several times. My 7mm is flat-shooting and accurate, but under such trying circumstances, nobody shoots as well as they do on the range.

"How far now?" I asked Joe.

"About four hundred sixty yards. I know you can make that shot; just take your time and pick out the largest part of the animal and squeeze it off."

I had time to look over the rams before they started to climb. The one

Rams need to be packed out from the rugged Brooks Range.

119

The author preparing the meat from his Dall sheep at Sewash camp, ten miles from base camp.

with the longest horns was magnificent. That was the one I wanted.

Two more shots and the ram still hadn't fallen, nor had it even stumbled. Joe was convinced I had hit it, though, and urged that we pursue the animal as it ran up the grassy slope and disappeared over the ridge. "Lud, we have to hustle to catch up to it," he said, as he took off up the hill without a breather.

Good luck, I thought. I was in pretty good shape since I ski all winter, but that ram was wasting no time. I barely kept up with Joe, and when we got to the plateau, he scoured the area for sign (tracks and spots of blood) while I caught my breath. There were different sets of fresh tracks there, but we locked on our ram's trail and followed for better than half an hour.

We didn't see any blood, and the slippery trail was becoming steeper and more treacherous. Joe was ready to admit that he had been wrong and quit the chase, but then he spotted dark-red spots on the snow. We followed the blood trail several hundred yards up the steep, snow-covered shale slope. Joe was certain the wounded animal was not far off and figured that if we climbed another thirty or forty feet, I would get a shot at a slowly moving ram no more than two hundred yards away.

When we looked over the ridge crest, the scene was better than we could have imagined. We peered into a steep, mostly open small valley, and there was the ram, an extraordinary specimen, lying in a shale bed thirty-five yards below. It was looking right at us. Joe reached in his pocket for his camera, but I was too quick with my reflexes. I dropped the ram right there. Joe had wanted to take a photo of the live ram, but I wanted to make sure it didn't get away.

Photos, skinning, and butchering took the rest of the day, and we carried everything down the steep shale to a frigid stream, placing the quarters and the rest of the meat in the part of the stream that saw no sun. That part was a veritable ice garden, a perfect spot to store the meat until we came back the next day.

With our bellies full of charbroiled sheep backstrap, we enjoyed the gorgeous starry night in camp that evening. The next morning, the weather was beautiful as we hiked back to retrieve the meat. Although the "old man" was quicker to the top of the mountain than I, it fell to my younger and stronger physique to carry out most of the meat plus the horns and cape. This chore made my trophy all the more valuable to me.

As we made the long hike out, I had time to reflect on several aspects of the hunt. First, it was a wonderful and unique experience not to see a soul other than Joe for ten days. Second, I had chosen a guide who was consummately experienced and knowledgeable, a true master of his profession. Joe was more a hunting partner and friend than a hired hand. Third, my previous sheep hunt had been a disappointment, not only because I had taken a small (¾-curl) ram, but also because I was sure my guide had flown out in his plane to spot the animal.

That is not a fair chase! I took pride in knowing that my sheep hunt, as well as my bear hunt, was conducted ethically, with the utmost respect for the animal. I was also proud of my 42-inch (1½-curl) Dall ram!

BIG SMILE, GIANT HEART

BY
LITTLEJOHN NAVARRO

In the hunting game, the rewards aren't always measured in trophies won or lost. To challenge nature, fate, and the wits of wild animals and find out what one is truly made of can be more than enough for both guide and client.

Last spring I received a call from a consultant with a booking for two moose and grizzly hunters, one around forty years old and the other around sixty. A short while later, when the deposits arrived with the completed questionnaires I ask my clients to fill out, certain information on the form signed by Allan Nygren hinted at some health problems and included a rather long list of prescription medications he was taking. Red flags instantly went up in my mind, and I quickly called the consultant for some necessary assurances before contacting the client directly. I was somewhat relieved to hear that Allan had been hunting cougars the past winter with his son-in-law, Walt Landi, my other client.

Knowing that I might have to return the deposits if I didn't feel comfortable with this health issue, I called Allan and was greeted by a man who certainly sounded healthy. Not one to beat around the bush, I asked him outright, "Do you think you can chase bears all over the mountains, and, by the way, what the hell is all that medication you're taking?" He was totally frank with me about his precarious health, matter-of-factly describing—in detail—three heart operations he had undergone in the past year. He used phrases like "busted valves," "internal bleeding," and "serious infection," and all the while I was visualizing a frozen corpse, evacuation helicopters, and hostile conversations with lawyers and insurance people.

Like any responsible guide, I asked him how he felt right now, this morning, to which he replied, "A little rough, but OK." After careful consideration I said, "Sounds good to me, let's go hunting!"

Over the busy months that ensued, I remember wanting to call him several times but never did, figuring "no news is good news." The first of August arrived, and I was off to my camp in the eastern Brooks Range to begin my season. Things started uneventfully—hunters arrived on the days they were supposed to, the weather cooperated, and we were fortunate to take some nice animals. Before I knew it, the fifteenth of September was upon us, time to prepare for the arrival of my last two hunters— "Allan—Heart Medications!" as I had scribbled in my book, and his son-in-law, Walt.

Feelings of anxiety flooded through me as I remembered the conversation we had had in the spring. Oh, well, maybe we'll get lucky and nobody will die, I thought to myself. As things happened, the weather deteriorated, heightening my feelings of foreboding, so I decided to leave the camp in the capable hands of my crew and fly into Coldfoot to meet my hunters.

Heavy fog had delayed them from making the morning flight, but by early afternoon it had lifted just enough for the Navajo pilot to complete a very nonstandard but routine NDB departure out of Bettles and into Coldfoot. When they finally climbed out of the aircraft and I shook Allan's hand, I noticed his Nebraska farmer's weatherbeaten face and a smile as wide as the Great Plains. He was tall, about six foot four, with a long, thin body, and was wearing a lightweight wool jacket and pants that, along with his hunting boots, had seen lots of miles. Walt, I decided at first glance, was a "no worry" hunter, young and strong.

I grabbed some gear and headed for the pickup with Walt at my side, and as I reached the truck I turned to see Allan taking very slow, deliberate strides. As he caught up he smiled and said, "I can get anywhere as long as I go slow," meaning, of course, that he had to hunt at that pace. I remember thinking while driving into town, *Moose, no problem, but how the hell am I going to keep a bear in one place long enough?*

The weather continued to worsen, so I decided to wait it out in Coldfoot, which seemed infinitely more desirable than diving through sucker holes between granite clouds. Before we ate supper that night, Allan pulled out a pillbox the size of Kansas, with all the days of the week on it, and proceeded to pour the contents into his hand.

Walt, noticing my stare, said, "He takes that many twice a day."

"What happens if you don't take some pills?"

There were some incredulous looks and no response.

"Better take the pills, I guess."

The next morning the weather was much the same, with solid fog. Great fun, waiting with hunters who have paid you tons of money, while they chew the corners of their moustaches and pace. I'd rather eat glass! Later in the day the weather improved enough to favor life after flight, so we took off. Two trips and some time later, we sat in the cook tent sipping wine and enjoying sumptuous food. Life was good again.

At 5:30 A.M. on our first day of hunting, as we sat in the cook tent with the Coleman humming and the obligatory rain dancing off the canvas, I asked Allan how he was feeling. He looked up from his plateful of hotcakes, eggs, and sausages and, with a twinkle in his eye, said, "A little rough, but OK." After giving some thought to his response, I told him we would be hunting from base camp, where the food was better. Without a word, he finished his breakfast and we were off.

The first day out is always a shakedown day to me, a time when the hunter and I begin to get used to each other. We walked slowly along the riverbank, scanning the bottom for moose and the opposing slopes for bear. Allan would need frequent rests, so we combined those stops with glassing. His long legs, not unlike those of a moose, could eat up the ground, and he never seemed too winded—a good sign, I thought.

After lunch we entered a stand of white spruce and birch that contained some fresh moose sign, so we began to still hunt, with Allan about two steps behind and to my right. After a few hundred yards we came upon a bull in its bed around thirty yards ahead. It rose slowly but hadn't seen or winded us, and Allan chambered a round and smoothly shouldered his rifle.

I looked at the bull and whispered, "Thirty-eight inches, a three-year-old." At that moment, without realizing it, I also voiced my unspoken concerns about Allan's physical condition when I added, "But he's legal in this unit, and you can take him if you want."

Allan turned to me, that big smile reappeared, and he said, "Nah, too long of a pack back to camp."

We both just stood and watched the bull amble off. As we walked on I found myself admitting that I was in the company of a hunter; the bud of respect had just sprouted.

The next ridge had a nice rock outcropping, so we stopped to glass. Within minutes, a really nice eight-and-a-half-foot boar grizzly climbed out of the brush across the river—around six hundred yards out—and began to slowly walk away from us. "He's a beauty and big; come on, let's try to get closer," I said excitedly.

Allan responded, "I'll try, but we'll have to go slow."

After five minutes, it was obvious that our pace was just too slow to intercept the bruin, so we stopped for a rest and watched it walk away. While we were glassing the bear, I was standing an honest fifteen feet from Allan and began to hear a very loud ticking sound. I turned to him and chided, "Tomorrow you've got to leave that watch back at camp. It's much too loud!"

He raised his left arm to expose his wrist. "This is a digital watch; that's the mechanical valves in my heart making all that noise. When I get tired my chest gets tight and my heart beats faster."

I didn't say a thing; my mind was racing as fast as Allan's heart, computing the most direct route back to camp so I would know which way to go while I wandered around in shock after watching a man die of a heart attack, something I was absolutely sure would happen momentarily. We made our way very slowly back to camp, and I was relieved that Allan would have the opportunity to quietly expire while sleeping that night. He had determined earlier to get some extra rest and sleep the next morning and asked me to wake him at six. I smiled and said, "No problem, Allan."

The next morning I realized one of the advantages of having employees: I sent Dan, our packer, to check on Allan. Ten minutes later Allan walked into the cook tent looking none the worse for wear! And so it went for the next four days—each night he looked done in, but by the next morning he was OK, so off we went. I couldn't be sure, but it seemed we were taking fewer rests each day, and he was talking more about hunting and less about hearts and operations.

On the sixth day I was beginning to feel good, and then it happened: Allan shot a nice bull, and it was a great day for both of us! The next day he seemed to be walking more upright with even a little spring to his step, so we decided to go see if that bear we saw on the first day had wandered back into the drainage.

We glassed all day, and around 5:30 Allan whispered to me, "Littlejohn, what's that black dot on that flat spot down the valley back toward camp?"

I looked through my eight-power glasses, and all I could tell was that it was a black spot around four miles away, so I grabbed my spotting scope. "It's a bear, but it's a long way off!"

I looked over at Allan, and his giant smile seemed to say, "Can we get him?" A lot of things were going through my mind right then, not the least of which was that although I have taken some really nice bears with hunters, none was so far away, and all the hunters were healthy. Still, the bear was almost facing toward us and the wind was in our favor, so I said, "Let's do it, but it'll be dark in a few hours, so we'll have to run."

The next two hours were really tough. We would stop every twenty minutes or so, and, while we weren't really running, we were eating up tundra. The bear was so cooperative, I couldn't believe it. It actually didn't move more than a few hundred feet the entire time we were approaching; then, just when I thought we might get close enough to tell what color it was through the glasses, it disappeared. I told Allan it had probably just walked over a little knoll, but I knew there was a better chance that bear was in New Mexico by now. We continued, mostly because I didn't want to tell Allan I had probably just run him to death for nothing, but I thought maybe, just maybe, if we were real lucky . . .

Ten minutes later we looked up, and there it was again—still three-quarters of a mile away but heading for a little horseshoe basin in which my first sheep hunter had killed a ram over a month earlier. I told Allan that if we could climb up there while the bear was still in the basin, we'd have a chance.

Although the previous two and a half hours had been very hard on him, Allan was still game. Forty-five minutes later we were at the mouth of the basin with less than twenty minutes of light remaining. We slowly sidehilled along and got to a point where I was sure we'd have to see the bear if it were there. But we found nothing but rocks and tundra. It was gone!

For the first time during that hunt I was really disappointed. I turned to Allan and said, "I'm really sorry. I was beginning to think we'd get that bear, and now he's gone!"

Allan was sitting with his head between his legs and muttered, "He must have gone up over the rimrocks." I couldn't believe that bear would climb those nasty rimrocks unless it had a reason, and I knew it had never winded or seen us, so I turned to look one more time, and sure enough, there it was, at the base of the rocks five hundred yards straight above us, sidehilling just as we had been doing.

I dropped to my knees and cried out, "Allan, there he is, shoot him!" Instantly regretting what I had just said, I reached around and grabbed his .300 magnum as he prepared to fire and said, "No, don't, he's too far!" We sat there and watched the big griz walk behind the only finger ridge in the basin we couldn't see over. I turned to my client and urged him on, but Allan looked at me and said, "I can't, I can't!"

I don't know exactly what I was thinking right then, but I knelt down next to him and, with my hands on either side of his face, looked him right in the eyes and said, "If you do as I say now, after all that work, we're going to get that S.O.B.!"

He started to shake his head in a negative reply, then stopped, a smile appearing as he said, "I'll try!"

We had at most ten minutes of light remaining. Shadows had already faded into the dark filter that swallows rocks and makes your eyes dance, desperately seeking reference before your brain is forced to accept the night. Down the last small draw, through the bottom alders, we came up on the finger ridge that jutted into the basin. I was now looking up, not because I thought the bear was likely to be above us, but rather because it was the only direction illuminated by the last faint glow of a sun that had set long ago. And there it was! The grizzly was digging on the very top of the ridge. I squinted, to make out, only barely, the outline of the bear around three hundred yards above us. Pointing for Allan, I let out a desperate, "Can you see him?"

Without wasting time for a reply, Allan sprawled down on the hill and slid backward, digging his boots into what had to be a sixty-degree slope, then resighted and fired. The bear went down, and just as quickly got back up. Allan fired twice more, and on the last report of the .300 mag, the bear rolled end over end into total darkness.

The stars were out and moonlight flooded the north fork of the Chandalar as we slowly descended several hours later. Although I couldn't see, I was certain I could feel Allan's smile on my back as we stumbled our way to camp. Sometime during that night, while walking, I made a silent vow that I would never again try to judge the amount of grit in a man's heart, especially by how much noise it makes!

PART THREE

HUNTING
THE INTERIOR

ADVENTURE NEAR LAST DAY LAKE

BY
JOHN HUTCHINS

In late August 1995, I packed my gear and boarded a plane for Anchorage, Alaska, where I was met by Middit Kvamme, the fiancée of my outfitter and guide, George Siavelis. I then met George, and we flew from Anchorage to Aniak, followed by a forty-minute flight in a floatplane that landed on what George and I called No Name Lake. George had already been back in the bush for a couple of days, setting up camp and scouting. He got me all worked up when he told me he had seen two big brown bears the day before—one he considered to be at least nine and a half feet. (Of course, that was before the season started, and all hunters know you scc all thc game in the world before you can legally hunt, but come opening day, there's nothing around!) At that point, we thought we were right in the middle of things and destined to have a great hunt.

We spent the remaining hours before the opening of bear season scouting for caribou, moose, and bear. We saw plenty of animals. In fact, during the two weeks I was in Alaska for bear season, George and I saw over a dozen full-grown black bears and caribou every day, including some that were fairly impressive. But because I didn't want to spook any trophy bears I believed to be nearby, I passed on my chances to shoot those animals.

Several days went by, spotting and glassing in miserable weather—a combination of snow, strong winds, and very cold rain. We stuck at it, but the days were sure long—out at 7 A.M., not back until 10:30 P.M. George is absolutely relentless: When you book a hunt with him, you're going to hunt, no ifs, ands, or buts about it. No amount of whining or pleading could convince him to let me stay in the tent while he went out and glassed for game. George's devotion inspired me to hunt no matter what the conditions.

On the seventh day, while glassing from a mountain, I spied what appeared to be a large deadfall in a patch of scrub across the valley. Upon closer inspection, it turned out to be a giant bull moose lying in the alders. Four hundred yards to the right were two more nice moose bedded down. I told George what I had seen, and he got pretty excited.

"Let me look!" he said, grabbing the scope. "John, those are damn nice moose, each one a wall-hanger."

The biggest of the three stood up and walked into the alder thicket. George estimated the moose to be at least sixty-six inches wide, with very wide palms. We had no trouble tracking it for the next couple hours because its huge antlers stood out like a sore thumb. We debated whether or not to pursue the massive bull, since my primary objective was a brown bear, but I also wanted a nice moose. That rack was a long, long way off—George figured at least five miles from camp. It could take days to pack it in, leaving little time to hunt bear. On the other hand, I could hunt the rest of my life and never get another chance at a 66-inch-or-better moose. After careful consideration, we decided to go for it!

George took off across the tundra as though he had rockets strapped to his backside, and I followed. Three miles later, huffing and puffing, we stopped to assess the situation on a little knob about five hundred yards from our quarry.

134

"The moose I want is over there in that thicket," I said. "How are we going to get him out?"

"Well, let's try to call him out."

"George, how are you going to do that? The rut isn't on."

George looked at me cockily. "He doesn't know that. He's only a moose."

We walked several hundred yards into the middle of the alders until we found a clearing, where George began doing bull and cow calls. A couple of minutes passed. I was standing at the ready with a shell in the chamber and my finger on the safety when I heard the most god-awful sound in my life.

The bull was responding! It sounded like King Kong coming straight at us. It was unnerving. We could tell the bull was going to emerge within thirty yards of us, and I stood ready while George hunkered down. As George had predicted, that randy moose emerged from the bushes ready for a fight. It looked straight at us, put its head down, and started rotating its massive headgear. It was making sure we knew how big it was.

The author's moose, which turned out to be a wide-palmed 67½-inch bull.

135

George Siavelis with the author's gigantic 67½-inch bull moose antlers.

George gave me a smile and shoved his fingers in his ears. I figured that was my cue to shoot. I shouldered my .300 Weatherby Magnum just as the bull charged for battle. I let the behemoth have it in the front shoulder. Given how close the moose was, and given that I was shooting with a high caliber, you would have thought all hell would break loose. No chance. It immediately took off. I chambered another round and hit it again in the front shoulder. It ran into a small thicket and stopped. "Shoot! Shoot!" hollered George. I could barely make out the bull's outline in the brush. George still urged me on, so

I repositioned myself and squeezed off another one, this time crippling its other shoulder and leg. Down it went. I ran up and finished the ol' boy off.

George confirmed that this was indeed a splendid trophy. With darkness setting in, we took some quick pictures and then caped and prepped it. We planned to return early next morning to begin the real work. We made a hellish, five-mile march back to camp, stumbling in the dark and getting drenched in the pouring rain. We didn't get back until the early morning hours. Too tired to eat, we just collapsed in our tents.

It was still pouring when we awoke the next morning. George contacted the pilot, and they decided to rendezvous at a landing strip about three miles from the kill, which would save a lot of time and backache, since we were over five miles from base camp. He also decided to have a meat packer brought in to speed up things. We got our gear together and headed out, prepared to make camp at the rendezvous strip on the way over to the kill site. By the time we got there, nightfall was already approaching, eliminating the possibility of packing any meat that day.

The next morning we awoke to cold rain again, and we were miserable in our perpetually damp clothes. Nevertheless, at first light we hiked out to the kill site, George cutting trail along the way. We butchered the moose, taking almost half the day to get all the meat ready for travel, and then we began the herculean task of packing it all out to the landing strip three miles away.

It took three grueling days, averaging 80 to 150 pounds per load, but we finally got it all moved. Imagine our state of mind when, on the last day, we were informed that the pilot had damaged a wheel on the plane the day before and would be unable to land on the strip. We would have to carry all the meat another two miles to a lake, where he would pick us up by floatplane.

The next day, we hauled two loads of meat back to the lake and spent the evening in base camp. When we made it back up to the kill site the next morning, we discovered that a bear, a very large one, had found the remainder of the meat, eating and spoiling a good part of it. We gathered up whatever scraps we could find and packed them along with the antlers, which George had wisely cached separately, and met our pilot, who was busy loading meat at the lake. We explained the situation, and he agreed to fly me back to Aniak in two days after all the meat had been brought in.

At six o'clock on my last full day of hunting, we spotted a brown bear, which George estimated to be over nine feet, on the side of the mountain above our camp. As our pilot, Rick, flew in again to get the last of the meat, the big bruin darted into the alders and vanished without a trace—disappointing, because the animal was in a good location for a stalk.

The next day would be my last chance for a big bear, but I wasn't worried. I knew something would present itself. Before turning in that night, we heard a grizzly roaring in proximity to our tent, which was unnerving, to say the least. We slept—not too soundly—with guns ready. But nothing

The author with his 8-foot, 3-inch, last-day Alaskan brownie.

happened. The next morning, we awoke long before light and, with our binoculars, went out to scout from the lakeshore. As daylight was breaking, I spotted a good-size brown bear up on the side of the mountain. George told me, "Johnny, there's your bear!" It was a fat, mature bear, one George figured to be over eight feet. Though not a nine-footer, it was still very handsome and in good condition. It would make a great trophy.

"OK, let's go!" said George. "If you just stick with me, we'll go up and get above him before the wind changes. If you can keep up, we should be on top of that bear in roughly forty-five minutes."

"I'll keep up with you, just give me some time to catch my breath when we get there. Don't bring me out with that thing fifty yards away and expect me to shoot in a snap when I'm dragging my tongue behind me."

"No problem. We'll work up on it, and we'll get you nice and relaxed before you have to do your shooting."

We followed a caribou trail up through the alders, practically running up the mountain. George was worried that the wind would shift and the bear would catch our scent, so we were anxious to get into position quickly. We sighted a rock outcropping and aimed straight for it. We made it there in exactly forty-five minutes. After shedding packs, preparing our rifles, and catching our wind, we cautiously advanced the last seventy-five yards. George whispered, "If you inch your way out over that little knoll, I think you're going to see the bear right below. When he's in the right position for you, let him have it. I'll be right behind to back you up."

After a slow belly crawl to the knoll, I looked down, but there was no bear. George and I became concerned, figuring the griz had gone into the alder thicket, in which case we might easily become the hunted. After crawling up to the next little knob, we spied the immense back of the bear by an alder thicket sixty yards distant. It was sitting out in the open, and I knew if I didn't make my first shot count, there would be hell to pay.

I waited for what seemed an eternity for a broadside, and then let go with the .300, hitting the griz in the shoulder. It roared and wheeled around on its haunches. It was ready to charge. My second shot hit the shoulder again, but the animal did not fall over. As I was chambering a third round, George fired his .375 H&H Magnum, concerned now that the bear would charge. The big bruin went down. I put one more in its neck to finish it off. We waited ten minutes to be sure it was dead, and then approached for an appraisal of my prize. What an impressive animal! And what a great stalk it had been.

The sun finally came out. It was a gorgeous day. From our point high up on the mountain, it seemed we were on top of the world, the ruggedly beautiful mountains and valleys stretching for what seemed forever. It was then that we renamed the nearby lake Last Day Lake, to commemorate my eleventh-hour success.

We skinned the carcass and prepared it for packing in about two hours. We packed up our gear and loaded the hide and skull in our packs, and then we headed down the mountain. At Aniak, they sealed my bear hide and looked at the meat and torn bags, and our pilot flew back to pick up George. We then butchered and froze all the meat. The following day I flew home with my meat, trophies, and a lifetime's worth of great memories.

George and I keep in touch, and I'm looking forward to the day when I can hunt with him again. Maybe George and I can rename another lake, river, or mountain!

TWO MAGIC HUNTS, SEVERAL REEVALUATIONS

BY
GEORGE SIAVELIS

It is still dark as I awake on this cold and clear mid-September morning. I reluctantly poke out of the warmth and comfort of my sleeping bag to light the stove, and then I quickly retreat back into that lovely synthetic world. It is the third day of Larry Goehring's hunt, which I am guiding. We spent the previous day watching a lot of bull moose from the knoll above camp. We watched five different bulls all over sixty inches, chasing cows or each other. We also decided before going to bed that the next day we were gonna make an attempt on the biggest boy down there.

With extreme caution, I slip a hand slowly out of my sleeping bag to check the temperature. The hand seems to return without damage, so, like your average Alaskan hunting guide, who hasn't a lick of sense (otherwise he'd have a real job), I unzip my bag to begin another day well before the sun has decided to do the same. After lighting the lantern and watching Larry retreat farther into his synthetic world, I know as I put the water on that there are some guides who would have had a hard time resisting chuckling at him.

Some guides would have been in pure ecstasy watching Larry inside his bag, wrestling with mental demons, emotional issues, and other forces concerning why he is on another big-game hunt. Now, it's a known fact that what makes some idiots take up guiding has nothing to do with loving the outdoors or its challenges or any of that nonsense. People become hunting guides purely because they are so sadistic that they love to watch other people suffer, and they are willing to suffer themselves so that they are able to watch others suffer on a regular basis. Myself, I love the outdoors and the challenges it brings, but I do notice the client's suffering and try not to take it too seriously. Sometimes their suffering is documented with photos or by other witnesses, which is the main reason guides hire extra help. Generally, the more persons a guide hires the more sadistic he or she is. Each year I hire only one or two employees, and I take only a few clients. I don't want to feel too guilty after the season about what I've witnessed.

I could tell Larry was trying to figure out why he had gotten himself into this situation again. I go through pretty much the same thing each morning, finally saying to myself that any job would be better than this one. But then I picture watching my client get up, and suddenly the great outdoors motivates me once again!

Finally, what would be one of the high points of the day for some guides occurs: Larry emerges from his sack with an unbelievable look on his face. Some guides would have a hard time not laughing out loud at this point. Larry's only mistake is not being awake and ready with a light and camera to document my emergence on any of these mornings. Like I said, some people just aren't that sadistic. Larry's one of those guys that's easy to guide, and fun to be around, and he doesn't try to document his guide's "love of work" (in town it might be considered suffering). It doesn't much matter, of course, how good a hunter is, and it's hard to change guides. My coffee sure is tasting good, and it's warming me up, too.

About the time Larry starts coming out of his bag and into the warm tent, I have to go do a number one. I have had to since I got up, but I pretend that I've been too cold until now, and I can't hold it any longer. I wait until Larry's completely out of his bag. Boy, does this little tent cool quickly when I open the door wide to get out. Poor Larry scrambles for his clothes while mumbling something about my leaving the door wide open. As I stand and relieve myself, I am thinking how a lot of guides—that is, those who guide for the wrong reasons—might be laughing at the noises coming from inside the tent at this point.

Larry and I begin to hear my assistant guide, Henry, in his tent nearby. It sounds like one hell of a wrestling match, and I wonder how many battles it takes to be an official war.

I re-enter the tent, and busily get breakfast and do other preparations. My suffering and possible enjoyment is lessened after Larry starts his coffee. Then Henry comes into our tent. Henry doesn't have any heat in his tent; employees aren't supposed to. Henry has a smile on his face and seems ready to hunt. Wow! It's just amazing how some hunters can disguise suffering.

The author's deluxe riverboat used on the second half of the hunt, from which the big bull caribou was shot.

After breakfast and during the second cup of coffee, it usually starts to set in that we have to leave the tent for the subfreezing and windy great outdoors. That's usually the second time in the day that I re-evaluate my choice of career.

Finally we're headed up the hill to our lookout. Quite seriously, it's good to be out hunting. Nowhere would I rather be right now. When we get to our spot to glass from, Larry sits down a lot closer to Henry. You'd think he was worried about me forgetting to close the tent door up here, too.

We soon spot the big boy. I'm sure the animal's over sixty-eight inches, and its palms are huge. Since the bull's a couple of miles from us, we devise a plan to work our way toward it through a lot of thick brush, keeping the wind in our favor while pretending to be another bull and a couple of cows. (Me, the bull, of course, and those guys the cows.) We head down the mountain toward the giant moose.

After we wade the river and work a little way into the thick brush, I start advertising that we're just a bull and a couple of cows on our way through the woods to see the king of the valley. Every little way, I bawl like a cow or grunt like a bull, and we make no real attempt to be super quiet. At times we make more noise than we need to by doing things like raking brush. Not very far along I hear an answer ahead. We stop and stoop down. The bull grunts, and I answer with a weak grunt. I add a cow bawl. The bull starts grunting continuously and is coming toward us. I can see antlers coming through the brush. We get the video camera out and get ready just in case it's the big boy. The bull keeps coming and steps into the meadow. The animal is about fifty-five inches. We film it as it continues toward us to about seventy-five yards. We enjoy the moment together. Ah! There's no better career in the world! Finally, the moose decides Henry and Larry ain't that cute and leaves. We push on toward our objective. We continue to call and act like moose (me being the bull) as we go through the brush and over the beaver dams.

I think I hear branches break! We stop and listen. I grunt softly. I bawl and then rake brush. I look back at my guys to make sure nobody's getting the wrong idea. Keep in mind that

Larry and packer Henry Fryer with Larry's tremendous 72½-inch Boone and Crockett moose.

my assistant has been away from his wife for some time. We wait. Nothing. I grunt louder. No answer. We wait. I bawl. Still nothing. We pick up our packs and move on. We're still quite a way from where we last saw the big boy. I grunt or bawl periodically on our way.

When we get to where I think the big boy might hear us, we stop and get ready, and I start calling. I grunt and rake a tree with a dead branch. We listen for a response. Silence. I bawl loudly, shaking hysterically. I grunt again and go silent. We wait and listen. Nothing. It seems no one hears anything. Larry waits patiently with his rifle ready, and I can tell he's really enjoying himself. Henry waits with the video camera, listening acutely for the slightest noise. I grunt again. Still nothing. After waiting a little longer we push on.

We stop again after another few hundred yards. I bawl like a cow. I pick up a dead branch and start raking an old, dead spruce tree. I bawl again. We sit still and listen. . . . I hear a bull grunt. I motion to the boys that we have gotten a response.

145

I grunt again and rake the spruce. I hear a moose coming toward us, and then a cow runs by and bawls. Briefly, I hear the moose grunting rapidly as it trots down toward us. I see movement and figure it's the bull, but it's another cow going by. The brush is so thick we can see only a few yards, and things are happening very fast. I hear other moose, but can't see them. I stand as tall as I can to see over the brush. Suddenly, there it is, thirty yards in front of us, standing and looking for the bull it thinks is nearby. I move out of the way, point at the monster, and say to Larry, "Him big enough; shoot him." All you can see are its upper neck, head, and antlers. Larry drops it with a shot through the spine of its upper neck.

When we walk up to the fallen giant, we are in awe of its size and beauty. Its size especially makes me reevaluate my career— the third time already this day, and it is early yet. Larry jumps across the moose and hugs me. He says, "George, a dream of mine has come true, and you're a part of it." About that time, I am

The author actually caught on film reevaluating his career direction.

hoping he knows I was only kidding about my being the bull and so on. Seriously, though, Henry and I are happy for him.

The bull turns out to be over seventy-two inches wide. I'm told it has officially scored very well in the Boone and Crockett all-time record book. It really couldn't have happened to a nicer guy.

While packing the meat out, I reevaluate my career several times. Actually, it turns out to be a pretty easy forty-five-minute pack-out to the river, where my jet raft will take over the honors. That night we toast Larry, the moose, Henry, Larry's huge cigars, the great outdoors, and even my career more than a few times.

The following day, after boating the meat up to the lake, we have the glorious pleasure of watching thousands of caribou migrating. We put the scope on quite a few of them and make some stalks, but none are big enough to take. Larry wants a book caribou. It sure is hard to beat watching thousands of caribou crossing the tundra all day. I don't reevaluate my career even once.

After we fly back to Aniak and get the meat, trophy, and everything else squared away, a much-needed shower is embarked upon. Even though a guide finds no enjoyment in seeing his client enjoy a hot shower in the middle of the hunt, there isn't much I can do to stop it. Between the clients and hired help, a guide must keep in mind that there's always the chance of a mutiny.

The next morning dawns clear again but much colder. We're talking single digits here, and small ones at that. After three distinct wrestling matches and three exorcisms, we come out of our bags to start another day. Larry and I launch in the big jet boat and head upriver again. We're looking for bear and caribou this time. The country seems to go from green to gold to bare-limbed in a matter of days. (Perhaps time to reevaluate?) The country, mountains, and river are truly beautiful. We stop and enjoy a little fishing along the way. I want to show my client and friend how to stop and smell the roses along the way, even though there isn't a live leaf in sight, let alone roses!

A few hours later I pull into a dead-end slough and park. We will camp on board the boat on this outing. Since it's a little

Larry's giant caribou shot from the boat at forty yards.

colder, there is more opportunity for enjoyment of the great outdoors. Larry and I enjoy a hot lunch and Larry's fine imported cigars. Larry's the type of guy who won't smoke a cigar in front of somebody without offering him or her one. He just doesn't have a sadistic bone in his body. He's got a lot to learn, I know, but you gotta forgive him. He's just a cheechako.

For the next three days, Larry and I enjoy watching perhaps five thousand or more caribou walk by the boat no more than fifty yards away. We have gone out looking for bear sign in the morning, but there is no salmon in the river this year, and the bears have apparently left by now. Finally, though, a giant bull comes trotting along, and I mention to Larry that he might want to consider putting down the camera for a moment and shooting this one. I'm not sure if it will make the book; in fact,

I tell Larry that the caribou is very close but probably wouldn't make Boone and Crockett's all-time book. Larry drops the bull at forty yards. I wonder if caribou ever reevaluate their direction in life.

We videotape and take pictures of the beautiful fallen monarch, which would score high in the SCI record book and might squeak into Boone and Crockett. After that we butcher the animal, and we merely toss the quarters into the boat. Ah! What a job! Somebody has to do it. We enjoy the constant sunshine, which is finally starting to warm up the day. We watch beavers and otters work their way up- and downriver. Life is magic! No reevaluations today.

We spend most of our remaining time together smoking fine cigars and filming caribou at very close range. The animals provide us with constant entertainment. One bold bull with impressive antlers walks over and hangs its head over the side of the boat and looks through the door into the cabin. The humans and caribou, separated by only four or five feet, stare at each other for a moment in time.

I wonder if some caribou are sadistic. I have seen them do things to each other and watch each other in a way that makes me think some are. Over the years, I'm sure I've caught them laughing at me more than once. Probably during one of my reevaluations.

ANTLERS AND ICE

BY
DR. RONALD LEBEAUMONT

In 1989 I was lucky enough to draw a coveted Shiras moose tag in Wyoming. Armed with bow and arrows, I hunted hard and ultimately harvested a young bull. During my Wyoming hunt, I had seen a much larger bull but was unable to get within bow range, so on the last day I opted for meat in the freezer. That was my first moose hunt, but it was not my last. I continued to dream of wide-palmed, massive monarchs lording over beaver ponds and willow flats. Then, in 1991, I ventured north to Alberta, Canada, with visions of big bulls dancing in my head. It was another hard, tough hunt, and I passed on the only bull I saw, a little "shoe-jack" horned youngster devoid of palmation. Over the next seven days, I saw no other bulls. As I drove home, I decided I had to hunt Alaska moose.

In fall 1992 I went to Alaska. I took a nice but rather lightly racked 61-inch bull. It was great to come home with meat and a nice trophy. Even more exhilarating was just being out in the bush, away from corrupt civilization, in some of the most unspoiled country on earth. Indeed, Alaska has become my

The author with his first Alaska-Yukon bull, which had a 61-inch spread.

Mount Hesperus and the Alaska Range, with Big River in the foreground. This area is close to where the 72^{1}/$_{8}$-inch moose was taken.

hopeless addiction. I have returned there every fall since 1992, savoring the crimson blush of tundra and the bold yellow of alder thickets, the taste of wild blueberries and caribou jerky, and the heart-pounding intensity of an encounter with the giant Alaska-Yukon moose.

In 1995 I hunted in Alaska with Bob Hannon at Big River Lodge near Big River. We saw some gorgeous country, including the snow-covered Revelation Mountains, which jut dramatically from the tundra: one moment, sea level; the next, 5,000 feet. The sunset and sunrise cast a ruby-red glow upon those snow-covered peaks. It was absolutely breathtaking.

But despite the beautiful scenery, I was wet, cold, and tired after ten days of pounding the tundra. It was time to go home, and we had not seen a good moose, though we did have a caribou in the freezer, thanks to my favorite hunting partner and wife, Dominique. Later, I learned that an Austrian hunter had taken an enormous Boone and Crockett moose from the same camp we had left only a few days earlier. I dreamed that someday I might be so lucky and made plans to return to Big River the following year.

The winter of 1995–96 was very mild in west-central Alaska. Most years there is deep snow, and the moose get bogged down. The wolves, weighing much less, are able to run atop the crusted snow without sinking, making moose easy prey for wolf packs. Old bulls, stressed from the rut, are often the first to be killed under normal winter conditions. But, given the mild winter, more of these old trophy-class bulls would probably be around come fall, when I would be there to hunt them. In addition, I had heard that native subsistence hunters had taken a 68-inch bull in August near where I was planning to hunt. The year 1996 was also looking like an excellent year for antler growth, with good winter survival of old bulls and a wet spring producing an abundance of browse rich in nutrients.

To prepare for my 1996 hunt, I spent many hours running, weight training, shooting, and organizing my gear. Finally, September arrived and I was off to Alaska! From Anchorage I flew to McGrath, where Kenneth Best had taken the former

No. 1 Boone and Crockett Alaska-Yukon moose. The bush pilot reported that he had seen more than the usual number of big moose in the area. I was feeling optimistic—until I landed at Big River.

Two of the hunting guides had to return home at the last minute for personal reasons, leaving only two experienced guides and two camp helpers for five hunters. As if that weren't bad enough, the weather had been unusually cold, windy, and snowy. That meant the moose would be bedded down in the spruce thickets, which meant we would be unable to locate them by glassing.

Over the next five days, we left camp and hiked two miles up a steep, slick, swampy trail, where the mud threatened to pull our boots off with every step and black muck was sometimes well above our knees. The weight of our rubber hip boots, packs, and rifles made us sweat. When we reached the top of the trail, we were on a broad, tundra-covered plateau where the wind-chill factor was well below zero, chilling our sweaty bodies. From atop this frozen plateau, we could glass the slopes of several mountains and look down into some willow-choked river valleys.

But nothing was moving. The only moose tracks across the snowy tundra were at least several days old. After five long, cold days of hunting, we had seen only two bull moose, but they were at least two miles away and headed away from us across the Gagarrayah River. Time was running out for everyone in camp. In fact, two of the five hunters left camp with rich memories of the Alaska wilderness, but with no moose.

The next day a brutal Arctic storm dumped a foot of snow at base camp, and its winds made drifts several feet deep. After a brief foray atop the plateau, we were forced back to camp by the near-zero visibility caused by the blowing snow. While we tried to warm our frozen bodies near the woodstove at base camp, we were surprised when senior guide Tommy Karshekoff returned with the two other hunters. Thinking they would be snowed in at spike camp, they had struggled through the heart of the blizzard for more than eight hours to make it back to base camp by nightfall. After they had eaten some delicious, hot moose

The author with a 72⅛-inch moose, which scores 504⅛ in SCI, and 227⅜ in B&C.

enchiladas and warmed their nearly hypothermic bodies by the blazing fire, Tommy mentioned that he had seen two good bulls, each with several cows. The bulls were less than four miles from base camp, and one of them was exceptional. At the time he spotted them, however, the weather was awful and his hunters so exhausted that his only option was to return to base camp.

The next morning, it was still snowing, but visibility had improved considerably. While the other hunters packed their gear for the long trip home, Tommy and I headed out. We decided to take an ATV, just in case we got lucky and needed it to pack out the moose. But the ATV caused us a great deal of agony because the ice-covered trail offered little traction. For about four hours, we pushed and pulled the machine repeatedly. At the trailhead, we abandoned it in a snowbank and set out on foot in the direction of the giant moose Tommy had seen the day before. The weather had worsened and visibility had deteriorated, but, mercifully, our efforts in the deep powder kept us warm in the twenty-degree temperature.

Snow was filling our tracks almost as we made them, and I was beginning to wonder if we would find the moose before the weather forced us to turn back. Tommy admonished me to step directly in his tracks so that we sounded more like a moose walking, and to be absolutely quiet. I nodded OK, glad that I was wearing my wool mackinaw, which is about as silent as you can get. After three hours, I had almost given up, when Tommy suddenly grabbed my sleeve and pointed off to the right. "Shoot, quick!" he whispered.

I saw a giant rack of antlers crowning an enormous brown body bedded down in the deep snow only one hundred yards away. Swiftly, I chambered a round in my Remington 700, .30-06 rifle, slipped off the safety, placed the cross hairs low on the chest, and squeezed off a shot. The great bull didn't flinch. I thought I had missed it, until it dropped its head into the snow. The 180-grain Nosler Partition bullet had done its job quickly and humanely.

The closer we got to the bull, the more impressive it became. Tommy said it was one of the biggest he had seen in over twenty years of guiding moose hunters. We made short work of butchering and caping the animal. We carefully laid each quarter in the snow to cool, and since daylight was running short, we elected to leave everything and come back in the morning. I placed the two tenderloins in my backpack and we began the long walk back to camp, leaving behind the ATV.

When we got back to camp, we were surprised to see the other two hunters still there, bad weather having canceled their trip to McGrath. They were eager to learn if we were successful. Saying nothing, I placed my backpack on the table to display the tenderloins. Instantly the whole camp's mood changed from depression to jubilation, and we celebrated my extraordinary good luck. The next day the guides and I headed back to retrieve the rest of the meat and the trophy.

The moose had a 72⅛ inch spread, scoring 227 ⅜ in Boone and Crockett and 504⅛ in Safari Club International, placing it into both record books. It was the No. 1 Alaska-Yukon moose in 1996 for the North American Hunting Club, and placed No. 3 in the Alaska Professional Hunter's Association/SCI awards for 1996. But more important than numbers on a scorecard are the memories of bush planes and spike camps, of stews cooked on a woodstove and friendships forged in the outdoors, of the adversity and challenge of hunting Alaska, and the rugged beauty of the Alaskan wilderness.

THE
GERMAN CONNECTION

BY
PETE BUIST

September 4. Eve of moose season. Sixty-three degrees. At 7 P.M. I drive over to see Assistant Guide Fred Bast. He has just finished fueling up the Bellanca Scout. Anja Götz, her father, Hans, and the packers, Bill and John Bast (Fred's sons), are already at Herman Bucholtz's cabin. Also along on the trip is Hannah, Fred's German wirehaired pointer. From Fairbanks to the cabin is a thirty-minute flight. It is fall, and yellow aspens, willows, red berry bushes, and dwarf birches are mingled among the dark-green spruces. Spirits are high as we fly into camp at Beaver Creek.

Hans's return to Herman's place at Beaver Creek is significant. He is the nephew of Herman Bucholtz, whom he last visited in the early seventies. At that time, Herman was still trapping the area on foot with a dog as his only companion. Soon after Hans's visit, Herman was diagnosed with Parkinson's disease and had to give up the line.

Herman's trapline was sold in two parts. The upstream part, including the Alpha Trail and the Winter Trail, was sold to Clair

Herman's cabin at Beaver Creek.

Lammers. The downstream part, including part of the Summer Trail and part of Beaver Creek north of Big Bend and Fossil Creek, was sold to Leroy Shank and Jerry Gappert. Leroy and Jerry had trapped it for only one year when Jerry was killed in a snow machine accident. Leroy then moved to Kantishna to trap, and in his absence he allowed Gary Thompson and me to trap the area during winter 1976–77. That was a busy winter, for not only did Gary and I take 213 martens and 5 wolverines, but my son, Jason, was born. All the money I had made trapping during that season went toward paying the hospital bill for Jason's arrival.

Several years later, I trapped Beaver Creek for two winters with Jon Gleason and "Bear" Wyse, and each winter we had some fifty miles of line.

After Herman died, his wife, Marie, stayed in Fairbanks for a while and then moved back to Germany to be with family. From time to time, Fred had checked in on Herman, and when Herman died, Fred bought the forty-acre parcel from the estate.

In 1980, when Beaver Creek was designated by the federal government as a wild and scenic river and the White Mountains National Recreation Area was established on the surrounding federal land, Fred wisely had the forty-acre parcel subdivided. He has no inclination to sell any of it.

I have not been to Beever Creek for more than ten years, and now as we fly in, a lot of great memories (and a few nasty ones!) return.

In the cozy "main" cabin (Herman has about twenty trapline cabins scattered throughout the country), we share tales of Beaver Creek in days past. Hans, who speaks very good English, is a prison guard in a youth facility; before that he was a master sergeant and tank commander in the military reserve. Anja, at seventeen, is far more limited in her English, but she seems to understand a lot. We all speak "hunting!"

Anja has passed the rigid hunting exams given in Germany, which include a marksmanship test. She has taken roebuck, but has dreamed of taking Alaska moose ever since she first heard her father's stories about Beaver Creek.

September snow at Beaver Creek.

I explain to Hans that my primary purpose as a guide on this trip is to do paperwork. This is because "nonresident aliens," as defined by statute, are required to be accompanied by a master or registered guide. I am now referred to as "Herr Paperwork."

The sporting goods store in Fairbanks that sold Anja her license and moose tag has neglected to furnish the required harvest ticket. Nor did they write the tag and harvest numbers on the license, as is required by law. Luckily, since I am an official licensing agent, and since I have brought the materials, I am able to finish the harvest ticket and render her legal once more. Then I write in the numbers and fill out the hunting contract. Now we are legal to hunt tomorrow.

It's clear and warm, actually too warm for good moose hunting. We turn off the oil stove and fall into our bunks. Fred, Hans, Anja, and I make good use of the four monstrous bunks. John and Bill, Fred's boys and our packers, occupy a big sleeping tent down on the airstrip. I sleep very soundly until about 3 A.M., when I go outside to urinate. I come very close to doing it in my pants when I nearly trip over a porcupine on the top front step. At least there are no bad snorers in this group, though Anja talks in her sleep. But if any secrets are revealed, it is only to Hans, because it's all in German.

September 5. Fifty-seven degrees. Opening day. I get up at 6 A.M., but the fog is down on the deck and visibility is nil. There is really no sense in going out to hunt. Everyone else is up by 8 A.M., and we leisurely eat a bacon and eggs breakfast. By 11 A.M. the fog begins to lift, so we get Anja sighted in along the edge of the airstrip. She is a very good shot with that borrowed .30-06. We make only some minor adjustments to the scope, and then Fred, John, Hans, and Anja float off downriver to return, according to Fred, at 7 P.M. Bill and I remain in camp for a lazy day. Several aircraft fly over while Bill and I read and nap. Meanwhile, Hannah attempts to chase all the red squirrels out of the area. Tough duty!

At 3 P.M., I go outside to sit in the "high seat," which Hans and Anja pronounce "*hoch sitz*." (We affectionately refer to the outhouse near the cabin as the "low seat.") Herman built this high seat in the '60s and shot several moose from it. It has a seat for one and a set of moose scapulae used to imitate the sound of two bulls fighting. From the high seat, you can see thousands of acres of moose habitat—from Beaver Creek to the big ridge dividing Beaver Creek from the Tolovana drainage. After an hour of futile glassing, I climb down and walk toward the divide on the horse trail. From my next vantage point I can see the mountains on the east side of Beaver Creek, but I spy nary a living creature, much less a bull moose. During the period when I trapped this area, and once when I flew over it en route to a sheep hunt much farther north, I saw sheep (even rams) on those very cliffs.

At 5:45 P.M., I begin preparing a twelve-pound salmon for dinner. I season the fish and stuff it in the oven to bake alongside some potatoes wrapped in foil. Fred and the crew return almost exactly at 7 P.M. They saw two rafters floating the river, but no moose. My dinner is a hit, as is the yellow cake with chocolate frosting that Bill made. We feast and get ready to head back out for the prime evening hunting hours.

Fred, Hans, Anja, and I leave at 8 P.M., crossing the river to a point on the opposite bank some two hundred yards upstream from the end of the airstrip. We climb a steep little bluff to glass the flats and benches behind the cabin, and we perch with our binoculars and spotting scopes until almost ten o'clock, when it becomes too dark to see. Then in darkness we stumble back down the bluff, across the river, and back to the warm cabin.

September 6. Thirty-seven degrees. Once again the fog is atrocious. We sleep in until 8 A.M., and then Hans and Anja go grayling fishing while the rest of us huddle around the stove. Fred finds some oatmeal that appears to have been left by Herman (it's that old) and cooks it up into a more than passable breakfast, and then he bakes bread. At 10:30 a plane flies over, but we cannot see it through the fog. Just the fact that someone would be flying in that stuff leads us to believe that the fog will soon burn off. It is growing lighter every minute. We plan to hunt moose upriver near Big Bend, while Fred flies back to Fairbanks to pick up his friend and business partner, Walt Babula.

The author with a 56-inch Beaver Creek bull.

We leave for Big Bend just after noon in two shifts. I will be in the second wave and thus am able to finish the bread baking detail. I also sweep out the cabin and wash the dishes, and then I take a bath and shave.

There is a lot of aircraft activity today. Fred floats back in at 4:30 P.M. after dropping the others at a good glassing point. Shortly thereafter, we are visited by the ADFG assistant area biologist Toby Boudreau and his friend Gerry. Toby, on leave from work, and Gerry, a vacationing Connecticut game warden, are hunting moose. They are going to float downriver for a pickup at Kenny Miller's homestead at Victoria Creek. Tonight they plan to catch a lot of grayling and try hard *not* to see a moose because they have flown today and cannot hunt. (An Alaska statute precludes a person from hunting on the same day he or she has flown.) The plane that flew over this morning was Sandy Hamilton trying to fly Toby and Gerry in. Unfortunately, they never had the visibility and had to return to Fairbanks and wait for the fog to lift.

We talk over coffee and fresh bread. Fred takes off for Fairbanks to get Walt, and Toby and Gerry float downriver to find a good camp for the night. I prepare some caribou burgers and sliced potatoes to put on the grill later, and then I head upstream to join the hunting party.

At Big Bend I see only Hans and Bill (and Hannah, the pointer) at the lookout. I learn from them that John and Anja are in hot pursuit of a big bull and a paddle-horn bull they spotted on a mountainside about one hour ago. I hook up with them, tying the canoes up in a small beaver slough and then heading out through swampy terrain.

The bull suddenly appears on the far side of a little tundra pond. Anja takes an offhand shot at one hundred yards, downing the bull. But it gets back up and jumps in the pond. The bull swims strongly all the way to the opposite side of the pond and lunges out onto terra firma. Anja gamely follows it into the brush. Thirty yards in she finds it, and two more quick shots put it down for keeps. That's the good news. The bad news is that it's now almost 9 P.M. and night is coming on fast. Moose have never been known to skin and gut themselves while the hunters go back to the warm cabin!

We gut the bull and proceed over to the river to the canoe. We begin our float in the pitch-dark of the subarctic night. After an exciting ride, we reach the cabin at 11 P.M. We gratefully accept the reheated supper, and we make a toast of schnapps to Anja and to her beautiful 58-inch bull with its wide palms and nine brow points. This young Diana and her first Alaskan trophy are both keepers! We finally flop into the bunks at 1:15 A.M., a tired but happy crew.

September 7. Thirty degrees. Clear. It is clear today; we do not need to glass. We are up at 7:30, and I wrangle up sausage and French toast. We will move the canoes and airplane up to the big bar and base our meat recovery project from there. Fred first flies Walt, who is going to help pack the moose out, and then me to the bar. We will use the airplane to pack most of the moose meat to Fairbanks.

We cannot see the kill from the air; nevertheless, when we land we decide to move the boats onto an old beaver slough that appears to be close to the site. We take the boats across the slough and enter the woods. It takes thirty minutes to locate the dead bull. I finally locate it by standing still and watching for birds flying above it. The bull is only 250 yards from the slough.

We take photos and some video and then dive into the butchering process. There appear to be plenty of flashing blades, so I head over to the slough, placing a few ribbons and cutting a few trees to clear a good route for packing out the moose. Back at the kill site, I help with skinning and cutting. We are done in an hour and a half, and that includes the moving of the meat to the slough. Fred takes about half the meat in a small canoe, paddles to the bar, loads the Scout, and takes off to Fairbanks. We go back to the landing and prepare to move the remainder of the meat and gear.

At the landing, we put some of the meat into the small canoe with Bill and Walt. The rest of the meat, the antlers, and the packs, as well as Hans, Anja, John, and I (and Hannah) load up into the other. The fact that we are too heavily loaded becomes evident as soon as we leave the sheltered water of the slough and enter the current of the open river.

Water pours over the bow. Being a master guide, I recognize immediately that this is a bad sign. John and I both holler, "Oh sh—"; Hans and Anja holler, "Oh *sheis!*" Holding the two rifles, Hans goes over the left side of the boat. I go over the right side carrying the bow rope. I make for shore. The water is up to my chest and very cold! Anja makes a valiant effort to save her moose antlers, but to no avail. She says, "*Mein elch, mein elch.*" The boat, antlers, and three bags (three hundred pounds) of meat are soon at the bottom of the river. The bow is resting on a sandbar, but the stern is three feet underwater.

Paddles, coats, and bags float merrily down Beaver Creek. We intercept most of it and throw it up on the bank. Next we strong-arm the boat to shallow water and begin bailing. After twenty minutes of bailing, the canoe is light enough to enable us to flip it over and dump out the remaining water.

The next major project is to recover the moose meat, which is now nicely chilled, having spent the last half hour on the river bottom. I strip to my long johns and dive to the river bottom for the three bags of meat. Being white, they are easy to locate. The antlers, however, are nowhere to be found, and I am afraid that the current has moved them much farther downstream. By climbing a little hill and peering down into the water, I finally glimpse a rather orange glow among the stones. One more trip into the freezing water and Anja's antlers are rescued from their watery resting place.

After standing around in soaked, heavy clothing on the gravel bar, we are all pretty cold. At some point I realize I have a dry bag as yet unopened. In it is a dry jacket. Feeling chivalrous, I offer it to the shivering Anja. Chivalry is rewarded by the wonderfully uninhibited young fräulein's peeling off of her wet jacket, shirt, and bra to put on my dry jacket. Her dad may still be shivering, but the rest of us are warm!

We transfer some of our load to the other canoe and float down to the big bar. We meet Fred, who has returned from his first meat flight to Fairbanks. Walt and Bill (both still dry) stay to help Fred load the remainder of the meat into the Scout. But before the loading, Fred flies Anja back to the cabin. She is very cold and shows signs of hypothermia. John, Hans, and I paddle off downriver toward camp, making it in record time. By the time we get there, Anja is dried off, has changed into warm gear, and is feeling much better. The unseasonably warm fall weather may have been bad for moose hunters, but it has been a blessing in the case of our inadvertent swim in Beaver Creek. The way my luck usually runs, it should have been snowing, or at least raining! We trundle into the cabin, change, and hang our wet gear from the rafters to dry over the stove.

For supper, we barbecue both tenderloins and enjoy them with some rice and steamed broccoli. Dessert is ice cream, whipped cream, and chocolate sauce, all of which Fred brought in from Fairbanks on his last trip there. Exhausted but eternally grateful to be in the warm cabin with nobody the worse for wear, we turn in at 11:30.

September 8. Forty-five degrees. High cloudiness. Without Fred's boys (they're asleep in their sleeping bags), we have a light breakfast. Walt spends an hour in the high seat, spotting two

The high seat.

small bulls on the hills to the west. The rest of us laze around the cabin. Most of the crew head to the woods along the river to select timber for construction of a new (and safer) high seat, to be engineered in the finest German tradition by Hans.

The remainder of moose season will be spent just existing in moose camp. We will get up early in the frosty morning if we choose. We will do the camp chores and improvement projects at a leisurely pace. We may take an afternoon nap. The finest of international friendships; the beautiful, crisp fall weather; and the smell of wood smoke, freshly split spruce bolts, boiled coffee, bacon, gun oil, and pipe tobacco will all combine to make this the exquisitely high-quality experience that those unfortunate folks who do not hunt are not privileged to know. We who hunt are indeed blessed.

ADVENTURES ALONG WOLF RIVER

BY

BERT VERHOEF

I arrive in Aniak, Alaska, on a flight with four other passengers. In my pocket are a caribou tag, a fishing license, and a black bear tag that I hope to use on a bear, wolf, or wolverine, whichever critter screws up first. George Siavelis, my guide for the next ten days, picks me up at the airport. My first impression of George is OK, possibly because when he laughs—which he does a lot—he reminds me of one of my colleagues back in Holland. George talks with great enthusiasm about the country he calls home. I am quickly captivated by all he has to tell about the country's wilderness, animals, and people. He is also a good observer and is quite intelligent.

In the evening we eat caribou—quite tasty—followed by strawberry cake and cream and and too much coffee. I'm back in the cabin by eleven, packing my gear for tomorrow's trip. I turn in at midnight, and George will pick me up at 6 A.M.

Though I've had very little sleep, too much coffee, too much excitement, and am feeling jet lag, I am up before six the next morning and ready for the adventure. The weather is overcast with low clouds (although that will change and the sun will shine

The author with one of the many Arctic grayling he would catch. This one was cooked on a rock for supper.

for the next two weeks while I'm here). We go down to the river and load the airplane. We taxi out to the middle of the river and take off. After traveling over some 125 miles of untouched wilderness, we land on a lake. One of George's boats, a custom jet raft, is already moored there. It's an aluminum frame with two inflatable floats without any real bottom, just places where you can lash bags. According to George, it is a unique design. It has a shallower draught than a standard jet boat, which makes it particularly handy in the shallows.

We head off downstream in the jet raft using the engine. After awhile we drift with the current, George steering the boat skillfully past shallows and rocks. The river is splendid; it meanders and breaks into two, three, and even four channels, all dotted with islands and gravel banks. Willows are everywhere, gnawed away by beavers, and there are numerous beaver lodges. Here and there the secondary channels are dammed. Only days later will I come to truly appreciate what an incredibly beautiful valley this is. It is unspoiled, primeval; it stretches for what seems forever, and is surrounded by mountains and other valleys that stretch hundreds of miles.

George steers us to shore at a gravel bar, where we'll pitch camp for the night. We take our gear out of the boat, prepare a meal, and then climb a hill to spy out the land with our binoculars. We see several caribou here and there in the valley and on the slopes. One hour later I see something black moving a long way off. When I look through George's large spotting scope, it turns out to be a bear—a large brown bear, according to George. After setting up the tent, I go fishing and catch my first arctic grayling. Later George broils it on a rock, and it proves very tasty. My first night's sleep in the wilderness is uninterrupted.

Over the following days we see caribou, black bear, and grizzly every day. These are days of relaxation, full of peace, spent fishing and also glassing for bear and caribou each evening and morning.

August 15, 1997. On this memorable morning, we once again climb the hill to spy out the land. If the black bear, which we have spotted three days in succession, shows up again, we will cross the river and wait near the spot where we saw it in the evenings. This evening, however, there is no black bear, for a brown bear has apparently chased it off. While we sit quietly watching, George suddenly becomes excited. He has spotted a wolf standing in a grassy spot between the low spruces on the opposite riverbank. A splendid sight, but the wolf disappears as quickly as it appeared.

In the late evening we go on watch again. There is one large, lone brown bear on the opposite side of the river, and on our side of the river, quite a way off, a grizzly with two cubs. This sow and one of its cubs seem almost white in the glow of the low evening sun just before it disappears behind the mountain. The other cub looks practically black. (We will come across these three bears two more times.) A bald eagle remains perched at the top of a black spruce. As I study it carefully through my binoculars, I suddenly discover its nest at the broken top of the spruce. The nest is gigantic, and in it is one almost mature eagle flapping its wings.

170

August 16, 1997. This day will turn out to be an eventful one, though I'm not aware of this as I wake from a peaceful sleep in our tent. George is a splendid storyteller and can paint with words to captivate his audience. In the morning, we sit contented on our lookout along the river, gazing at the slopes bathed in the morning sun and the caribou, or whatever else is out there. Suddenly I hear a sound that reminds me of a ferry's horn a long way off. George says, "Wolves." We gaze through our binoculars, and suddenly there they are in our sights on top of a bluff across the river. The valley is transected with old dry river courses surrounded by bluffs. Then something that George has witnessed only once before in his lifetime develops. More and more wolves appear on top of the bluff—six very large wolves and two slightly smaller ones. Eight wolves playing and chasing each other in the hot sun.

The alpha wolf is clearly distinguishable, being extremely large and powerfully built. The other wolves behave like young dogs around it. The entire pack lies bathing in the sun on the old bluff, some of them occasionally playing with each other and with the alpha. It is such a wonderful sight that it brings tears to my eyes. George has a great deal of respect for wild animals, especially wolves, and he teaches me much about them and their behavior. I had hoped to see just one wolf in Alaska, if only for a few seconds, knowing that the chances were slim to none. But here I am, watching a pack of them for nearly an hour.

Suddenly, the alpha wolf gets up and trots off the bluff into the willow bottom. Almost in unison, all the other wolves follow in single file down the trail and into the willow bottom. I tell George that I can't believe what we have been watching. George just stares across the river, watching to see whether any of them come out of the willows.

Out of the blue, George asks if I would like to go on a long hike on this beautiful day. He tells me that he believes the wolves will bed near the bluff, as it is already very late in the day for them to be out and about. George suggests that we cross the canyon and spend the evening on the bluff overlooking the willows the wolves went into. He admits there's only an outside chance of successfully stalking wolves on foot when they are over a mile away, but he says we need a hike, the weather is beautiful, we have seen bears on that side every night, and maybe—just maybe—the wolves will show themselves, come evening. I agree, and so we're off.

We use the raft to cross the river, and then I follow George as we make our way through the willow bottoms and old creek beds, circling downwind of what we hope will be stationary wolves. We have to make a big two- or three-mile circle around them. This hike proves easier than we had thought, since there are caribou and moose trails everywhere. Around 1:30 P.M. we are eight or nine hundred meters from the bluff. We stop here, eat, and lie dozing in the sun for the next three hours or so. Then, stealthily, we cover the last distance and inch our way over the crest of the bluff. According to George, there is little chance of our seeing the wolves, and even less of getting a shot at one, "but you never know," he adds. We sit down, each looking a different way, and wait for about two hours.

Suddenly, one of the wolves appears in the dried-up riverbed, no more than sixty meters away. Two seconds later, a second wolf appears. We hardly dare breathe. George whispers so low in my ear that I can hardly hear, "It's a small one; wait for the big one." We expect to see more wolves any second. There must be more in the vicinity. The wolves come closer and closer until they are barely twenty-five meters away. One of them gnaws nervously on a branch. They then disappear, one by one, in the low willow shrubs. We wait another half an hour, worried we won't see them again. Then they reappear in the open between the willow shrubs. A splendid sight—the two wolves in the old riverbed. Once again they come to within twenty meters. The first, a male, now appears to sense something's wrong and gazes penetratingly at the bluff where we are sitting as quiet as statues, with cramps in every part of our bodies from not moving an inch in the last three hours. It is getting late, it might be a long hike back to camp, and the cramps are getting unbearable.

The second wolf comes up the creek bed unsuspectingly. "Take him," whispers George softly. A large red spot appears on

The author with his wolf (shot from twenty-five meters) after his and George's successful three-mile stalk.

the wolf's shoulder. One leap and it is lying still among the willow shrubs. The other wolf darts off like a bolt of lightning, and then reappears in the low undergrowth and looks anxiously around.

We take pictures and then George begins to skin the wolf. He does it skillfully and is apparently a dab hand. When he is halfway through his work, we hear wolf howls from two different locations close by. We look at each other, race to reclimb the bluff, and wait. Nothing happens. George wants to finish the skinning because he wants to return to the river before dark. We take the shortest route back to the river. There are wolf tracks and droppings seemingly everywhere. The pack has evidently spent some time in this maze of woods and dried-up riverbeds. The wolves howl a lot that evening. They are singing the blues, according to George.

The next morning I feel thoroughly rested. I have slept well, though I did wake up thinking of wolves. We take our time as we eat breakfast and gather our gear to travel upstream by boat to the lake. George wants the wolf skin in the freezer back in Aniak as soon as possible, and he says the pilot will be flying to the lake today. The ride upriver is as beautiful as was the ride down. Rick, the pilot, does indeed fly in half an hour after our arrival at the lake. According to George, you can wait twenty minutes or twenty days for bush pilots to turn up.

We head downriver again and decide to camp at a tent we put up a few days earlier. We eat dinner, with coffee of course, and then climb a hill and spy out the land. After awhile, George crosses to another hill and beckons me to join him. There's a young fox cub watching us eighty meters away. In no less than ten minutes, there are five young fox cubs and a vixen sitting in a row staring at us, a delightful sight. I take a couple photos with the 300mm lens—too far away, of course, and too dark. However, later in the hunt, George and I will photograph these foxes at less than one meter.

When I've finished taking the photos, George, who has returned to our old hideout, beckons to me again. Two caribou are walking on the tundra a long distance away. One of them is a bull, not a particularly large specimen, according to George, but a mature adult. We study them through our binoculars, and slowly but surely they head in our direction. The bull appears bigger the nearer it comes. It is a good bull, not one for the record book, but who says we will come across a better specimen in the coming days? After further deliberation, we decide to have a try. The hunt is on.

I keep looking around as I trudge behind George, and I suddenly see the head of the cow surface from behind a hillock. When I hiss "George," he quietly stops, looks up, and sees the caribou. He crawls back, but it seems the caribou cow may have seen us. We turn back and after 100 meters stalk again from another angle. We watch until the cow lies down, and the bull soon follows suit, lying next to the cow. We can easily approach to within 300 meters unobserved, using the terrain. George asks about the range of my rifle. When I say 100 meters, he wonders what to do about the other 200 meters. George thinks we can head along a line of hillocks on our side, and we

The author and George with the author's bull caribou shot near the river and the boat.

do so. After awhile we come to a small notch-between. As we look over the edge, we see them lying on the opposite shore of a small pond only 200 meters away. The bull is lying very close and partially behind the cow. The distance between the cow's head and the bull's shoulder is less than half a meter.

George asks if I can make the shot, apparently concerned that I might hit the cow. I reassure him, yet I take up the aiming position three times before I am able to fix my sights steadily. I finally whisper "OK" to George. As soon as I shoot, I clearly hear the bullet strike home. Nothing much else happens. The cow doesn't even look at the bull that, with a bullet in its shoulder, cannot stand. A shot in the neck finishes it off.

That night I crawl into my sleeping bag feeling contented. George recounts enthralling stories about the mad trapper of Rat River, but I slip into a dream about the infiniteness of Alaska, and about the tundra, rivers, mountains, creatures, and peoples of this fascinating, intact, unspoiled land. I will dream about Alaska on countless occasions after I return to my native, overpopulated homeland, the Netherlands.

Meanwhile, for the next week, George and I boat, float, hike, and fish this magnificent river. We talk by the fire in the evenings, stalk animals for close-up photos, and thoroughly enjoy this awesome land. Alaska—a land to dream about, and a place I hope to return to frequently.

TRAPPING THE ALASKAN WOLF

BY

PETE BUIST

My pulse quickened as I noted seven large sets of wolf tracks coming off a lake and starting up the slough along my snow machine tracks. A quarter-inch skiff of powdery snow had fallen since my last trip around the line, and this dusting helped paint a clear picture of three adults and four youngsters. The adults were keeping pretty much to the trail, while the pups cavorted along the edges, checking scent posts, galloping up to beaver lodges, and engaging in mock combat. Three miles ahead I had a surefire wolf trap in place. If the pack stayed on the slough trail, I stood an excellent chance of taking at least one of them. I was so confident, I started worrying about where I had stored my wolf boards the previous spring!

For more than a mile, the pack kept to the trail, but then, on a long, straight stretch, my hopes were shattered, because the tracks showed that the wolves had left the trail. Why? Had they scented a moose or caribou? Had a plane flown over and spooked them? Fifty feet in front of where the wolves had left the trail was a stob of driftwood about twelve inches

Author just finished checking eighty-two miles of trapline by snowmobile on a minus 30-degree day on the Tanana Flats.

high and one and a half inches in diameter. Protruding from the icy slough at a 45-degree angle, the driftwood was a perfect spot for a urine post-set. The lead adult had recognized the stick as a place where a trap might be, and it led the other wolves off the trail. Am I giving too much credit to the intelligence of these animals? After more than twenty years of trapping them in the subarctic, I'd say, "Definitely not!" Thirty yards past the stob, the tracks showed that the wolves had returned to the trail. I continued to follow the tracks, but I wasn't feeling nearly as confident.

As I rounded the willow patch, which was right before one of my wolf traps, I saw drag marks on the slough that went up the far bank. I took out my .22 rifle. Once I topped the bank, I saw a large black wolf standing less than ten yards ahead in the willows. An adult female had one of its legs caught in my Newhouse No. 114. Despite the pack's obvious experience with traplines, one of my nonconventional sets had produced again.

* * * * * *

Trapping wolves is truly the pinnacle of a trapper's achievement. I remember my feeling of accomplishment after I had taken my first fox. Later, I got to where I could consistently catch coyotes, but it took a lot longer to learn how to catch wolves.

Though the rules for trapping the canids (which includes wolf, fox, and coyote) are the same, when going after wolves, there is no margin for error. To successfully trap a fox, for example, some human odor can still linger near the trap. Not so with wolves. All gear must be super clean. Serious wolf trappers seldom use the same gloves, wire, and trowel that they use when setting traps for other species. Catching wolves is serious business. If you are not clean, you will not catch wolves.

All my wolf gear is kept separate from the rest of my trapping equipment, and I also change my attire frequently when setting the wolf sets. When I go out for even a short winter's day (only four hours of daylight) of setting wolf sets, I take along at least two dozen pairs of clean cotton gloves. As soon as one pair

The author sets traps and snares around the carcass of a moose recently killed by wolves. The wolves always return to their kills, though they don't necessarily eat from them again.

starts to get damp, I change to a new pair. I might change gloves four or five times in forty-five minutes. I also always start a set with clean gloves, and I never place snares or traps with gloves that I've used to operate the snow machine. I'm especially careful to avoid getting gas or oil on any part of the gloves, or on gear and bait.

Wolf traps must be heavy-duty. A wolf can—and will—render a Number 4 Longspring into a collection of parts in short order. The only "small" trap I have ever had hold a wolf is the old Sterling MJ600. The trap preferred by most serious wolfers is the Alaskan No. 9. It was designed by a trapper-machinist concerned about the frailty of some of the larger jawspread traps. The Alaskan No. 9 is a coil-spring trap with 9-inch offset jaws, the maximum jawspread allowed in Alaska. The traditional favorite is the No. 114 Newhouse, which is a heavy double longspring with offset jaws and an

8½-inch jawspread. This trap has probably taken more Alaskan wolves than any other model.

Many modern wolf trappers are putting more emphasis on snares. Snares ordinarily kill wolves outright. That is why the old-timers avoided them, even though snares are lighter to carry than traditional traps. In those days, a man used snowshoes to get around his line and so had to skin any wolf he caught, there and then; he couldn't pack it. Skinning a warm wolf that you have just dispatched is preferable to dragging a frozen one ten or fifteen miles back to your cabin.

* * * * * *

I once bought a half dozen No. 114 Newhouse traps from a retired trapper. From the photos on his shed wall, I could see he was a pretty good wolfer. I asked what his secret was. "Put the trap where the wolf is going to step," he said. Having trapped some wolves myself, and being young, I laughed and forgot what he said. Now, many years later, I realize that his tip was sound.

What the old trapper meant was that if you become a student of wolf behavior and can figure out where a wolf is likely to step, you should place a trap there. Most trappers who are novices try to pick a place for a trap, and then "force" the wolf to go to it with bait and lure. Though this might work on less intelligent animals, wolves are generally too smart to go where you want them to.

The best sets are those placed where a wolf will probably go anyway. Sets on wolf trails commonly fill the bill. Here in interior Alaska, we seldom trap near towns, so burying a trap in a wolf trail is OK because there's no chance of a person coming along and stepping in it.

The drag is normally buried well away from the wolf trap. The drag should be of green wood, six to eight feet long and at least six inches in diameter. Ten to twelve feet of extension chain, which is attached to the drag, is appropriate, and all coupling devices must be welded shut. Heavy grapples or wood drags are then attached. A 140-pound wolf is a big, strong animal, so gear has to be strong and mechanically sound.

One of my favorite sets came about by watching how wolves react to the presence of a team of sled dogs that is in their territory. For many years, I used dogs as trapline transportation. The wolves eagerly followed the tracks of the sled dogs. Where I had stopped to rest my dogs, the wolves had stopped to roll and urinate in the snow. Now that I use a snowmachine, I have to simulate a resting dogteam. To do this, I carry a box with scrapings from someone's dog yard (containing brown and yellow snow) and bits of chopped fish, because sometimes I would feed chopped fish to my dogs after their rest. Just off the trail, I pack down with my snowshoes an area about thirty feet long and six feet wide, distribute the contents of the box, and bury randomly two or three wolf traps in the area. I use a clean, heavy-duty cooking spoon to bed and cover my traps in the snow. Another tool I would not be without is a pair of setting clamps. You don't want your finger caught in a No. 114 Newhouse or an Alaskan No. 9!

* * * * * *

While snared wolves are normally frozen, trapped wolves should be shot with a carefully placed .22 or .22 magnum round. Wolves are killed quickly with a shot to the heart, and such a shot causes little pelt damage. With a good market for skulls, it also precludes damage to the head. I plug the bullet hole with absorbent material to ensure that little or no blood gets into the fur, thus saving me later cleanup.

Trappers can make good money trapping wolves, and they can also be proud that they are helping to maintain big-game prey populations. In many areas of interior Alaska, moose, caribou, and Dall sheep are preyed upon heavily. In fact, wolves and bears take, on average, 80 percent of the yearly harvest. By contrast, human hunters take only about 2 percent. By helping to keep wolf numbers in check, trappers help keep big-game meat on dinner tables.

SLEEPS WITH WOLVES

BY
JIM HARROWER

In the movie *Dances with Wolves,* Kevin Costner's character shares social behavior with a wolf. In early April 1997, I had a similar experience while hunting grizzly bear in Alaska with Harold Arnold.

Harold and I had spotted two dead moose while flying into a hunting area. They were recent kills lying half a mile apart in the current of a river that was mostly frozen, and we figured they had been killed by grizzlies. As we started the descent to a sandbar, several wolves ran across the bar and into the bushes by the river.

By the time we had put up our small tent and secured the airplane, it was late in the day. The days are long at that time of year, and it must have been nearly 11 P.M. when Harold and I took a walk. After walking about a hundred yards, we saw wolves crossing a small, frozen pond at the edge of the brush. We saw up to six at a time. Though aware of our presence, the wolves were not sure what we were. They barked like dogs, howling and yipping in short bursts. Though we never saw more than six, there must have been twice that many in the immediate vicinity. Other wolves began to bark and howl from upriver, downriver, and from behind us. The light was fading as we slowly worked our way back to our tent. We saw wolves at the edge of the bushes and on both sides of a small clearing. Although their size varied, they all had a light-gray coat that was full and unrubbed. They were beautiful.

The barking and yipping began to turn into a mournful howl. More wolves joined in, and it began to sound like the Mormon Tabernacle Choir. When darkness fell, we went to bed, but the valley remained full of howls. The wolves were all around Harold and me. It's difficult to say, but there may have been as many as fifty out there.

The howling continued without interruption for more than two hours. When some wolves ceased howling, others began. The wolves' howling was never discordant to Harold and me. We felt privileged to be the only human audience to that wonderful wilderness symphony. Neither of us had ever heard anything like it.

After several hours, the howling stopped as if on cue. However, with the first suggestion of daybreak four hours later, the wolves began again until the day was firmly established. Harold and I were in the area for several more days after that, but we heard no more howling.

Why had the howling occurred? Harold and I had camped between the wolves' two moose kills, which the animals had probably killed just before we arrived. We had landed the plane right in the middle of the pack, breaking it up as wolves ran in different directions. But I do not think the howling was solely for relocation and reorganization purposes. The howling sounded like an organized production, as complicated as the harmonies of a full choir, or those of a church organ. The wolves, through their eerie and primitive howling, were baring their souls to the heavens.

Harold and I have slept hundreds of nights in wild country, but no other experience comcs close to that night when we slept with the wolves.

PART FOUR

HUNTING
SOUTHERN ALASKA

MOUNTAIN CLIMBING FOR RAMS

BY
DENNIS F. DANNER

"Don't shoot, he's not the big one!" whispered my guide as I watched a full-curl, thirty-six-inch ram walk slowly out of my scope sight and disappear from view. Almost immediately I began to question the wisdom of that decision. This was the third time I had come to Alaska to try for a full-curl ram. The two previous trips were unsuccessful for several reasons, but mostly because of bad weather and bum luck. I shook my head in disbelief, hoping I would not regret passing up that fine ram.

This hunt really began two years ago, when I booked with R&R Guide Service in Anchorage. Having hunted Dall sheep before, I knew what to expect and what I would need in gear and what preparations needed to be made. But nothing could have prepared me for the actual experience of the final stalk.

Upon arriving in Anchorage on 8 August, I met Rob Jones, my outfitter and guide, and we made a bumpy hour-and-a-half flight into base camp near the Alaska Range. We had small cabins with heat, and our camp cook, Lloyd, served meals as good as you would find anywhere in Alaska.

Because the next day was wet and foggy, we were unable to fly into spike camp, but on the following day—10 August, the opening of the season—we had flyable weather. The flight was about twenty-five miles, and then we backpacked five or six miles to the base of a 6,800-foot mountain, where we camped for the night. My guide had previously scouted these slopes and had seen two legal rams, along with two smaller ones, safely tucked higher up on the mountain. A quick reconnaissance in the Super Cub confirmed that the rams were still there.

Since Alaska law prohibits hunting on the same day as flying, our plan was to reach our preplanned campsite and lay strategy for the stalk we would make the following day. On our way in, we had to be careful not to expose ourselves to the keen-eyed sheep watching the open valley. We even waded streams so that the alders on the banks would screen us from the sheep's view. After several hours of overcoming obstacles, including waiting while a large grizzly finished feeding in the area we had planned to hike through, we finally made it to spike camp. A short walk around the base of a hill confirmed that the sheep were now bedded exactly where we had last seen them. We were confident the sheep would still be there in the morning. Our plan set, we tried to get a few hours' sleep so that we would be fresh to begin our stalk at first light.

The day of 11 August began misty and foggy, making visibility poor. Rob said that sooner or later the fog would lift but that in the meantime the fog might actually help us. We knew where the sheep would be, and we knew the sheep wouldn't travel very far in the fog. We began the stalk believing the odds were in our favor.

The sheep were unaware of our presence. The wind, even though it was swirling, seemed to be right, and the mist and the fog allowed us to move quietly. After several hours, we reached the first viewpoint on a steep ridgeline. Rob crawled over it and, using my Bushnell 800 range finder, located the rams, despite the fog, at 400 yards. Even though I had spent endless hours at the rifle range shooting long distances and knew my 7mm magnum would drop exactly 16.1 inches at 400 yards, I told Rob I didn't want to take such a long shot into the stiff wind. I knew I could hit the ram, but I wasn't sure of a clean kill. We decided to get closer.

Rob believed that if we climbed higher and were able to get to a rock outcropping, we might be able to close the distance. We managed to reach our objective, but even from there the range was a long 365 yards. I passed on this shot as well, because of the distance and wind.

We slithered back over the ridge, where Rob stated flatly, "Here's where the going gets tough!" Tough wasn't the right word. Our only alternative was to come down over the top. As we climbed higher, the wind velocity really picked up, and when we "peaked" the ridge, it was howling like a banshee. For several hundred yards we crawled like—well, like sheep, clutching the ground for handholds. The ridge was like a jagged knife-edge. It was very intimidating. I had been on steep mountains before while hunting sheep in the Chugach Mountains in southern Alaska, but that was when I was younger and dumber. Now, common sense told me to be very aware of every step I was taking. It turned out that our ridge-walking was only a warmup for what was yet to come.

Having closed the distance on the rams to about 250 yards, we now faced a dilemma. The only way to continue the stalk was via a chute that went about two hundred feet almost straight down the rock face. Rob looked me in the eye and said, "Well, this is the only way to get any closer. It's steep as hell, but I think we can make it. I'll go first. Don't follow until I reach that ledge two hundred feet below. Hold on, and before you let go with a hand or step with a foot, make sure you have total control." Before I could respond, Rob plunged down the chute.

This was mountain climbing without ropes. It took Rob thirty minutes to safely negotiate his way to the ledge. Now it was my turn. I tried not to think what would happen if I lost my balance. I tried not to think that one slip would mean falling over a thousand feet to certain death on the rocks below. Rob kept motioning me to follow, and I slowly lowered myself down the steep rock wall. I got stuck on the

View of sheep country.

steepest section because I couldn't get solid footing no matter how hard I dug my toes into the loose, rocky surface. My gloveless hands were bleeding from using them as if they were ice axes.

Rob saw that I needed help and started back up the chute. Using his outstretched hands as support, I was able to descend the last few feet I needed to get sure footing. From there it was only a short distance to more manageable terrain. Even though we had no time to rest, I could see a sigh of relief on Rob's face, but both of us knew we would eventually have to deal with getting back up. Rob motioned to our packer Kenny, staring down from the top of the chute, to stay put. Rob didn't want to deal with getting him to the ledge right now.

Still on extremely steep terrain, we crawled and clutched at rocks as we closed the distance between the rams and us. We could see the head and horns of only one of them, but luck was still with us because that animal was lying down, unaware that less than two hundred yards away was a hunter seriously intent

After a lot of climbing, the author finally got his ram.

on filling his tag. For several minutes I studied its horns. Rob told me it had good fourteen-inch bases and was definitely legal.

The ram stood up; the moment of truth had arrived. I was all set to take it as my prize, but Rob stopped me because he had just caught a glimpse of another ram with far bigger horns. We waited anxiously for that animal to emerge from the rocks. An hour passed. Nothing happened. In my mind, I relived the experience of climbing down that treacherous chute. It would be even worse climbing up it empty-handed.

Rob said that he was going to circle around to see if he could spot the rams. We would then decide whether to move or stay put. That decision came quickly when coming into view to my right was a small ram followed by the big boy. As I put my scope on the giant ram, I could see it was about 110 yards away. By that time, Rob had made it back, and he didn't have to tell me that this was the ram for me. It was a straight downhill shot, so I held low behind the ram's front shoulder. I waited till it walked away from the edge of a steep drop.

My ram never knew what hit it. The solid impact of my 140-grain, trophy-bonded bullet knocked the animal completely off its feet. It slid off a fifty-foot cliff and then off another cliff almost as high. Rob and I despaired as we saw the ram drop out of sight, knowing that if something didn't stop it real soon, we would be picking up pieces at the bottom of the mountain. When all was quiet, Rob went down for a look.

Rob hollered from below that he had found my ram, but I needed to get to him immediately to help secure the ram's position. I slid down quickly and held the big sheep's feet, while Rob carefully wedged rocks under it to keep it from sliding any farther. The ram was only thirty feet or so from a drop-off that would have taken it thousands of feet down.

I finally had my trophy ram, and we started taking pictures, but we didn't have much time because it was starting to rain. Rob quickly skinned the big sheep and boned the meat so that we could get off the mountain while we still had daylight left. He then went back up the hill and somehow got Kenny down the chute; Kenny had with him empty packs for the meat and horns. As a hard rain fell, we pondered our ascent up that life-threatening chute.

Rob went first. I could see him struggling, but he finally made it. Next went Kenny. He really struggled, and almost lost it twice, which made Rob think it was too dangerous for me. I had already started climbing the chute when I heard Rob yell, "Dennis, stop! I think I have found a better way!" I could not imagine words more welcome. The new way looked easier, except for a thirty-foot section, where I would have to inch my way along a foot-wide ledge, and then climb straight up a four-foot wall. Since Kenny was already on top, he would be able to pull me up when I reached the wall.

This approach definitely seemed better than the slick chute, so I made my way carefully up the new route. Everything went OK until I reached the ledge, where I began to inch my way across, hugging the wall so tightly I could barely breathe. I remember looking down at two hundred feet of sheer rock and praying I wouldn't lose my balance and fall. Giving my hand to Kenny, I took a deep breath and said, "Let's do it!" and ascended the four-foot wall with ease. Knowing that we were all now safe on the upper side, I took the opportunity to savor the moment.

The rest of the climb down the mountain and the backpacking to the plane seemed anticlimatic. I barely felt my pack, even though it was heavy with camp supplies. At one point, I turned to gaze at the mountain and briefly reflect on the ordeal I had just gone through. We had been one slip away from falling to our death. I felt great appreciation and respect not only for the majestic sheep that navigate those mountains, but also for the untamed Alaskan wilderness.

A WALK UP THE CREEK

BY
JIM RILEY

It's not often that hunters are asked to bag an animal at the request of a spouse. That request was made to me in November 1994. I had just returned from a successful mountain goat hunt in southeastern British Columbia. I was sharing the adventure and photographs of the trip with my wife, when she asked, "When am I going to have a say about the animals you hunt?" I asked her what she had in mind. She said that she was tired of looking at deer, elk, and those ugly Cape buffalo from Tanzania. She wanted me to bag something pretty such as a sheep.

Being a considerate husband, I took her request seriously. I told her of the four types of sheep found in North America, what they looked like, and where they lived. She said that she thought the Dall sheep was the prettiest and asked if I would hunt that one. In January 1995, after speaking to outfitters in Alaska, the Yukon, and the Northwest Territories, I selected AAA Alaskan Outfitters of Anchorage to guide me for Dall sheep. The Dall sheep hunt was booked for August 1997.

I had two and a half years to prepare for my hunt. My guide, Roger Morris, was very helpful in providing a detailed list of equipment I would need for chasing sheep in the Wrangells. One piece of equipment he recommended was plastic sheep boots. Roger and the other AAA guides use Koflach plastic boots. I purchased a set of ASOLO plastic boots from Cabela's. Another piece of equipment I planned to use was a "sheep" rifle. During my B.C. goat hunt, I had carried around a 10¼-pound rifle. By the end of my sixth trip up the mountain, I had decided I needed a lighter rifle for my next mountain hunt. I bought a used, left-handed Remington 700, a 26-inch Krieger barrel, a PME three-position safety, and a Shilen trigger. I sent those pieces along with my 6.5 Wolverine reamer to Lex Webernick of Rifles, Inc., in Cedar City, Utah. He put together a rifle that weighed only 7 pounds (which includes the weight of the 2.5–8X Leupold scope, Butler Creek scope caps, 1¼-inch nylon sling, and four rounds of ammunition).

On the evening of 7 August 1997, I boarded a Northwest Airlines flight from Detroit to Anchorage. After a restful night in the hotel, I met in the lobby the next morning three other sheep hunters booked with AAA: Jim Van Hook from Michigan, Bill Green from New York, and Ray Moore from California. The four of us were greeted by Brent Jones of AAA, who drove us from Anchorage to Chitina, where we crammed into a Cessna 206 for the flight into AAA's Bryson Bar base camp. At base camp, we repacked our gear for each of our spike camps and checked our rifles. On 9 August at 1 P.M., the four of us were shuttled by Super Cub to our individual spike camps. The spike camp that Roger and I would share was set at the base of a mountain. It consisted of a ten-by-ten Eureka tent, a Coleman stove and lantern, a latrine, a cache of food, cots covered with Thermarest sleeping pads, and North Face sleeping bags.

My gear was in the tent quickly, and my Swarovski ST80 spotting scope was set up outside. As I focused on the mountain to the north, four white objects three miles away materialized into young Dall rams. For the rest of the afternoon and evening, I watched for sheep. At 7:30 P.M. a group of fifteen sheep, including four legal rams, walked across the mountain and dropped into a valley on its western face. That's when I consulted with Roger about our plan of attack for the next day.

"Tomorrow morning," said Roger, "we'll walk up the creek, cross the glacier, and hike up the back side of the mountain. We'll arrive at the top and be above the sheep sometime between noon and two. We'll scope the valley, pick out the best ram, and then you'll shoot him."

It didn't take an alarm clock to wake me the next morning. Roger fixed a great breakfast of eggs, bacon, sausage, potatoes, hot cider, and juice. We left camp at eight and started up the creek. It had rained all night and was still raining as we worked our way through dense willows toward the creek bed. For the next five and a half hours, it was a steady climb up the creek, over the glacier, and up the back side of the mountain. Even though I regularly work out on a treadmill and hike a six-mile mountain bike trail with a 45-pound pack on my back, I was winded from the climb at this altitude. But after a couple of hours, my body adjusted to the altitude, making climbing easier.

Higher and higher we went. Around 12:30 P.M., we stopped on a shale face to eat lunch, and then we continued to climb through the rain. Finally, around 1:30 P.M., we reached a bench at the mountaintop. Roger took off his frame pack and told me to chamber a round in my rifle. We got down on our hands and knees and worked our way over to the edge of the bench and looked into the valley below. Ewes and young rams, about ten of them! We continued to glass but could not locate the larger rams we had seen the evening before. We moved farther north along the bench so that we could glass the head of the valley. Reaching the north end of the bench, we peeked over the edge and saw four legal rams bedded down over four hundred yards away. Roger motioned for us to move back so that they wouldn't see us against the skyline. He said that all the rams were legal, but that he wanted to go back to his pack and get his spotting scope so he could better judge which one was the best.

After ten minutes, he returned with his pack and the spotting scope. As we eased our way back to the edge of the bench, we noticed that the four rams were moving toward the other sheep, now grazing farther south down the valley. We quickly grabbed our gear and ran around the back face of the mountain in an attempt to position ourselves across the valley from where the rams were headed. Around 2:10 P.M. we saw the rams join the larger group of sheep. Roger quickly set up his spotting scope, and I got ready for a shot.

The sheep were across the valley and below us. Roger began evaluating the rams, while I followed his description through my binoculars. "The ram on the right is a tight-curl, with some flare at the tips. He'll go thirty-six to thirty-seven inches. Now let's see, the ram in the middle, facing away from us with his head down, is a very deep full-curl with dark horns. He's about thirty-seven to thirty-eight inches. The ram on the lower left . . ."

We finally agreed that the middle ram was the best of the group. I took a distance reading with my Leica Geovid binoculars, and it showed the animal to be 353 yards away. I would have a downward, twenty-five-degree-angle shot. My trajectory chart for

Master guide Roger Morris and the author with his Dall ram.

my 140-grain bullet said to aim four inches low at that distance and angle. I held the cross hairs of my 2.5–8X Leupold scope on the center of its chest and squeezed the trigger. For reasons I still don't understand—maybe it was my hold, maybe it was the effect of the balloon over the muzzle—the shot went three inches over the animal's back. The report of the rifle sent the sheep moving up the valley toward the mountain. I cranked a fresh round in the chamber and followed the ram through my scope. A second ram then walked next to the quarry, obscuring my shot. After what seemed like an eternity, the second ram stepped clear and I fired again. The ram collapsed with a broken spine, anchored where it fell. I cranked another round in the chamber but didn't fire because the ram didn't move.

Roger congratulated me on the shot, and I thanked him for planning a perfect stalk. We gathered our gear and began a slow descent to the sheep. Before descending, I took a final reading with my Leicas. It was 419 yards from where I had shot to where the ram lay. The climb down took a little more than thirty minutes. As we approached the ram, I was struck by its beauty. Dall sheep have an elegance that is lacking in the rugged mountain goat and the menacing Cape buffalo.

After cleaning the ram up, we took two rolls of pictures. Roger skinned it for a life-size mount, and then deboned it and loaded the meat and horns into his frame pack. At 6:50 P.M., we started the hike back to camp. It was amazing to watch him traverse rock slides and other mountain terrain with 125 pounds on his back. At 9:15 P.M., we dropped our packs in front of our tent. It had been over thirteen hours since we had walked up the creek, and all but the last fifteen minutes had been in a steady Alaskan rain.

I'm looking forward to another walk up the creek. This time on the Alaska Peninsula!

A GOAT FOR LIZ

BY
ROBERT P. HARDY

Elizabeth Sowers is a small woman full of youth, enthusiasm, and curiosity. Her love of the outdoors and everything in it is evident in her lifestyle and the goals she has set for the future. A willingness to work hard and solid ethics have made her a devoted, respectful hunter.

These are the qualities that caught my attention when I began searching for an apprentice guide and wrangler to complement my guiding operation. Elizabeth possessed all the talents necessary to become a topnotch guide, and she was committed to the long haul. So in spring 1997, my wife and I brought her on board to work as an apprentice and wrangler until she was fully qualified to be an assistant guide.

As part of her payment for the 1997 season and at her request, I agreed to guide Elizabeth on a mountain goat hunt after all the clients had gone home for the year. I looked forward to the "vacation" we had planned together and began to count the days. After a lesson on fleshing, salting, and meat care of the two goats my clients had taken a few days prior,

In her quest for a record-book mountain goat, Elizabeth had to make several dangerous crossings of this glacier-fed river, including one nighttime fording.

Elizabeth and I said good-bye to the two visiting hunters and watched them depart in the Super Cub. Now it was her turn. Anticipation grew into excitement as she realized her dream was becoming a reality, and I couldn't help but smile when I saw the emotion in her sparkling blue eyes. This was going to be a great hunt.

We spent the remainder of the day doing camp chores, packing our gear for the next day's hunt, and talking about the fickle late-October weather. On occasion, she and I stood behind the spotting scope to keep tabs on several billy goats perched among the cliffs above us.

On the following morning, dawn came clear and cold, perfect for goat hunting. After an entire season of Elizabeth greeting me with a hot cup of coffee and a warm fire in the early morning, I decided to do her the favor in return. We were soon on the trail to new adventure.

We both wanted to see new country, so we struck out for the gorge below camp. After traveling a mile, we spotted a goat on the opposite rim of the gorge about four hundred yards away. It was an ancient nanny with splendid horns, but

Our goat camp was nestled in a high valley that gave us a commanding view of the surrounding mountains.

Elizabeth wanted a billy. The day was young, so we continued on. Another mile down the old horse trail, she and I came upon a small group of goats gathered along the edge of the gorge, alternately feeding and resting as they absorbed the faint heat of the sun. This group contained one very nice billy, but as we studied it in the spotting scope from two hundred yards, Elizabeth decided to pass it up in hopes of getting a crack at one of the granddaddies on the mountain overlooking camp. For the rest of the day, we watched a group of goats interact, and I instructed my apprentice on the peculiarities of goat behavior. It was a learning experience for both of us.

On the second day, we found a commanding view of the mountain and set to the task of locating our billies. The overcast sky and the flat light on the snow-covered slopes made spotting difficult, but within a few hours we had located three candidates. Unfortunately, all the billy goats were in a bad position for a stalk, and instead of risking broken horns, we decided to wait for them to move onto more gentle terrain. Late in the day, two of the goats had moved onto a gradual ridge 2,500 feet above camp, and it looked like they were going to stop there for the night. With satisfaction, we gathered our things and proceeded home for the evening. Along the way, Elizabeth and I bumped into a rather large bull moose, and we lingered until dark discussing the good and bad characteristics of its antlers.

I was having a blast. My hunter was not only a partner in this endeavor but also a keen student who took in everything around her. I hadn't paid much attention to this side of Elizabeth over the course of the season, and I was encouraged by her attitude, not to mention her lively personality and energetic charm. It dawned on me that I had lost some of that youthful wonder over the years, in the name of success rates and the pressure to satisfy paying hunters.

On the second-to-last day of our hunt, I awoke to low clouds and fresh snow. Not much hope of spotting a goat in that! We lounged around camp that morning, waiting for the weather to break. I was entertained by Elizabeth's ideas on training her saddle horse, and she listened to my tales of goat hunts in years past. By early afternoon, the clouds had started to break, and we earnestly began to scan the slopes for goats. It took about an hour to locate the two billies we had put to bed the night before on the gentle slope above camp. If it weren't for their fresh tracks in the snow, we probably wouldn't have spotted them. At the time of year when goats begin to rut, the old billies develop wallows and cover themselves in mud, grit, and stench. Their mottled brown-and-white coats blend well with the surrounding snow and rock. Elizabeth called it the "Bev Doolittle look," and that's exactly what we were dealing with.

The day was getting away from us, and in late October in south-central Alaska, darkness comes early. Elizabeth grabbed her rifle, and we both grabbed our pack frames and set off for the mountain. I didn't think we would have enough time to climb up to the goats and bring one down before dark, but you'll never succeed if you don't try, so up we went. About halfway up the mountain, I glanced at my watch and then to the sky to assess the incoming weather. We discussed turning back, knowing full well that tomorrow we might be shut down entirely. Elizabeth and I agreed to push on and hope for the best.

After steadily climbing for an hour, we were within a couple of hundred yards of the two billies. But there was a problem—a band of Dall sheep had moved between the goats and us. We watched the sheep, and the sheep watched us. I told Elizabeth that if we didn't pay too much attention to the sheep as we circled around and away, they probably wouldn't spook toward our two goats on the ridge above. She was eager to try it.

We got around the sheep all right, but now we faced another dilemma. The slope was becoming very steep with some nasty cliffs sprinkled throughout, and everything was covered in new snow, making for slippery and dangerous climbing. In the rush to begin a stalk, I had inadvertently forgotten our crampons back at camp, and now we were both wishing that we had them. My mountaineering boots were adhering to the slope fairly well, so Elizabeth got in front of me while I braced my ice ax across her behind to stabilize her whenever she lost a grip on the icy mountainside. Up we went slowly.

Elizabeth Sowers and the author beside Elizabeth's Boone and Crockett goat.
Determination, persistence, and a lot of effort helped make Elizabeth's dream a reality.

By then we both knew the two big billies were very close to us. We had last seen them bedded on a little flat just beyond a rise, which was now directly in front of us. Elizabeth inched ahead as I whispered instructions. Suddenly, I spotted a pair of goat horns silhouetted above a snow berm forty yards in front and slightly to our left. I reached ahead and grabbed Elizabeth by the belt to stop her forward progress. On my coaxing, she raised up slowly, looked in the direction of the goat, and quickly dropped back down. She had seen the billy! The goat was lying in its bed looking in our direction, but it acted like it hadn't seen us, or didn't care that we were there. We did not want to shoot it without first getting a close look at its partner. Elizabeth and I mulled it over and decided that we would sneak out of sight and come around behind and above them to get another look. Slowly we moved to our right and inched our way upward.

We eased over the rise cautiously and peered beyond. Directly in front and not more than fifteen yards away lay two magnificent goats! Elizabeth bolted a cartridge into the chamber of her .30-06, as both goats arose to their feet and began to feed, still not the least bit concerned. I looked from one goat to the other. Although both goats' horns were nearly equal in length, the billy on the right had horns that were more massive all the way out to the tips. Without hesitation, we chose to take the older goat on the right. Elizabeth's rifle boomed once and the patriarch of the mountains lay still.

We had done it! All the waiting, dreaming, and anticipation had boiled down to that one triumphant moment. I was jubilant. Elizabeth was awestruck. There lay a Boone and Crockett goat, and beside me stood one of the finest hunting partners I've ever had the pleasure to be with. The torturous trek half in the dark down the mountain with loaded packs and the nighttime crossing of the glacial river were exciting, to say the least.

Such experiences, accomplishments, and camaraderie are what drive me to be a guide. Elizabeth's memories of that hunt, and the decisions she made, will enable her to grow as an outdoorswoman and eventually to become an accomplished guide. Our goat hunt is something she and I will always treasure.

DREAMS OF A BLOND BEAR

BY
RICK HAYLEY

Exhausted and out of breath, my guide and I paused momentarily before I made my move. We knew that "Mongo," Rob's nickname for the humongous, silver-tipped grizzly that had lured me to Alaska, stood just above the ten-foot gravel bank we'd been stalking along. Attempts to calm myself having utterly failed, I nocked an arrow and began to crawl up the bank. At any moment I expected to be confronted by that snarling mountain of a bear, rearing and raking the air with its massive paws.

I was daydreaming, but something was still out of whack. Before my eyes was a midnight sunrise. Then I realized that since my Delta flight was approaching Anchorage, Alaska, in mid-May, I was observing early-morning twilight. Yes, the stalking of a giant bear was only a dream, but the bright midnight sky outside my airplane window definitely was not. I knew then that this trip was going to be an adventure in which anything could happen.

My guide, Rob Hardy, and I packed several horses for the start of our twelve-day horseback grizzly bowhunt in the scenic Talkeetna

The pack-in was a six-hour horseback ride. The author's guide, Rob Hardy, led the way through Boulder Creek, about ninety miles northeast of Anchorage.

Mountains of south-central Alaska. Rob had called a few days earlier to inform me that his previous two spring bear hunters, both riflemen, had struck out. The first hunter missed an eight-foot-plus grizzly in April. The second hunter became ill and was flown out, and it was during that hunt that Rob spotted Mongo. It was now up to me, a southern Texan bow hunter, to save face for an exceptionally hardworking guide who was 0 for 2 for the spring grizzly season.

My watching the Discovery Channel regularly for six months prior to the hunt had led me to believe that stalking grizzlies would be a walk in the park. Wrong! Hunting the brown bears that feed on salmon streams and beaches near the coast of Alaska is light-years away from glassing bears from a mountaintop with nothing but a bow and arrow to get the job done. In fact, finding grizzlies without the help of salmon-packed streams or some other natural draw is no easy task. I soon learned that mountain grizzlies shouldn't be compared to the Discovery Channel's brownies. Mountain bear must hunt harder and longer for food, and they're faster and generally more aggressive than their giant coastal cousins.

For four days straight we climbed the mountain opposite our gravel bar camp, negotiating the eight-hundred-foot climb up and down the 60-degree slope through slippery moss and berry bushes. Once atop, we glassed for twelve to fifteen hours each day. We saw numerous moose and countless Dall sheep. In one spot near camp, a cow moose had hung out for three days, and on day four it delivered a calf.

"Once a calf is born," Rob said, "a grizzly will sometimes pick up the scent and come running." Not long after that, around 8 P.M., we spotted a grizzly boar trucking after a moose a mile to the west. The moose ran toward the cow and calf, and then all three bolted to the top of the mountain and out of harm's way.

Realizing the wind was not in our favor, we scooted down the mountain parallel to the grizzly's path. We were hunkered among some trees just seventy yards from the big bear's path when the animal suddenly whirled 180 degrees upon smelling our camp and galloped by us around thirty miles per hour. Within minutes it vanished. I never had a chance to shoot. It had taken four days to encounter one grizzly bear, and the episode had lasted merely minutes. Now I understood why, according to the Alaska Department of Fish and Game, bow hunters have taken only eleven mountain grizzlies in Alaska since statehood.

On day five we glassed all day, and at 10 P.M. Rob left the hillside to take care of horse business and to start our dinner of pork chops and pasta. I had decided to stay and glass a little longer, and twenty minutes later I spotted a fine eight-foot boar a mile away. I signaled Rob, and we quickly met at the gravel bar. Rob had not seen the bear, but I told him the griz appeared to be following the same trail as the bear had the day before. Since we had a good wind, we waited between the gravel bar and the side of the mountain behind camp. Before long, the unreliable bruin crossed our gravel bar and was going up the mountain toward our glassing position.

Since the wind was still good, I raced to get in front of the bear. While struggling through a snow mound at the bottom of a twelve-foot embankment, I nocked an arrow and paused before

This is how most of the day is spent when bowhunting in Alaska.

crawling cautiously to the edge of the bank. I was surprised to find that the bear had already passed by and was now climbing along the mountain slope facing us. In a moment, the bear was within fifty yards of our glassing knob, but when it caught our residual scent there, it was gone in seconds. I couldn't believe it. Here I had charged off that mountainside after the bear, only to watch it pass within bow range of where I'd been glassing from for the last several days. Even though I felt discouraged, I've always believed that things happen for a reason. I eagerly awaited the next opportunity.

By day seven, Rob decided we should saddle the horses and check out East Fork, eight miles down Boulder Creek. I questioned his reasoning, since our area had become something of a grizzly hot spot. But Rob explained that grizzlies travel about twenty miles per day. We probably wouldn't see those same bears again for another four or five days, and our chance of seeing a third griz so soon was remote. I yielded to my guide's knowledge, and we rode to East Fork.

By 3 P.M., the weather had grown windy and the sky threateningly dark. We had found minimal grizzly sign, and I was beginning to write the day off as a scouting trip. Then, at four o'clock, Rob pointed toward a cliff a mile away. His expert eyes had spotted a shaggy blond bear that had curiously chosen a cliff face for its midday snooze. The big bear appeared to be getting edgy, as if it might strike off, and Rob suggested that we make our move. Our only hope for a shot was to get the wind in our faces by making a difficult circular stalk. As usual, timing would be critical. But even if the stalk worked, I would have to make a thirty- to forty-yard shot at a 45-degree angle down the cliff face.

I was used to the strain of my guide's pace by now, as we began the laborious uphill stalk. Along the way, we had to cautiously push two full-curl Dall rams downwind to avoid spooking blondie. At the midpoint of our stalk, Rob checked the bear's position once more. As luck would have it, the bear had moved. It was now facing toward the spot from which I'd hoped to shoot. We momentarily pondered the situation before deciding to keep heading along the same path. I thought perhaps I could maneuver to get a better angle.

When we were a hundred yards from the bluff, we completely lost sight of the bear, but we could see a cloud of dust rising above the top of the cliff. At first, we thought he had bolted. Then, a few steps later, we saw him still there. If I could sneak out on that point and deal with the 30-mile-per-hour crosswind and 150-foot height, I'd cut five yards off the range and gain a better shooting angle. As I reached the top of the cliff, I suddenly appreciated my previous close calls: They had been warmups for this moment.

Although the sight of a seven-and-a-half-foot blond grizzly took my breath away and made my heart race, my previous hunting experiences had prepared me for the shock. I successfully completed the risky walk out onto the point. There I stood, seemingly bared to the world, wind blowing in my face, trying to steady myself for the shot. I glanced at the face

*The author and Rob shook hands after all was said and done. The bruin was
perched on the cliff behind them when the author struck it.*

211

of the cliff, mentally calculating twenty yards, and then another ten, and then five more. But, given the steep angle, I would aim for thirty yards rather than for thirty-five.

I drew my 70-pound Hoyt Deviator, anchored my knuckles under my jaw, and gradually settled the glowing fiberoptic pin on the bear's ribs. Just as I was about to touch off the shot, an enormous gust blew off my aim. I struggled to bring the pin back to the grizzly's midsection. Still at full draw, I pushed the 30-yard pin over the last two ribs of the bear's chest and squeezed the thumb-released trigger. In the blink of an eye, the arrow buried to the fletching in the bear's heaving chest. The bear paused and then let out a hair-raising roar. It rushed off, circled downhill, and collapsed eighty yards away.

This once-in-a-lifetime, textbook shot came as a result of tremendous teamwork. Glancing back at Rob, I wasn't sure which of us was more excited. "I'll remember that shot until the day I die," he said. I will, too. This was no dream. This one was for real.

THE ELEVENTH-HOUR BULL

BY
RICK HAYLEY

"Get your gear and get your butt on a horse! Now!" yelled my guide, Rob Hardy. Still wiping sleep from my eyes, I shoved my bow in the scabbard, attached my hip quiver, and jumped on Duchess. I followed Rob across the river, where we milled around on a tundra hill. Then we headed back to camp.

Later that day, I asked Rob, "What exactly were we going after this morning?"

He looked at me, his arms extending wide, and said: "There was a sixty-five-inch, once-in-a-lifetime Boone and Crockett bull, and we missed it by about five minutes."

My nerves quivered and my heart skipped a couple of beats. "Damn!"

* * * * * *

Four months earlier, I had gone on a spring bowhunt for grizzly in the Talkeetna Mountains in south-central Alaska. My guide for that hunt was Rob Hardy. After I had returned to Corpus Christi, Texas, Rob called to ask if I could join him in the fall on a combination moose-and-sheep hunt, due to a late cancellation. It took me five seconds to jump at the offer. Still trying to calm down from my once-in-a-lifetime Alaskan grizzly hunt, I couldn't believe I'd just committed to my second Alaskan big-game bowhunt in the same year. It was a dream come true.

Flying to Bucking Horse Ranch base camp in a Super Cub was quite an experience, to say the least. We flew through gorges and spotted game from above, and we landed on a makeshift runway in the middle of a gravel bar in a huge canyon.

It was rainy and foggy on the second day of my hunt. I wanted to pursue Dall sheep, but drizzle made spotting and stalking the upper elevations impossible. We spent the next two days glassing for bulls across the river from camp. Moose sightings were plentiful at first, and I actually passed on bulls in the fifty-three- to fifty-eight-inch range. Even though Rob knew larger bulls were in the area, he seemed a little surprised that I was so picky. If hindsight were 20/20, I wouldn't have been so selective. Many of those bulls would've made Pope and Young.

The author's guide, Rob Hardy, evaluates their approach before they stalk the big bull.

On day four, the weather finally cleared and visibility was good, and I saw firsthand how quickly weather changes from day to day, even from hour to hour, in Alaska. With clear weather we switched gears and started evaluating sheep. Over the following days, we rode about sixteen miles a day, checking out Dalls when we spotted them. But we found only sheep with three-quarters and seven-eighths curls (Alaska requires a full-curl minimum to be legal).

By the ninth day, Rob figured the larger rams must've started their winter migration early and that it would behoove us to concentrate on moose, since my eleven-day hunt was nearing its end. Meanwhile, Elizabeth, our assistant guide, had spotted a real whopper five miles upstream from camp. We saddled the horses and rode over to take a long, hard look. Around midmorning, Rob located a legal bull (50 inches or more), grazing the same hillside that we were sitting on. He estimated the moose to have a fifty-three-inch spread, a Pope and Young animal. Since I had passed up on a fifty-eight-incher on day two, I couldn't see myself going after this guy. (Oh, how I wish I had taken that fifty-eight-incher!) Rob reminded me that the clock was ticking and that I might consider lowering my standards a bit, if I didn't want to go home empty-handed.

The long look on my face inspired Rob to throw me a little crumb of hope. "It's not time to worry yet. The fat lady hasn't even begun to warm up her voice." Then he told me that many of his clients had taken game during the eleventh hour of their hunts. One hunter actually shot an animal two hours before his flight home. There was time enough only for him to take a photo, jump on a horse, ride to camp, grab gear, and run to the landing strip. I hoped my hunt wouldn't be an eleventh-hour one.

On the morning of day ten, Rob told me that the rut had started ten days early. Instead of seeing bulls calmly grazing and browsing, we'd see them cavorting about looking for cows in heat. He said we would have to intercept a bull's path, or spot one trying its luck with a cow. With the rut on, my challenge had just stepped up a couple of notches. After breakfast, we loaded our gear and rode up the mountain above timberline to glass across the canyon. We spotted a few cows about three and

On day nine, Liz pointed out where she had spotted a huge bull moose the day before.

a half miles away across the river. Around one o'clock, I had a cow pegged through the spotting scope when suddenly a really big bull popped out of the alders and started chasing the cow. The bull had good width, long palms, and incredible brow tines. We loaded up and rode to the other side of the canyon.

After tying our horses to a tree (where Liz stayed to watch the bull in case we missed it), we stalked downhill and stumbled upon the big guy seventy yards distant. We had to hold our spot because its potential mate had us nailed. I couldn't believe how long that cow stared at us without moving! Finally, it started walking away, and the bull followed, its nose close to the cow's backside. It was obvious the bull wasn't going to leave the cow for a while. Rob decided to try calling, but it had the opposite effect of what we had hoped. Probably feeling it was a little too old for a sparring match, the moose responded to the call by pushing the cow farther down the mountain. Rob said that our timing wasn't very good and that we might consider backing off and trying again tomorrow. I could hear that fat lady warming up. Tomorrow was my last day to hunt!

Day eleven began as usual. We rode above timberline and started scouring the canyon. We spotted a couple of cows but no bulls. For about an hour, I left the spotting scope pointed at a cow, checking it periodically to see if a bull had showed up. Soon I saw what appeared to be an antler reflection seventy-five yards above the cow. The image was blurred and difficult to determine (often the case when you're three and a half miles away). It looked like it could be a bull lying in tundra brush but obscured by limbs and leaves. Rob looked through the scope and said that it might be heat distortion but that I should keep watching. For the next thirty minutes, I focused my eyes entirely on that blurred image. The reflection would sometimes darken, and then lighten up again. I thought that if it was a bull, maybe it was rocking its head up and down.

Finally, I saw what I was hoping for: brow tines. I ran to Rob and said that the blurred image was definitely our bull and that it was now far enough from the cow for us to attempt a stalk. As we rode to the other side of the canyon, I hoped that we'd get there before the moose started courting again. Fortunately, the cow probably wasn't yet in estrus, because it showed no interest in the bull's antics.

We got off our horses, and I followed Rob as he scampered downhill toward the area where he thought the moose would be. After about two hundred yards, Rob slowed his pace and then began to crawl. In each direction was waist-high tundra bush for several hundred yards. After we crawled through an opening in the bush, I could tell by Rob's eyes that he sensed that the bull was nearby. As we reached the little clump of trees, he whispered, "Stay put," and he cautiously peeked around the left side. Suddenly Rob froze, waved me over, and pointed. There it was, thirty yards distant, lying down. Spotting it from so far away was deceiving. The bull's size astonished me.

I had no shot because vegetation obscured my view. The wind swirled slightly, and I knew the bull would pick up our scent soon and stand. When it did, we gambled that it would move to our left. Within seconds it did just that. The moose approached the edge of the trees. Its antlers were swaying back and forth as I came to full draw. But it stopped, spun around, and started off the other way. I let down but immediately re-drew when I noticed two possible shooting lanes if it continued along its path. I laid my sights on it, but its pace was too fast to allow for an ethical shot through such a narrow opening.

I was overwhelmed. I began to hyperventilate. *What is happening to me? I've never had this happen to me before!* Rob had guided me to a Pope and Young grizzly bear only a few months earlier, and on that hunt I had showed nothing approaching the anxiety I was now experiencing. Rob looked at me quizzically, as if he thought I'd pass out any moment. When I finally caught my breath and calmed down, he waved me over to set up for a shot.

The bull came into view with its nose up, having caught our scent. It was 4 P.M. on the last day of my hunt. I was facing the last possible opportunity to bag an animal, and felt ready to explode. Talk about pressure!

I took my shot. My bow delivered enough energy to thrust a Spitfire broadhead twenty inches into its side. The bull crouched at the sound of my bow, and then it ran forty yards and stopped, looking around in confusion. I nervously snatched another arrow from my quiver. Rob stopped me. "Another shot would be overkill," he said. "Let's let the arrow do its job. You made a lethal shot. If we risk pushing him, we might lose him." The bull continued to walk as if nothing had happened. Then it disappeared down the hillside.

Rob immediately started looking for blood, and he found some in the area where my arrow had hit the moose. We found a trail, but it only went fifty yards. Since my shot was a little high, I figured most of the bleeding was occurring inside the animal's body cavity. What we had found was blood from the flesh wound. We analyzed the sequence of events in order to determine the animal's probable path. Then it started to rain— and blood trails don't last long in rain. Though discouraged, I

Although the hunters are feeling relaxed and happy, they still have a long road ahead. Processing an animal this big requires quite a bit of work. Thank goodness for horses!

was determined to find the moose. If my shot was lethal, the moose couldn't have gone far.

The short blood trail pointed to a line of alders 150 yards distant. We agreed that the bull probably went that way. Rob suggested I follow the bull's trail so that I could get a second shot, if necessary. He and Liz would search the lower area, and we would meet on the other side.

I took one step into the alders and froze. My knees went soft. I was in shock. My monstrous bull moose lay ten yards away. It was actually bigger than the horse I was riding! I pulled my arrow out and spun it on my finger. Still tuned! After checking the moose over, it appeared that it had been lying there the whole time. I'd been a nervous wreck for nothing.

By dark, the three of us had packed out a shoulder and a hindquarter. My bull's cape, antlers, and quarters weighed about eight hundred pounds. Rob estimated the bull to be fourteen years old and probably too lean to live through the upcoming winter. It was comforting to know I had harvested a moose that was past its prime.

After the kill, I had to leave Alaska right away, so I couldn't stay for the processing of the animal. The next day, I flew back to Corpus Christi, and as I sat on the plane I kept reliving how I had harvested a record-book Alaska-Yukon moose at the eleventh hour!

DREAMS DO COME TRUE

BY
HANS-JURGEN KREUZKAM

Alaska fascinates many German nature lovers and hunters. For years, my friend Reinhold and I had dreamed of hunting Alaska. We read books and magazine articles on Alaskan hunting, and in 1997 we decided to make our dream come true. We first needed to select the outfitter and the hunting area. After much research and deliberation, we decided to hunt on horseback with master guide Ray McNutt of the Wrangell R Ranch. An acquaintance, who had hunted with Ray twenty-five years ago, highly recommended Ray's operation. Wrangell R Ranch was located in the Wrangell-St. Elias Mountains near the Yukon border. Reinhold wanted a trophy Dall sheep and a moose, and I just wanted a moose. Besides hunting, Reinhold and I longed to experience and take photographs of the state's unspoiled nature. We also wanted to learn more about hunting in Alaska.

We arrived in Anchorage in early September 1997, and shortly thereafter made the scenic and awe-inspiring flight to Wrangell R Ranch. We met Craig Rose, our guide, and Jason and Tom, the assistants, at the airport, and upon arriving in camp, we were welcomed by Ray and Randy, the cook. The log kitchen, where we had our meals and social gatherings, was at the center of the camp, and our accommodation was a comfortable tent with wood floor and heater. In the afternoon, we tested the rifles (everything was OK). We quickly learned that in camp everything went according to a certain schedule. At 6 A.M., Jason and Todd gathered the horses and drove them into the paddock. They saddled the horses, and at 8 A.M. the hunting started.

On the first day, we saw Dall sheep on the mountain slopes of nearby Wiki Peak. Our horses were easy to ride, but I felt uneasy when we crossed icy Beaver Creek with its torrential current. Without horses, the crossing would have been impossible. We got as close to the sheep as we could on horseback, and then we tethered the horses and continued our stalk on foot. When we got within a thousand yards, Craig and Jason discovered two legal rams, but we couldn't get any closer without spooking the other sheep. We stopped the sheep hunt for that day and went to a vantage point for a wide view of the valley. In the evening, we saw two moose cows, one moose calf, and a moose bull that might be worth hunting.

The next morning we wanted to get closer to the bull, so we got up at five to begin our stalk on foot. We reached a small hill not far from where we had seen the moose the previous evening. There Craig tried to stir things up by doing his moose call. After ten minutes, Reinhold discovered the bull in a group of five. It was a marvelous sight—the giant bull standing between the multicolored spruce and birch. The moose's palms were prominent, and pieces of velvet were still hanging from them. Craig tried to lure the moose closer, but then we noticed that the moose bull wasn't big enough to be legal, so we went back to camp.

After breakfast, we resumed our sheep hunting on Wiki Peak. Probably because of the weather, which had deteriorated to intermittent rain and hail, we saw only ten animals. Among them were three animals that Craig identified as rams, and one was fairly impressive. After getting as close as we could on the horses, we dismounted and started to climb. Craig led us toward the group, using every possible bit of cover. One ram was legal, so the tension was rising, but it was still too far away to shoot. The three rams, eating and moving slowly, drifted up toward the summit. We headed for the pass to overtake them. Though tired, we moved up the slope fairly rapidly. Reinhold, trying to save energy for the big shot later, fell slightly behind.

We were thirty yards from the pass, waiting for Reinhold, when the three rams coming from the other side saw us. Panic on both sides! The big, dominant ram escaped into the valley, while the two younger rams sprawled across some scree toward

Reinhold Holzapel (left) and guide Craig Rose with the nine-year-old ram. Everyone appreciated the beauty of the outstanding trophy and the surroundings.

the summit. Suddenly, the dominant ram changed its mind, turning and following the two younger animals, giving Reinhold, who had closed up the distance, an unexpected shot. Reinhold rested his rifle on a small rock to steady for the upward shot at the fleeing ram. The distance was about one hundred yards. My comrade fired. The big sheep ran one hundred yards and fell dead on the rocky slope.

223

We exulted in our good fortune. Our exhaustion was replaced by sheer joy, and the ordeal of the climb, the hail, and all our doubts were quickly forgotten. The ram was nine and a half years old, an outstanding trophy. We crouched around our prize and took in the fantastic surroundings—the unrestricted view of Horsefeld, the soaring mountains of the Yukon, and, to top it all off, the magnificent rainbow in the sky. Time stood still as we looked upon a landscape that seemed to stretch to eternity. We enjoyed it as long as we could, but then we had to get down to business. Craig skinned the ram and carved up the meat, and we all went back to camp elated. The next day, Craig and Jason packed the meat and the trophy, Reinhold stayed in camp to rest, and Todd and I went on a photo trip on horseback.

On 7 September we began moose hunting. Though the nights were getting colder, the days remained warm and sunny, and the willow trees and the aspens were in fall colors. We were riding on an old trail along Beaver Creek, and we made stops at good vantage points to look for moose. During lunch we spotted two moose, one of which was a young bull. Early fall is normally the beginning of the rutting season, and there should have been some movement among the moose. At 6 P.M., we saw a good bull one to two miles away moving toward Beaver Creek. Craig urged us to go for it, but when we did, the moose proved too clever and eluded us. Craig was so disappointed he skipped supper.

The next day, Craig made every effort to find the big bull, but it was futile. That evening we developed a new strategy. Ray figured our best chance was to go to the outcamp on Carl Creek, so on 9 September we headed out with five saddle horses and five packhorses. The outcamp was in a forest of small spruce, and it consisted of a small, low-ceilinged cottage with a heater and a two-man tent in which to sleep. After lunch, Jason and Todd left to strike a sheep camp, while Craig, Reinhold, and I hunted moose. Though we saw only a cow moose and calf that afternoon, we had great hopes for the morning.

Despite the rain and snow, which had been falling every night, and problems with the horses, we set out at 7:30 for a forty-five-minute ride to a good vantage point. Craig went alone to climb a small hill in order to get a better view of the valley. After barely five minutes, he hurried back to report seeing a good-looking moose moving over a hill.

We rode about a mile, tethered the horses, and began walking carefully. We climbed a steep slope, and from the top we saw the bull 350 yards away in a small valley. Since the moose looked promising, Craig did his moose call. As if electrified, the bull stood still and looked in our direction. Once again, Craig gave a blast of his moose imitation. The testy beast moved toward us. With every step, the bull called and Craig responded like a lusty rival. We were fascinated. Reinhold was ready to shoot but couldn't quite see the animal, even though it was no more than 120 yards away. We stood breathless.

The big bull emerged slowly into full view—first the top of the palms, then the mighty head, and finally the whole body. Reinhold quickly took aim and fired. The big moose ran fifty yards and broke down. Reinhold shot a second time. It was all over. The big beast lay framed in golden willow and fire-red dwarf birch.

After an appropriate time of reflection, we returned to the outcamp to get Jason and Todd and packhorses for the big job of bringing the moose in. It took hours to skin and carve up the huge animal. That evening in camp, we had a tremendous meal of fresh moose meat. The next morning, the horses were saddled and packed and we returned to the main camp, and that afternoon Craig and I returned to outcamp to begin looking for a moose for me. This time out I rode a new, well-trained, older horse, which was quite to my liking. At outcamp, we saw nothing but sheep for the next two days. I was considering changing my trophy plans, but Ray advised me to stick to my original objective. With all the snow we'd been having, he explained, sheep hunting was getting more difficult, but moose hunting was getting easier. It would also be difficult to get a sheep license at this time.

By 13 September, we were back at main camp to try for moose. When we crossed Beaver Creek that morning, what we had most feared occurred: Craig's horse stumbled and pitched him into the cold, torrential water. Fortunately, there was no serious impact. Both horse and rider were OK.

That morning, we saw one nice bull from the first observation point, but the bull eluded us after our long and hard stalk. We returned to the vantage point. The weather had improved, and by evening we had spotted moose in three different areas, two of which had been rutting areas the previous year. We decided to check those areas in the morning for any fresh sign. If we didn't have any luck there, we'd try hunting from outcamp again. The next morning, we reached the first rutting area after a one-hour ride. We saw no fresh moose sign. Nevertheless, we decided to stay there awhile, since the area gave us a good view of the surrounding valley.

Shortly thereafter, Craig and I heard a slight cracking sound coming from the opposite slope. There was movement between some aspens. It was a moose! Craig gave his bull call, luring the beast into open view, but the bull was not quite up to size. Meanwhile, the moose kept coming closer and closer, curious about Craig's call. My hands were wet with excitement, and I managed to take many photographs when the moose passed us to amble to the lake. The beast began drinking at the shore, and we could hear drops falling as it dipped its enormous head in and out of the shallows. It was fantastic.

We finally left that area to check out the other rutting area. Craig was ahead of me and nearly there when he suddenly dismounted and ducked for cover. Jason and I also dismounted, and we led our horses into thick brush. About a thousand yards away, a good-looking bull was poised on the edge of a spruce thicket, and Craig thought it might be worth hunting. We couldn't see any cows nearby, and between the moose and us there were enough small birch and willow for cover. Craig decided on a direct approach to get us to within shooting distance, but after only one hundred yards of stalking, two cows erupted from the brush to the left and ran into the spruce. Our big bull pursued them.

Craig and Jason were swearing now, but fortunately I didn't know enough American expletives to understand most of what they said. They had barely quieted down when I spied the same bull standing in a clearing on the other side of Beaver Creek. The animal seemed calm and was moving slowly, obviously not making any connection as to the cause of the prior disturbance. In a scraggly stand of jack spruce, it stopped to lie down. Here was our lucky break! We waited an hour to make sure the moose was completely calm, at the same time keeping it in view with our binoculars. Then we began our stalk. We circled around to Beaver Creek via a wide bend and tethered the horses to the bank. We climbed one hundred yards of steep slope to get a view of our quarry, our hearts pounding from exertion and excitement. Was the giant bull still bedded down in the spruce? Yes! But the distance to it was much greater than we had expected, and there was scant cover between the trophy and us. The only choice we had was to narrow the distance.

At three hundred yards, we halted our stalk, since our cover had petered out and the ground was rising, giving the bull an excellent view of the area. I positioned for a shot, straining for a glimpse of the big head with its enormous palmed antlers, all the while knowing it might be awhile before the enormous bull got up. Craig was certain the moose would move as soon as the afternoon sun overheated it. He was right. With no warning, the hefty monarch rose to full height between two spruces, and I quickly took aim with my rifle. Craig urged me to fire, but I wanted to hold for a better shot. He repeated his command, afraid

Guide Craig Rose (left) with the author and the moose measuring almost sixty inches. As is the German custom, a sprig of evergreen was placed in the mouth, symbolizing its last bite.

(Left to right) Assistant guide Jason Morgan, Reinhold Holzapel, master guide Ray McNutt, the cook, guide Craig Rose, and the author.

the moose would move away and all would be lost. It was a long shot, but I aimed for the heart and squeezed the trigger. There was a thud, and the big bull turned and stood perfectly still. Blood ran from its nose, and I knew my shot was fatal. Craig urged me to quickly follow up, but I had problems with my rifle's action. My guide and the assistant stepped in to finish the job.

For that hunting area, it was a very large moose, nearly sixty inches. I got hearty congratulations from Craig and Jason, and I thanked them repeatedly for a job well done. As is customary in Germany, the moose got a sprig of evergreen in its mouth to signify its last bite. Then we reflected on the hunt. Slowly the tension was replaced with total joy. I had read and heard so often about happy hunting adventures in Alaska. And now I had experienced it firsthand!

TRIALS AND TRIUMPH ON AN ALASKAN MOOSE HUNT

BY
LESTER A. KISH

Alaska is vast, wild, and remote. Mere mention of it conjures up images of paradise to a hunter. But on this day, Alaska didn't look too hospitable. Snow—a lot of it—covered the ground. It began falling soon after our departure from McGrath, a bush community on the banks of the mighty Kuskoquim River. My wife, Jo, and I were en route to a section of the western Alaska Range on a mixed-bag hunt. Even though this region is home to a variety of game and contains some of the state's finest moose range, we had seen zero moose so far.

As we flew over the Kuskoquim lowlands, distant mountains loomed above the tundra. Soon the diminutive plane banked and began to circle. A group of wall tents covered with brightly colored tarps came into view. It was John Runkle's hunting base camp on the broad, braided plain of a riverbed that was now nearly dry. The bush plane made its descent, stalled, touched down, and bounced past camp on the snowy runway, rolling to a stop near a group of rusted fuel barrels. With a squeak the plane door opened. Cold air poured in, followed by the profound silence of the Alaskan wilderness. This was the end of our two-day journey north and the beginning of a trilogy of hunting adventures.

Base camp, called Silvertip, was situated at the foot of the Alaska Range. It consisted of a log cabin headquarters, a large cookhouse, a log steam sauna, a woodshed, and a log-frame structure for hanging meat and capes. There was also a gas generator, which supplied power and allowed us to charge camcorder batteries. Radios maintained contact with the outside and kept bush pilots apprised of local flying conditions. Hunters stayed in wall tents with wood floors, stoves, and bunks with foam pads. After each day of hunting, we'd fire up the stove and hang our clothing and hip boots out to dry. Staying warm and dry is a priority when hunting in the bush. A cold, wet, and miserable hunter cannot hunt effectively for very long.

Unlike most outfitters, John Runkle and his family are year-round residents of the area. In addition to the summer-fall hunting business, John runs a trapline from his home in Nikolai to his hunting concession. In March, he guides hunts for bison in the Farewell Lake area. He also raises sled dogs for recreation and for transporting himself along his traplines.

The first morning of the hunt dawned bright and clear. After breakfast, we began packing for the trip to spike camp. Einar Douglas and John Paul Nikolai (J. P.) were our native Alaskan guides. They proved to be entertaining characters to hunt with. Einar and J. P. readied the ATVs and hooked a travois to each, to which our gear, bundled in a tarp, was lashed. This setup, referred to as a Japanese packhorse, is an efficient means of transporting hunters and gear in big-game country.

The ATVs are indispensable tools for game retrieval in Alaska. A moose is a mighty big animal. I had heard horror stories of backpacking moose over miles of spongy tundra. In fact, I know people who claim their backs start hurting whenever they so much as hear the word moose! Backpacking moose even makes sheep hunting sound easy.

This is a spectacular region of Alaska. The trip to spike camp took us through a variety of terrain: open tundra, willow

Base camp, with Mount Silvertip in the background.

flats, scrubby spruce forests, riverbeds, and rolling hills. The wide variety of wildlife habitat makes it a sportsmen's paradise, with moose, Dall sheep, black and grizzly bear, caribou, wolf and wolverine all inhabiting the same area.

Spike camp, called Ridge Camp, was situated in a patch of stunted spruce. Immediately above camp was a knoll, which provided a panoramic view of the superb game country. Most of John's spike camps were situated near areas to spot from. We settled in, unloaded our duffel, built a fire in the stove, and made some tea. Soon thereafter, we strolled above camp for an afternoon of glassing.

Einar and J. P. soon located a band of caribou on a distant ridge. There were five or six bulls in the group, one of which looked particularly good. Just as we were about to move in for a closer look, a lone black wolf burst over the ridge and scattered the herd. We decided to head there anyway, just in case the caribou hadn't been spooked too badly. But the weather would not cooperate; we had scarcely gone fifty yards when the snow swallowed us up. The ATVs got stuck repeatedly in the newly fallen snow. After extricating ourselves, we got back on the trail used to access our spike camp, and then we dropped into an adjacent riverbed. The plan was to run downstream, hook up with another drainage, and then run back up and locate the caribou. No dice. A good plan. But it didn't work.

More snow, more pushing, more extricating. I thought ATVs were supposed to be ridden! The brush closed in and that ended our stalk of the caribou. Our options temporarily exhausted, we retraced our tracks back to Ridge Camp.

Once, in the open where the going was good, we took off in our ATVs at a mad dash, racing up the riverbed and plowing down brush and small trees along the way. Then we met some brush that wasn't so forgiving. The rig stopped abruptly. Einar nearly pitched over the handlebars. I wasn't so lucky; the ATV and I parted company. I picked myself up, none the worse for wear, in time to see Einar look over his shoulder and with a big grin say, "Throttle must of got stuck!"

Back at Ridge Camp, I wondered what the devil we would do if we spotted any worthwhile game. Although we could see an incredible amount of country, we couldn't get to the game. Our only hope was to have game come to us.

Since moose was on the agenda, Einar started doing his moose call. He was using one of those coffee-can-and-rope contraptions, where you wet the rope, put the can between your upper arm and body, and pull the rope really slowly through a hole in the can's bottom. After a couple of pulls the can emits a mooselike *Wuuhh! Whuuuhh! Whuuuuhh!*

It was a clear, windless day, and the sound carried well. Moose began to appear some miles distant, clearly responding to the call. A nice cow and calf appeared, followed by a fifty-inch bull with nice palms. Two more bulls moved across a distant ridge, but they looked small. Another bull came out of a nearby brushy riverbed. We watched it plod along, head cocked in our direction, using its dishlike antlers to funnel sound to its mocassin-size ears. It looked to be in the fifty-inch class.

Because we had glassed the surrounding country so extensively, the country was beginning to look very familiar. Stringers of spruce and clumps of brush were recognizable at a glance. A couple of miles out, another bull approached across a hillside, and it looked like it might even be a sixty-incher. "Why don't you guys take a look at this?" I said, as I handed the scope to the guides.

There was no doubt it was a big bull, and all we had to do was run like hell through a couple of miles of knee-deep snow in bulky hip boots. J. P. and I took off, trying to keep any available cover between us and the bull's line of sight. We made it to a small clump of head-high spruce, hunkered down, and took a peek. The bull, still some distance off across a timbered creek bottom, was peering in our direction, maybe because it thought we were wolves. When Jo and Einar came trudging up, they were told of the situation and decided to stay put in the scrub spruce and call to the bull while we tried to intercept it as it moved up the drainage. When the bull stepped behind some

(Left to right) Einar Douglas, the author, J. P. Nikolai, and the moose.

trees, we ran across an open flat, reaching the creek bottom. We had a tough time making it through the snow-laden alders. In some places, we were walking on the alders, a full three to four feet above ground. The wind was in our favor when we broke through the alders and onto the flat tundra.

Picking our way along the edge of cover, first to a stunted tree and then to a bush, we spotted the bull lumbering toward us. Head rocking slowly and rhythmically from side to side, the moose walked with the arrogant swagger of a big bull, intrigued by the call emanating from across the creek bottom. Then the animal disappeared into a patch of spruce. We waited . . . one minute . . . two minutes—and then saw movement—some hide . . . an antler. The moose stepped out, looked our way, and turned toward the knoll from which Einar was calling.

"You ready?"

"Yup."

"Wait till it steps well clear of those trees."

The giant bull stood statuesquely, and then, finally, it moved away from the trees.

"Take him," whispered J. P.

The rifle cracked, followed by the resounding *whomp* of a bullet striking home. The bull reared on its hind legs, spun around like a saddle bronc, landed on all fours, and continued plodding along. I shot again. And again. The big bull faltered but kept going. J. P. slipped in a couple of rounds from his .338, and I added a couple more from my .30-06. The moose dropped, but not before making it to cover. What a tough animal! It was like a Clydesdale with antlers.

Einar and J. P. field-dressed it. We were miles from camp, and evening was coming upon us. On our hike back to camp, we created a trail that the ATVs could use to retrieve the bull the next day. We walked side by side, pounding out a trail. We shuffled along like a quartet of penguins, on our slow, meandering trek to Ridge Camp. It was an absolutely gorgeous evening, with a breathless silence over the countryside. The view of the Alaska Range was stupendous, its peaks basking in alpenglow. Even Denali (Athabascan for "the high one over there"), the crown of the continent, was visible some sixty miles distant.

Less than twenty-four hours after shooting the bull, it was butchered and packed out to Silvertip. The cape was fleshed, salted, and hung out to dry. Pretty efficient.

Before I left that day, Jo quipped that I couldn't shoot a moose unless its rack was wide enough for her to lie across. Well, Jo, there it was, all 68-inches' worth! We celebrated by taking a sauna.

THE INCIDENTAL GRIZZLY

BY

LESTER A. KISH

It has been said that the surest way to bag a grizzly bear is to hunt for something else. Sure enough, that's what happened to me a couple of years back on a hunt in the western Alaska Range near Denali. It was mid-September, the season of the caribou rut, and winter had come early. Several feet of snow blanketed the mountains and foothills, extending clear to the lowlands of the Kuskoquim River. Grizzlies could be anywhere this time of year. Prior to denning, the great bears range far and wide in their search for food, trying to fatten up that last little bit before the winter season. They might be working blueberry patches, prowling the lowland streams for late-run salmon, or digging out parka squirrels high up in the mountains.

It would not be easy to take a grizzly this year. First, the berry crop had been a bust in southwestern Alaska. Second, we were a long way from a salmon stream. Third, the parka squirrels were buried under a lot of wet, heavy snow. Considering the conditions, the prospects of running into a grizzly didn't look too good, and I wondered if I would have to eat the $500 grizzly tag carefully stowed in my shirt pocket.

Woodshed with antlers.

My native Alaskan guides Einar and J. P., my wife Jo, and I had spent the first few days of the hunt chasing moose. With a moose already taken, our attention shifted toward securing a caribou for Jo. I had conceded that the grizzly would be a wild card, an incidental take on our hunt for antlered game.

Dall sheep, the only wild white sheep in the world, are abundant in the craggy peaks of the Alaska Range. So when I spied tracks descending a steep mountainside, I naturally expected to spot a band of rams. Surprise, surprise! The spoor turned out to be that of a mountain grizzly, striding across the barren face of the mountain. Einar and J. P. surveyed the situation and formulated a plan of attack. The stalk was on!

We dropped into Hard Luck Creek and made a run upstream. The curve of the mountain would lead the bear closer to the creek bottom. We hoped to get out in front of the bear before starting our climb. With a little luck, the griz would continue on its present course and walk right into our laps. Our climb led us through a patch of creek-side alders and then to a broad, flat bench, where we stopped for a blow and to watch the bear's progress. The

237

bear was high up the mountain, moving aimlessly and now and then pausing to dig for parka squirrels. A hundred yards behind it, a lone wolverine nosed along the grizzly's trail, looking to scavenge a free meal. The bear was able to locate parka squirrels even in the deep snow; maybe it could smell them, or maybe they betrayed their presence by squeaking when the bear rumbled by. At any rate, the grizzly was having a heyday. It had already torn up several room-size areas in its search for dinner.

When you climb mountains while wearing hip boots and rubberized Helly-Hansen rain gear, your traction is nil. Nonetheless, J. P. and I set a steady pace through the knee-deep snow, clinging to the mountainside and dropping in and out of gullies. As we gained elevation, we lost sight of the bruin. Its tracks crisscrossed the slope, but the folds of the mountain hid the bear well. Down the mountain, Einar and Jo had an easier time keeping the bear in sight. J. P. and Einar communicated via hand signals. Using his binoculars, J. P. would watch Einar, make a motion, asking *Where is the bear?* and Einar would flash signals that meant *up above, to the left, still feeding,* and so on.

Sunset near base camp. ATV tracks head off toward the horizon.

We soon cut across the bear's trail. I glanced down at the track, and it was then I realized that this animal was the real McCoy. Wow! A smoking fresh bear trail with a real live grizzly on the other end! J. P. cautiously moved ahead to the edge of a gully, stopped, and backed up. The griz was still up feeding.

Bear hunting has been described as several days of boredom followed by ten minutes of sheer terror. Whoever came up with that gets my vote for cliché of the year. Suffice it to say that I have never been more aware of my senses than I was during that hunt.

We caught the bear's trail and followed it up the back side of a narrow spine, and we continued climbing to get above the animal. "I think we're in good shape. Shoot as soon as you see him," said J. P. Creeping ahead cautiously, I looked over the spine of the ridge. No tracks. I glanced uphill. No tracks. Downhill. Nothing! I thumbed the safety and took a step over the ridge, exposing myself to whatever was out there. Gun up and ready, I took another step, this time a small step. I

The author, Jo, and the grizzly.

saw two brown ears cocked in my direction. Eye contact and only forty yards of pure Alaska air were between us. The bruin reared up on its hind legs, jaws moving and nose twitching as it desperately tried to catch my scent. It then dropped to all fours and disappeared from view. "J. P., I think he's coming!" I said.

"Shoot!" was J. P.'s curt reply.

I moved toward the ridgeline and saw the bear rear up again. I aimed at the middle of its chest and fired. The bear dropped, somersaulted down a slope, and landed on all fours. It tried to run. Another shot, this time to the shoulders. The bear rolled again, setting off a small avalanche, and skidded to a halt on its back. Twice it tried to right itself, and twice more I fired. All was still.

J. P. and I congratulated each other on an incredible stalk. Once convinced there would be no more shooting, we motioned for Einar and Jo to join us. The bear was a beautiful silver-tipped mountain grizzly. It was more than I had expected, for it had impeccably luxuriant hair for a fall bear. Einar and J. P. did the skinning, neatly rolling the hide and stuffing it into a grain sack.

While we were en route to base camp, we heard in the quiet late-afternoon twilight a familiar sound coming from a brushy draw: *karukukuk, karukukuk, karukukuk.*

"Hear that?" said Einar. "It's a ptarmigan arguing with its old lady."

We pressed on, confident that there would be no arguments with the other hunters at base camp about who had bragging rights at the dinner table that evening.

NO EASY CARIBOU

BY
LESTER A. KISH

"There's caribou on those hills. Can you see 'em?"

"Which hills?"

"Those across the creek bottom."

I looked through my spotting scope and, sure enough, there were thirty or forty caribou spread out on a bald-faced hill some four miles distant. The caribou looked like ants.

It was the first day of a mixed-bag hunt in the western Alaska Range. Our Inuit and Athabascan guides, Einar Douglas and J. P. Nikolai, both of whom work for outfitter John Runkle, had packed my wife Jo and me into a spike camp, which overlooked an expanse of mountains, foothills, and tundra. Jo hoped to collect a barren ground caribou while I hunted moose and grizzly. We had just settled in for an afternoon of glassing when our guides located the caribou.

The southwestern part of Alaska is not known for having large caribou herds. That honor goes to the Mulchatna and North Slope country. Nonetheless, this area does in fact support a nice caribou herd, which migrates right past our base camp,

Noon break while searching for caribou. (Left to right) Einar, on the radio, Jo and guide J. P. boiling tea.

making the bagging of one seem like a lead-pipe cinch. But when a lone black wolf burst over the ridge to scatter the herd like billiard balls on a pool table, we should have suspected that we were in for a long hunt. Days passed before we saw another caribou.

Winter had come early, even for Alaska, making hunting more difficult and perhaps also influencing the caribou's movement through the area. Although we had ATVs for transportation, they often foundered in the deep snow. It seems we spent as much time pushing them as we did riding them. Jo suggested we buy an ATV when we got home so that we could push it around the neighborhood to keep in shape.

On the fourth day we located some caribou, but as we were about to make our stalk, I spotted a grizzly (see chapter 32). The bear tag in my pocket pulled rank. The caribou would have to wait.

The next morning, we continued hunting the Fox Knob area. The caribou were where we had seen them the day before, spread out on the broad, flat ridge, feeding and carousing. There were about forty animals in the herd—cows, calves, young bulls, and one overworked herd bull. The herd bull had a nice, though not exceptional, rack and long beams. We had five more days, so it was no use burning up a tag on that one.

We saw moose nearly every day. The calendar was edging into late September, and the moose were well into the rut. We often were followed by bulls, especially after we initiated contact by grunting at them. Some were trophy class, and many were immature. Weather, wolves, and grizzlies permitting, it looked promising that I'd bag a bull on my upcoming moose hunt (see chapter 31).

It was on day five that I began to wonder what would happen if one of the ATVs got a flat. After all, we ran them on riverbeds carpeted with shards of rock. Sure enough, a tire on an ATV got a little soft and then went completely flat. Now what? Einar and J. P. went to work. A three-inch-long, pencil-thick piece of rubber coated with goop was inserted into the

Jo stoking the stove at spike camp.

puncture. A little air and voilà! We were back on the trail in ten minutes. Einar and J. P. never removed the tire.

The wind was extremely strong that night, sucking the stove cold in short order. We burrowed deep into our sleeping bags, fearing that massive snowdrifts awaited us come morning. In the morning, we heard footsteps crunching through the snow. "Come on out, it's not near as bad as it sounds," said our outfitter, John Runkle. When I emerged from the tent, I found that coffee was on and breakfast was almost ready, and though the wind was still blowing hard, the clouds were breaking up. Nevertheless, day six turned out to be a day of rest. Our ATV had been running rough, and Einar spent most of the morning working on it under nasty conditions. When we finally got rolling, snowdrifts kept us from getting far from camp. We barely made it to Grandpa's Knob, a nearby vantage point, because blowing snow had drifted the trail shut. Since we didn't relish floundering through snowdrifts and constantly digging out the ATVs, we gladly called it a day.

Day seven was tough sledding. Though the wind had finally let up, it was now snowing hard. We covered a lot of country but saw no caribou. One of John's clients entertained us by stalking and taking a mid-sixties-class moose. The day eventually cleared, and that night we were treated to the sight of the aurora borealis.

The next morning dawned clear and cold, day eight of the hunt. For a change of pace we decided to hike up the creek that flowed past base camp. It was a long drainage, which John had used earlier in the season to guide clients after sheep. Sheep sign was abundant, their tracks crossing and following the creek bottom. We saw ewes and lambs but no rams in this very scenic sheep country. We had hoped to catch a caribou lingering here, but caribou had vacated the drainage. Several large flocks of ptarmigan, their plumage now mottled with white, fed and chattered in the thickets flanking the creek. We also saw a sow grizzly and its cub moving toward the high country in preparation for denning.

That evening, one of John's guides radioed to inform us that a large herd of caribou had been spotted in the vicinity of our first-day

Jo and the author with trophy caribou.

spike camp. The guide then broke off the radio conversation so that he could photograph a big bull that was walking right past the camp.

Sleep came hard that night, and anticipation ran high as we hopped aboard the ATVs early the next morning. We had scarcely left base camp when we saw caribou tracks on the flood plain. During the night, about a dozen caribou had filed by about two hundred yards from base camp. They had paused and bedded some miles downriver, but were now up and moving. Their tracks led up into rolling timber that extended to Windy Fork.

Following the caribou on foot was out; however, many years back, a trail had been bulldozed through the area. That trail was now overgrown with stunted spruce. It was a rough, swampy mess of hummocks that challenged all men and machines venturing upon it. We hung on for dear life as the ATVs crawled through the quagmire. When we broke from cover and onto the broad, flat plain of Windy Fork, we were surprised by the absence of snow. This was the first bare ground we had encountered during the trip. It was a good sign. I hoped the caribou would stop to feed here after plowing their way through miles of deep snow.

They did. Out on the flood plain stood a group of caribou, all cows and calves, feeding on the knee-high willows. We hid behind the trees, watching, waiting, and hoping for a straggling bull to appear. A cup of tea cut our morning chill, but no more caribou came through. We solemnly considered our options, as we bucked our way back over the cat trail. We decided we would glass from Grandpa's Knob after lunch, figuring the herd had split into several smaller segments and that their normal seasonal movement would eventually lead them north past camp.

After hours of diligent glassing, we spotted a line of meandering tracks through the open scrub timber. Funny we hadn't noticed those tracks earlier. Several miles below camp there was a recent burn. The open stand of dead timber presented the caribou with an alternative migration route. We pulled out and went downriver, retracing our morning tracks. We found more caribou tracks where the burned timber pressed against the flood plain. Indeed, there were several tracks, some distinctly larger than the others, and they were headed (where else?) to Windy Fork. We stared at each other in exasperation. Not again! Our butts couldn't possibly tolerate another jaunt over the cat trail.

"We better get going," suggested Einar. We had no choice. If Jo wanted a caribou, we had to travel that bumpy trail one more time. It was getting late and we were on day nine of the hunt. With caribou scarce, any representative bull would be a hard-earned trophy.

When we reached Windy Fork, we again stopped at the timber's edge. Looking up- and downriver, we saw nothing. "If they come over, I think they will go downriver," said Einar. We proceeded to slowly poke our way downriver, with J. P. and Jo leading the way. After a couple of hundred yards, J. P. and Jo stopped. Caribou were filing out of the timber. The first bull to come out looked good, and familiar. It was part of the herd that had been spooked by the wolf on the first day of our hunt.

Jo, J. P., and Einar began the stalk, while I stayed behind to videotape the action. The cows and calves were busy feeding, and the bull was preoccupied with a demonstration of virility, thrashing willows with its antlers. Guides and hunter crawled on their bellies to within seventy-five yards. Alert but unconcerned, the bull turned to face them. At the sound of Jo's shot, the bull dropped its head, its nose close to the ground. Jo's second shot dropped it. We all had worked very hard for that caribou, and we had the bumps, bruises, and muscle soreness to prove it.

The trip back to Silvertip base camp was slow. We occasionally stopped to pull spruces aside so Jo and J. P. could squeeze through with the caribou rack. It was impressive watching J. P. weave the ATV through the timber as he and Jo peered through those beautiful antlers lashed to its front. They were enjoying the trip, grinning from ear to ear.

We spent the last day relaxing, and the trophies were prepared for shipment. Guides, outfitter, and hunters recounted the past several days. When we had originally booked the hunt, we had hoped for more than a hunting trip. We wanted adventure. I'd say we got it!

PART FIVE

MIXED-REGION HUNTS

MEMORIES OF AN ALASKAN HUNTING GUIDE

BY
WENDELL RUNYON

The stonewashed Glacier River fingered its way around silty sandbars, and on both sides of the river, towering peaks rose above lush alpine valleys and high mountain passes. Two miles ahead, the thin gravel landing strip came into view as I looked out the window of the Super Cub. As the small plane banked left for the approach, I spotted a group of caribou that had just crossed the river. They stood shaking themselves on a sandbar strewn with drift logs.

The plane set down smoothly and taxied to the far end of the makeshift runway. In just a few minutes, all my gear was unloaded, and the Piper bounced back down the strip, popped into the air, and was soon out of sight. I stood and turned 360 degrees, taking in the beauty of this pristine wilderness. I had been scouting the area for some time and thought it to be a good place to conduct the sheep hunt I had lined up, to take place five days later.

After base camp was set up, I walked out to the swiftly flowing river and pulled up a comfortable seat against the roots of a

Alan's 10-foot, 2-inch Kodiak brown bear.

toppled giant spruce that had once stood on the deeply cut bank. A small fire of spruce twigs broke the mountain chill as I watched the full moon rise into a starlit night sky. I remembered what old-time guide Nick Botner told me. "If you do choose the guiding profession, you will never regret your choice of occupation." He was right. As tiny flames danced from the spruce embers, a few memorable hunts came to mind. . . .

It was an early September sheep hunt. I could see two wolverines below, working the scent trail of four sheep like beagles after a rabbit. My hunter Richard and I were on a high ridge around five thousand feet, looking for a Dall ram. Richard had a tag for a wolverine, so we began the descent to the area where the animals were hunting. We lost sight of them as they trailed the sheep over a ridge and into steep rocky cliffs. Richard and I moved halfway down the ridge and into the cliffs where I had seen two ewes with lambs disappear, followed by the wolverines. We sat down and started to look.

Out of the corner of my eye I caught the movement of something behind and just above us, about ten feet away. I stood up and turned around, telling Richard I thought the "skunk bear" was behind us and to get ready. I slung my rifle over my shoulder and climbed the rocks behind us. As I pulled myself up onto a grassy ledge, I saw the wolverine lying in a bed lined with hair, feathers, and moss, which it had obviously used many times before. In the same instant, Richard said he could see a wolverine thirty yards below him in a rockslide. I said, "Yeah, and there's one here five feet in front of me." The animal crouched, glaring at me with savage eyes, and snarled its disapproval at my being so close. Richard's Weatherby boomed. The wolverine in front of me turned and jumped from the grassy ledge, over a small willow bush and into the gravel draw some twenty feet below.

The shot had sent the wolverine staring me down into a head-over-heels retreat. The lambs and ewes stepped out of the cliffs just twenty-five yards away to see what all the

The Frenchman's 9-foot, 4-inch brown bear.

commotion was about. Richard's wolverine from below had fine markings and was beautifully furred. After skinning the rare trophy, we headed in the direction of camp, searching the mountaintops along the way.

The next morning we spotted three sheep in a basin at the 4,700-foot level. One looked worth investigating. As we started our climb, a marmot whistled its alarm above us. I was worried it had spooked the sheep, but we kept climbing.

When we reached the basin, it was just as I thought. The sheep were gone. There was a cave behind the basin. I pointed it out to Richard as we glassed, looking for the rams that had been there earlier. The climb was steep, causing us to work up quite a thirst. A small creek ran clear and cold below, so I took the water bottles and went to fill them. I drank the refreshing fluid and searched the area carefully for the sheep. I glassed the cave, the cliffs above the basin, and the surrounding ridges, but saw no sign of the sheep. I took another long draw of the mountain water, and then the sheep materialized 250 yards above me, lying in front of the cave. They must have been hiding inside. I tried to get my hunter's attention one hundred yards away, but he had his binoculars to his eyes and was looking everywhere but at me. Finally, after several minutes, Richard glanced in my direction, and I waved him toward me and motioned him to go low and slow.

There were not three rams but five. Two were full-curls. The largest was lying down behind the others and didn't provide a shot.

Richard asked, "How long will they stay bedded?"

I said, "I don't know. It could be three hours or three minutes."

As soon as I got the words out the rams stood up. Richard fired and had his ram! The other four rams took off into the cliffs and were out of sight. We then headed for the ram, which had rolled nearly to the stream. It was a beautiful ram with high, wide, spiraling horns and heavy bases.

The mountaintops were bathed in purple light from the late afternoon sun as we began our descent, heading back to camp in this beautiful Alaskan wilderness.

The mountain animals inhabit some of the most breathtaking scenery on earth, I reflected. Then I recalled a goat hunt that took place in the rugged mountains of northern Kodiak Island. I was with Anthony, the same hunter who would be joining me for the sheep hunt in five days.

We began the hunt by climbing up through the alders toward the goat cliffs. When we reached the high alpine country, we stopped for a break and looked down to the beach where we had started. Pods of sea otters bobbed in the bay. The Alaska Peninsula was visible across the Shelikof Strait. We made it to the base of the cliffs and set up our camp in a sheltered bench just below the snow line. An ice-cold stream flowed out of the snow-covered mountains nearby. Large icicles had formed on the banks of the stream and hung from the cliffs and rocks above.

Late that afternoon I spotted two billies one thousand feet above our camp. Their dense, shaggy coats waved as gusts of wind carried a snow shower around the mountain. Both goats had long, heavy horns and were first-class trophies. We watched them for another half hour until it was nearly dark and the chill and hunger sent us to the warmth of a hot meal and our sleeping bags.

The next morning thick clouds covered the mountains and surrounded our tent while we ate breakfast. Wind-driven sleet stung our faces as we headed out. We tried to use our binoculars, but wet, heavy snowflakes covered the lenses as soon as we brought the glasses to our eyes. We subjected ourselves to the harsh elements as long as possible. At noon, we started back to camp. When we got there, the tent was covered with a sheet of ice and snow. Piping hot soup had Anthony and me feeling much better. The inside of the tent was quite cozy, and there we weathered the storm. Sometime during the night I got up and went outside. The sky was ablaze with stars, but a bone-chilling wind blew fiercely from the northwest. When morning came, the sky was sapphire blue and pure, but the wind continued cutting through us like a knife. It looked like several inches of new snow covered the high country.

Around 10:00 A.M. we spotted a bear. Its hide was a rich chocolate brown, and a single fat cub tagged along with it. They were digging roots a little less than half a mile away, at the top of a deep, alder-choked ravine. Pretty soon I spotted two goats. They were bedded out of the wind, one about a hundred yards above the other. They weren't as heavily horned as the first two we had seen, but the upper one was a respectable representative of its kind. Anthony said he wanted to try and get up to it.

We made our way along a gametrail that followed the creek, which came down from the peaks. Then the steep slope and deep snow forced us into the stream. We kept following it up over ice-covered rock and frozen falls. Halfway to the goats, we found a navigable draw. Leaving the water route, Anthony and I continued up the draw and came out in a bench that led around the mountain. Two sets of goat tracks plowed through the deep snow. We followed them to where they crossed the crest of a low ridge and into a snow-covered rocky basin.

Chambering rounds and inching our way to peer into the basin, we found the two billies slowly walking fifty yards in front of us. They were so close in size, it was almost impossible to tell which was the better of the two. For some reason, the one on the right looked slightly heavier. Anthony set his sights and fired. The majestic beast fell. The other billy trotted a short distance, then climbed a rock outcropping and stood there watching us. It was a fantastic sight! The goat looked like something left over from the Pleistocene period. Its long woolly hair was blowing in the wind, and the goat was slightly veiled by swirling snow against a background of icy rock.

Anthony's goat was a real trophy. The horns measured 5³/₄ inches at the bases and 10 inches in length, a Holy Grail of its species. As we packed the cape for a full mount and packed the meat off the icy mountain, I thought of warmer weather hunting at lower elevations. The events of a previous moose hunt flooded back. . . .

The early morning fog lay heavy in the trees. A mink swam across the beaver pond, then disappeared into the jumble of logs along the bank. A raven yelled *"Ku-luk, ku-luk"* as it flew high overhead. This was definitely moose country. Sign was abundant, and I knew of a trophy-class moose that was hanging around the area, but the terrain wasn't easy. The brush engulfed us, and visibility was maybe thirty yards at best. As stealthily as possible, we hunted.

By 10:00 A.M. the fog had burned off, and the annoying whitesocks began to swarm over John and me. The winged creatures lit without notice, then left with pieces of our flesh. Our plan had been to hunt in the morning, return to camp for lunch, then head back out for the prime afternoon hunting. The weather seemed like summer that afternoon. The pungent aroma of mid-September Labrador tea filled my nostrils. We followed a gametrail to an open ridge where heavy rutting activity took place year after year. I led John to my favorite glassing spot. It was a large siwash spruce, just under the crest of a scarlet ridge. Heavily used gametrails converged nearby, and visibility was perfect in all directions.

Richard's grizzly.

The vast Alaskan landscape.

Whiskey-jacks sounded off from a stand of spruce seventy-five yards distant. We could see a cow, moving through a blueberry patch, heading toward a willow-filled drainage a mile away. Then . . . *whaccckkk!* The sound of two bulls doing battle. Their antlers collided; tines raked back and forth on palms. I could hear hoofs being set to brace for the struggle. John and I stalked to within thirty-five yards of the dueling moose. They were both fine meat moose but not the trophy quality we were looking for.

Glancing in the direction of the cow, we saw a good-looking bull moose. It was in a willow swamp among scattered black spruce with streams of old-man's beard hanging in the branches. John and I wanted a closer look, so we left the two smaller bulls sparring and made our way to the far hillside. Sneaking along the edge of the willow swamp in the cover of spruce, I caught a glimpse of the top of the bull's right palm and pointed it out to John. In an instant the bull was gone, swallowed up by the tall willow. We stalked the area until dark, but that was all we saw of the bull.

By midmorning the next day, we had carefully glassed the ridges, draws, and thickets but hadn't seen a single animal. I knew of a good gametrail that led through the heavier spruce timber and alders, and we began following it toward the higher ridges at timberline. We had just made our way around three small ponds and were climbing a spruce-covered ridge near its crest. A reflection of the sun shining off moose antlers caught my eye. The bull was across a brushy draw, bedded near thick alder, among a scattering of spruce trees around six hundred yards away. Picking out some landmarks, I marked the bull's location. The old gametrail would put us very close to the bull, if we could remain quiet enough. The hot and dry Indian summer had created noisy walking conditions.

We were able to keep an eye on the bull as we moved along a forested bench that led to a narrow neck of the brushy, wet willow draw. An open blueberry ridge led up the other side of the draw and halfway up became covered with buck brush four feet tall. On top of the ridge stood several large spruce trees, and there our moose was bedded. John and I made it to where the berry patch gave way to dwarf birch and took off our packs. Chambering rounds, we began the final stalk on the bull one hundred yards away. A steady five-miles-per-hour breeze blew in our faces and helped disguise any sound we made. At sixty yards we spotted the wide-antlered rack with good brow palms, tilting slowly from side to side. Occasionally the bull would nod off and the big rack would bob down and then pop back up. We stood frozen. Three cows that had gone unnoticed stood guard around the bull. They paced slightly, then lay down and were out of sight.

We inched our way forward and cut the distance to forty yards. Still, the only part of the moose that was visible was its rack. The cows also were still hidden. I told John to aim just above the bull's rack, saying that I was going to make the bull stand up. When it did, he was to settle the cross hairs and squeeze. When John was ready, I gave out a low "Ungh." The bull jumped to its feet, pausing for a split second. The sound of the .338 broke the early afternoon calm. The cows came out of the buck brush, their ears thrown forward as they looked all around and then hightailed it for the alders. I heard the solid thump of a good hit. The bull reared and disappeared behind a spruce. I got off a quick snapshot but didn't have any faith in it.

We stood and listened. You could hear the animals crashing through the alders that were as thick as fleas on a hound's back. At one time I thought I heard the bull go down. We stood in its bed and waited a full twenty minutes. One of the cows bellowed from deep in the alders, calling the group back together. John and I retrieved our packs, topped off our magazines, and began following the blood trail. It was an easy one to follow. I was sure that just a few yards farther we would find our trophy. The heavy blood trail continued through the half mile of alders, across an open ridge, and into another section of dense spruce, alder, and willow.

The author hunting on foot

The bull had traveled almost a mile, and the blood trail began to thin. Turning up a draw that led to a wide timberline bench, we found our moose. It was a well-earned trophy, with four long points on each wide brow palm and a 63-inch spread. I showed the animal honor and respect. Closing my eyes, I stroked its massive neck and thanked it for letting me share the land in which it lived, where its spirit would always remain. John shook my hand and spoke, "My brother said you were a good guide. I just had to see for myself. Thanks for a wonderful hunt."

Two years earlier, I had hunted with John's brother Richard. The excitement came on the fourth day of his hunt. It was a gorgeous day—crystal blue skies with fluffy white clouds floating overhead. The red, orange, and purple colors of the fall foliage, with the snowcapped mountains for a background, painted a picture everyone should see at least once.

We had been sitting under a two-hundred-year-old spruce on a blueberry ridge overlooking a high mountain creek that meandered through the vast Alaskan landscape. We had spotted an eight-foot grizzly earlier and were trying to relocate it. Scanning with my binoculars, I saw the bear six hundred yards below us, gorging itself on the overripe blueberries that were extremely thick that year.

We got within one hundred yards of the last place we had seen the bear. Dropping our packs, we crept along a trail the caribou had carved into the earth's surface over thousands of years of migration. I told Richard to crank his scope to its lowest setting. The spruce trees were getting thick, and it was probably going to be a pretty close shot. We stopped where the bear should have been. I knew we were close; I just had that feeling. As we strained our eyes for any movement among the spruce branches, the bear stepped into view, bobbing its head, stripping the bushes of their weight of berries. The bear was just forty feet away! Two quick shots were all that were needed. Richard had taken a prime eight-foot Toklat grizzly in spectacular wilderness where the great bears flourished in unblemished habitat.

Then there was the time up in the Talkeetnas. Andy had booked a fourteen-day sheep and grizzly hunt with Jim Bailey. I was to be his guide. Jim flew us to a lake just before dark. We had eaten supper at the lodge, so we set up our camp and crawled into our sleeping bags for the night. Before daylight I got up, put on a pot of coffee, and made some bacon and eggs. The plan was to try and spot a full-curl ram at first light and make our climb. Just as we finished our last cup of coffee for the morning, nine rams came into view about two miles away. It looked like three of the rams were full-curl, with one exceptional ram in the bunch, but we needed a closer look.

We crossed the valley, climbed five hundred feet, then moved into a side valley where the sheep were. We got within one thousand yards with no chance of getting any closer. I looked them over with my 30X spotting scope and could see that four of the rams were full-curl, one of them an exceptional trophy. The only way to get to them was to backtrack out of the valley, move around the side of the mountain, climb to the top, then hunt down to them in a hollow that would provide cover.

Everything went well until we were five hundred yards from the sheep. They had all been bedded, but the amount of time it took to get to them was enough for the rams to get up and start moving again. Two half-curls crossed the hollow just below us. A couple more were climbing the mountain off to the left. The largest ram remained bedded, but all the others were moving. It was going to be very difficult, if not impossible, to get to the biggest ram. All of a sudden, a full-curl ram moved into view 150 yards in front of us. Andy said the ram was OK and that he wanted it. He made a very good shot, and the first part of our hunt was over. We could now concentrate on grizzly.

It took us two days of glassing to spot a bear. We saw it a mile and a half away on the other side of Christine Creek. The bear was eating blueberries and looked like it was going to stay put. We made our way to the creek, found a place to cross, and climbed the opposite bank. We looked everywhere for the bear, but it was nowhere to be found.

It was long after dark when we got back to the cabin we were hunting from. All the next day we glassed but only saw caribou, moose, and one black bear. Dawn came again, and a full day of glassing showed everything but a grizzly. Then, just at very last light, we spotted a beautiful silvertip. The bear was a half mile away, and we took off at a run, but it was pitch-black before we could get to where the bear was.

The next day we walked to the lodge, packed more food, took a shower, and returned to the halfway cabin for the afternoon hunt. Just after starting to glass, I spotted seven sheep up on the mountainside. There were hundreds of caribou grazing the tundra. A bull moose that would go around sixty-five inches stepped out of a spruce thicket. A black bear and two grizzlies were all in view at one time. Well, Andy and I took off after the closest grizzly, but when we got there, it was nowhere to be found. We looked in the direction of the second bear, and it was no longer in sight either. We hunted for them until dark with no luck.

The next morning at first light, right after breakfast, I spotted another grizzly. This one was on the other side of the creek, close to where we had seen the first bear. It looked content eating berries. We covered the ground, made the climb out of the ravine, slipped through some alders, and found the bear seventy-five yards away, still eating berries. Andy fired five times at the bear and hit moss every time. I saw he was disgusted that he had made an excellent shot on the sheep but had missed the bear. We sat there until just before dark but only saw moose and caribou.

The next day was Andy's last day to hunt, and we found another bear, a blond with black shoulders. We would have to move quickly to cut off the bear, but it was possible. We got into position on a ridge, but the bear never showed up. After looking for it the rest of the day to no avail, we packed up and headed for the lodge. Andy didn't get a bear, but he did get a trophy sheep.

Nothing is more heartbreaking on a hunt than to have your equipment fail. This includes everything from your socks to your rifle. I had a hunter from Michigan who took a 65-inch moose and a fine black bear in the first part of his hunting during warm, sunny weather. Then the rain set in. We were after grizzly and needed everything in our favor. After four days and nights of steady rain, we found a bear. We had just left our camp and saw a nice silvertip go over a tapering glacial moraine. On the other side was an expansive valley. We ran up onto the glacier deposit, hoping to find the bear in range, but it was nowhere in sight.

The highest point of the ridge was only twenty yards away, and would provide a much better view. Walking south to this point, we met the bear walking north. The distance was only twenty yards! I had Williams peep sights on my Sako .375 H&H and instantly had the bead steadied on the bear's chest. I told Dennis to shoot. No shot came. Again I said, "Shoot . . . shoot!" Well, that was all the grizzly could take. It sprayed gravel fifteen feet as it dug in its claws to turn and flee. The next time we saw the bear it was 250 yards away, weaving in and out of the thick willows that grew along the creek. Dennis's scope had fogged at the most inopportune moment.

I had another rifle in camp, and after making the exchange we were back in business. During the next four days we got two more chances at a beautiful grizzly of eight and a half feet. This bear had hair the color of straw. The legs from the elbows down were jet-black, sometimes called a toklat or a mountain grizzly. Many people feel this is the most gorgeous color phase a grizzly could have. But both times, just before our stalk put us in range, the wind changed 180 degrees, eliminating any chance for a shot. Sometimes I guess it just isn't meant to be.

The adrenaline really starts to flow when you're close to these great bears! Their size and strength, accompanied by their will to do what they want when they want, is enough to send shivers down the strongest of spines. The giant bears of Kodiak have provided me with some hair-raising encounters. I remembered one bear that was hellbent on doing great bodily harm. It all began during a deer hunt. . . .

It was late afternoon, on a clear and cold day. The sun was settling out of sight behind us as the heavy, dark-antlered blacktailed buck moved through the cottonwoods across the creek eighty yards away. The deer stopped to survey the area, and my hunter fired. The big five-by-five buck dropped. As we neared the creek on our way to the downed deer, we came upon an eerie sight. The beavers had built a new dam on the creek. This created a pool, and the late run of silver salmon were stockpiled like I had never seen before. I mean they were thick! Well, a bear had claimed this spot for its own. Huge muddy bear tracks were everywhere. There were several trees four to six inches in diameter that were broken three feet off the ground. The bear had torn up the ground in many spots, clawing up the small willows and alders with its four-and-a-half-inch claws. There were cottonwoods two feet in diameter that were stripped of bark nine feet up the trunk.

I quickly dressed the deer. With darkness approaching, I loaded the quartered meat and cape into my pack and hurried my hunter toward the beach, vowing to return in two days when bear season opened. On opening day, Harold and I were sitting on a concealed outlook searching for the bruin. Around noon I spotted the shimmering of sun on bear hair. It was a small, light-colored bear, probably a sow, moving in the stand of cottonwoods five hundred yards away. It looked like it was heading for the fishing hole. It was a beautiful bear with a prime hide but definitely not the bear that had marked the territory.

A few minutes later it left the creek on a run, looking back over its shoulder. I figured the larger bear had arrived and had run off the light-colored bear. Harold and I eased into our packs, chambered rounds, and slowly headed into the brush along the creek. The sound of the water's current was occasionally interrupted by the splashing of a salmon on its way upstream. I listened for the sounds of a fishing bear and tried looking everywhere at once, as we slowly stepped down the enormous bear trail that ran beside the creek. One second everything was quiet and slow; the next it was fast and furious. All of a sudden we were face-to-face with an enraged brown bear that looked like it meant business! The hair on its neck and shoulders bristled, and it was running right at us. At twenty feet it turned broadside, snapping its teeth together and bouncing on its front feet. The glare in its eyes was evil. Growling, it turned to face us and continued its charge.

My hunter was ready and fired. The .300 Winchester Magnum knocked the bear to a sitting position but did not stop it. Its head swayed from side to side, and in an instant it was on its feet, quartering away from us. My shot hit the Kodiak just behind the right shoulder, but it still did not fall. The bear turned sharply to the left and tried to put the small ridge, which ran along the salmon-filled stream, between itself and us. My hunter shot again, and the enormous bear rolled to the stream's edge. The late run of silvers splashed in panic to the opposite bank. Harold had taken the trophy of a lifetime on the first day of his hunt!

This was my favorite valley to hunt. Visibility was great from several vantage points, and the bear population was very high.

The prior spring my hunter got a bear that squared 10 feet, 2 inches, and the rough green measurement of the skull was 29 inches. Twenty-eight inches will place the bear in the Boone and Crockett *Record Book of North American Big Game Animals*.

It was the first day of Alan's hunt also. He and I had been glassing the mountainside all morning from what we call Seal Island. Around noon the incoming tide forced us to leave our rock. We got in the Zodiac and cruised to shore, climbed a small knoll, and continued our search. Within fifteen minutes, I spotted a good-sized bear walking in the snow at the 1,300-foot level, around a mile and a half away. We watched the bear for forty-five minutes. The bear looked to me like it was looking for a place to lie down in an alder patch.

It was around 1:00 P.M. when we began our stalk. We had cut the distance between us and the bear in half, then lost sight of it, but continued in its direction until we were 450 yards from the last spot we had seen it. Creeping into an alder patch that provided a good view, we began glassing for the bear. My eyes kept going back to a dark spot in the middle of an alder patch. Then it happened! The bear raised and turned its head, testing the air. It looked huge. I knew it was a very large bear. The wind was good, and I thought we could get within one hundred yards of the enormous animal. We slipped down through the alder patch, crossed a small creek, and began the final approach.

We started moving very slowly, and my hunter chambered a round in his .375 H&H. Just a few more yards and the bear would be visible. Then the snow gave way beneath us with an audible pop. We both looked in the direction of the bear and saw it sitting up looking at us, eighty yards away. Alan aimed and fired, and the bear fell and disappeared.

We walked up and admired one of the largest bears either of us had ever seen. The fur was perfect, chocolate brown and long. Jim Bailey, the master guide I was working for, said it was probably the finest hide he had ever seen, and with nearly thirty years of guiding experience, he had seen many.

Hunting brown bears isn't always as easy as it sounds. It can happen the first day or the last or sometimes not at all. Take, for instance, a spring hunt a couple of years earlier. My hunter was from France. He was a very nice fellow and a real hard hunter. We climbed to the top of several mountains on snowshoes in our search for bear "of at least nine feet." Day after day we looked at smaller bears and sows with cubs. We glassed in the pouring rain with fifty-miles-per-hour winds. We crossed rivers that were well over our hip boots, only to have the bears elude us. Finally, on the twelfth day, the last day of the hunt, we found a fresh set of tracks on the beach. I guessed by their size that the bear was a nine-footer.

It was another rainy, foggy day, and tracking the bear seemed impossible, but I tried. I cleared my mind of all things except what I thought the bear was doing. We left the beach in the direction I thought the bear had taken. There was no way to see a track in the grass; I just focused on what I thought the bear had done. We were on a deer trail that led into a dwarf birch thicket. There, in a sandy area, was a track, almost washed out from the heavy rain. We slowed the pace and looked hard. Nothing. Continuing around a small lake, through a stand of cottonwoods, there was no sign of a bear. Then came the thick alder patches and devil's club, but no sign of the bear having been there. Then another sandy spot and a track.

We moved onward, ever so cautiously, and came to the base of a mountain. Standing there, I concentrated harder than I

267

ever had. *Did the bear go up the draw or on around the base?* Many times I had spotted bears up that draw in those alders, almost too thick to penetrate. I stood—I looked—I thought, and I looked again. The fog was much thicker, and the rain was coming down heavily, pounding the mountainside. We moved around the base, slower and slower, until we came to some beaver activity on a small stream. We crossed on a dam and started climbing a small knoll. Halfway up, I told my hunter to chamber a round. Inching our way to peek over the crest, we saw the bear, not thirty yards away! One shot and the Frenchman was a very happy man. The hide measured nine feet, four inches, and the skull was $27^1/_2$ inches.

Experiences like that will definitely increase your heart rate and leave you with a cold clammy feeling, but one of the most exciting episodes I ever had with brown bears happened with a hunter named Ludo, from Belgium. We were glassing the mountainsides and basins of a valley a couple of miles from camp. Sitting on a ridge well above the valley floor, our view was incredible. The sun was shining brightly overhead, making glassing conditions perfect. Black-tailed deer moved from one alder patch to another, browsing on the early May buds. An occasional vole scurried through the grass at our feet, searching for a few dropped morsels.

Late afternoon turned into early evening, and around 7:00 P.M. I spotted something that looked a lot like a bear lying at the edge of an alder patch. I had the spotting scope on it but just couldn't confirm it to be a bear. I was trying to distinguish movement and locate tracks in the now-shadowed snow. All of a sudden a bear walked up to the object I was watching, and the object raised its head and stood up. It was a mating pair! They nuzzled one another, pawed at each other, and generally just frolicked up there in the snow. It was too late in the afternoon to make a stalk. I figured they would be in pretty much the same area the next morning, so we climbed off the ridge, crossed the river that ran through the valley, and headed for camp. We would fill up on carbohydrates, get a good night's sleep, and go after our quarry before daylight.

The next morning we were up at 4:30 A.M. We ate some pancakes and were headed for the bear before sunrise. Upon entering the valley at first light, I set up the spotting scope and found the bears almost immediately. They were in pretty much the same spot as the day before, around three and a half miles away. We followed the river until we came to a spot where it ran through vertical rock cliffs. Climbing up into the alders, we soon had to strap on our snowshoes due to the deep snow. We got to the place where the bears were but didn't see them. Their tracks were everywhere in the snow. Moving up the mountain slowly, we came to a very steep drop-off. This portion of the ridge was bare of snow. The grass was standing and dry, and the alders would provide cover while we searched for the bears. It was around 11 A.M., and the morning sun had already raised the temperature to around 55 degrees. We sat down and began to glass.

There was a forked gorge below us, one that would be nearly impossible to cross. All of a sudden, the two bears came up out of the gorge. The blond sow led the way. The big dark boar followed, biting at her neck. At around 130 yards, I told Ludo to fire. At the shot, the boar roared, fell, and rolled into a hole. It was just as if half a dozen fifty-five-gallon drums had been sitting there all winter, stacked three wide and two high, and someone had come along and moved them, creating this unusual depression in the snow-covered landscape. The bear was still alive. We could hear it roar but were unable to see it and get a finishing shot. Hating to have any animal suffer, we needed to finish what we had started. The only way to get down there was to sidehill around the mountain, away from the drop-off, and then approach the wounded animal. We had gone only thirty yards when we met the sow head-on, only twenty-five feet away! We looked at each other for what seemed an eternity. Then the sow turned and left at a run. We continued toward the downed bear. We were fifty yards away but still could not see the bear because it was in the depression. We just had to get closer. At thirty feet, the bear stood up and provided the shot we needed, then fell back into the hole and out of sight. We stood there, listening and watching. Nothing! Ten minutes passed. The only sound was the magpies and finches flying from bush to bush.

Creeping a foot or so at a time, and standing up on my tiptoes, I tried to get a view of the bear. I inched closer and closer, but I was still unable to see it. I was ready, chamber loaded, safety off, and my finger on the trigger. I took another step to the edge of the hole. My weight caused the sun-softened snow to collapse, and I began to slide . . . right in on top of the bear! As I slid, I was backstepping, trying to turn my snowshoes into wings to lift me out of there. I felt the grizzly underneath my feet. Instantly realizing that there was no movement from the bear, I let out a huge sigh of relief. Ludo came running to me as I scrambled up to meet him. He helped pull me out of the hole and gave me a tight embrace. I was thankful it was from him and not the bear!

Following Alaska's game trails has given me many exciting adventures to remember. It has rewarded me with an unequaled lifestyle.

My fire turned into a small mound of powdered ash, and the sound of the river weighted my eyelids. The full moon was shining overhead now, lighting my way to the tent.

ALASKAN HUNTS, 1992–1996

BY

MAARTEN JURGENS

When we were almost at the top, I saw its brown head and hump clearly outlined against the blue sky. Fred froze when I pulled the leg of his trousers and pointed at the brown bear forty feet away. While climbing through the thick alders, we had drifted too far to the right, and too close to the quarry. Seated on my rear and facing the bear, I pushed myself backward, balancing the rifle in my lap. I then saw the blond bear lying next to the brown. Its head looked huge. My two fingers in the air and the expression on my face informed Fred that I had seen the blond. I continued my retreat, knowing that at any second the sleeping bears might awaken to find a stranger in their midst.

* * * * * *

I bought my first bear tag in autumn 1983. That year I combined a backpacking trip and a moose-and-goat hunt in the Rocky Mountains in Canada. The outfitter, Karl Prinz, had told me many times that, as far as he was concerned, backpacking and hunting did not go together. But I insisted, and off we went on a ten- to twelve-day trip above timberline. Karl and I hardly spoke—which was fine with me—but while we sat at the campfire on the evening of the second day, Karl made his point.

"Let's say that tomorrow you shoot a bear," he said. "The hide will weigh about fifty kilos. Are you going to carry it out?"

I did not respond.

"So we are not going to shoot a bear—" said Karl.

"Nor a moose nor a goat," I added.

"Not unless you decide to return to base camp," he said.

But I didn't want to return to base camp. There were two other hunters and guides there, and I had booked a wilderness trip to get *away* from the crowd. We returned to base camp, all right, but after ten wonderful days in the Canadian wilderness.

The author killed a trophy moose on the second day of his 1992 hunt.

One morning on the trip, I discovered bear tracks around our tent. I was also lucky enough to spot a grizzly, and while we were making our way around it, we blundered into another brownie. It looked at us for a long time, only fifty yards away. Then it disappeared into the brush.

* * * * * *

In autumn 1992, I joined a couple of friends on their hunting trip to Alaska. My joining them was a last-minute decision that I'll never regret. The two weeks spent in Big Salmon Camp (just west of Denali National Park) made me fall in love with the Last Frontier. The trip was enhanced by my guide, Fred Cook Jr., who at the time was working for outfitter George Palmer. Fred and I hunted Alaska together five more times and became close friends.

I took a big trophy moose on the second day of my 1992 Alaska trip. Fred was delighted because my early success left us with a fresh carcass and ten days to hunt bear. Our camp was near a riverbed used by bears traveling to their winter dens. We saw several bear tracks and fresh dung, and one day we saw a bear. It was spooked by the airplane when George flew in to check on us. We saw it gallop in our direction down a hill toward a tributary of the main stream. The bear was about five hundred yards away when it disappeared into the brush. We went after it, but it passed us in the thick brush. We never even caught a glimpse of it, though I did smell it.

Soon afterward, Fred and I found a track, and that evening we saw a bear far upstream and on the other side of the main riverbed. It was moving away from us, and we had only about an hour of daylight left. It looked like the same bear to me. We ran after it, but it went out of sight as we crossed the riverbed. We never saw it again. It was pitch-dark when we returned to our small tent.

The next morning, the whole valley was white with snow. We remained in spike camp for another day, but because it kept snowing and getting colder, we spent most of our time in the wall tent, which had a stove. I was lucky that George managed to fly Fred and me to Mystic Lake Lodge before the snow got too thick for his plane to land. Two of my friends had to stay at spike camps for a week before a floatplane could arrive to pick them up.

* * * * * *

In August 1993 Fred guided me in the Brooks Range. We got a nice caribou near base camp, but once in the mountains, we were weathered in for most of the time and did not get our ram. I had brought nothing to read—I never do, except for field guides—and we talked a lot about Dall sheep and bears.

* * * * * *

I booked a 1994 spring bear hunt with Fred, and I decided not to shave on the hunt until I took a big brown bear. During the 1993–94 winter, I had read and reread every book I could

Fred Cook Jr. (right) and the author in the Brooks Range. August 1993.

find on bears. I fell in love with the species, just as I had fallen in love with Alaska in 1992. I hoped to get close to a brown bear, though I knew that would be hard to achieve. Excitement is a major reason why I hunt dangerous game, and it is when I am near the quarry that the real excitement begins for me.

Fred had booked two other hunters, Chuck and Don, for the 1994 spring bear hunt, and they each got a big bear. On the morning of the first day of the season, Fred and I were getting our packs ready when I heard shots, and I knew then that we would not

The author took this picture of a bald eagle landing on its nest.

be leaving base camp that day. Early in the afternoon, Chuck and his guide, Dennis, walked into camp with a hide of over eight feet! We partied that night, and Fred spent most of the next day turning ears and claws.

Not until the third day did Fred and I set out into the valley on our backpacking-hunting trip. Six days later, we were driven back to base camp by continuous heavy rain, which made it impossible to spot game. During the six days in the field, we had spotted eleven bears, including two sows with five cubs between them. When we arrived in camp there was nobody there. On a table was a note from the two other guides, both named Dennis: "Two days after you guys left, Don took a nine-foot bear three hundred yards from camp. There are plenty of steaks in the cooler in case you are tired of freeze-dried. Happy hunting."

We enjoyed the steaks, and, because the weather did not improve for five days, I learned how to play cribbage by losing about a hundred games. We left camp twice. The first time was to visit the kill site of Chuck's bear. It had been eleven days since the bear had been taken, and there was nothing left but the bones. Probably the sow and its three one-year-old cubs, which we had seen earlier, had feasted on the bear carcass. The second time we left camp was to take a look at the carcass of Don's bear, easily located by proceeding to where a flock of bald eagles were perched in cottonwoods. Don's bear had not been touched.

The last day of the 1994 season was one of the most beautiful I have ever spent in Alaska, though I may have been unduly influenced by its being the first day of sunshine after almost seven days of rain. We went down to the beach at low tide. We saw ground squirrels, marmots, sea otters, seals, and

The extremely low tide allowed the hunters to walk the beach to the next valley.

a fox, and we ate shellfish right out of the sea. Every living creature seemed to be enjoying the sunshine and the beautiful view of Mount Augustine. But we saw no bear, which left me with an uneasy feeling for a day or two.

* * * * * *

Because spring bear season in Fred's hunting area on the Alaska Peninsula is open only during even years, I did not hunt with Fred in 1995. Instead, I went on a ten-day hunt to Zimbabwe and bagged five African species, including a nice Cape buffalo after a beautiful stalk. Africa was a great experience with more game and sunshine than Alaska could offer in a lifetime. But I prefer to hunt Alaska and to carry a backpack over rough terrain, all the while knowing I might lose half my hunting days waiting in a small tent for the weather to improve.

Though I did not hunt Alaska that year, I still saw Fred, who came to the Netherlands (my native country) for Christmas. We had four shoots between Christmas and New Year's Eve. Fred met many of my hunting friends and shot driven pheasants for the first time in his life. Roe deer season opened on 1 January, and Fred bagged two with my .222 Remington, which is not enough caliber for big game in Alaska or Africa but is perfectly adequate on roe deer. Fred stayed till the end of January, and it was great to have him.

* * * * * *

On 1 May 1996 I arrived in Anchorage for bear season, which would open on 10 May. We wanted to fly in early to make camp at Kirschener Lake. By 7 May, the ice had melted enough for our pilot, Jon, to land his floatplane on the lake. It was windy and it looked like rain, causing us to put up the wall tent hurriedly. But the rain never came. In fact, we were to enjoy nine sunny days in a row.

By the time Dennis, a guide, and Harold, his hunter, flew in on 9 May, I had already spent many hours glassing the valley, spotting at least seven different moose and an eight- or nine-foot bear. I saw the bear on 7 or 8 May in the evening on a slope a mile from camp. Harold and I spent the evening of 9 May glassing on the same lookout knoll, but the bear did not show up. The lookout knoll was about eight hundred yards from camp; nevertheless, Harold said he could hear Dennis and Fred, both of whom had stayed in camp, talking.

Because there is no better bear repellent than the human voice, Fred and I decided not to speak a single word on our upcoming backpacking-hunting trip. On 10 May Fred and I left base camp. During the trip, we used a blue notebook to scribble down our "conversations" with each other.

In Alaska your eyes do most of the walking, and we spent many hours glassing the country from one spot. On the first night, we pitched our tent on a spot overlooking a hillside, where we had seen three full-grown bears in 1994. There had been much more snow that year, and I recall that I had seen at midday a blond bear lying spread-eagled on a snow patch to cool off.

One evening, we stalked a big dark brownie, but the alders were too thick and we had to abandon the stalk. We saw no

It was wonderful up there with the eagles.

bear on that mountain for the rest of the hunt, having spooked them out of the valley.

On the morning of 10 May, the wind was wrong for us, which meant we couldn't move farther into the valley. So we decided to climb the mountain. Late in the afternoon, we reached the top and enjoyed a wonderful view. Fred pitched the tent in a grassy saddle that offered some shelter against the high winds. We melted snow to get water to prepare our freeze-dried meals and to make tea and coffee. That same evening I spotted a big brown bear. It was feeding on the new grass popping up between the thick alders three to four hundred yards below. The next morning at first light I relocated the bear. In an entry in the blue notebook, I scribbled a note to Fred. "It's well over 8 feet—sooner or later it will feed in the open where we can work it—the question is when—staying on top is best—weather permitting! Besides, it is wonderful up here with the eagles."

Later that day I spotted fresh tracks in the snow on the opposite mountain. Soon afterward I located the bears that had made them: a mating couple a mile and a half away. I slept a few hours during the day but, apart from that, spent my time watching the two bears. The blond sow was obviously not ready to mate and furiously fought the brown boar off every time it tried to mount. I saw a fox as well. It was curled up in the snow, sleeping, and after an hour or so moved casually away. That evening, I spotted another bear right below us, working the banks of a small stream. It had a light coat and a chocolate face and was about seven feet long. It was obviously aware of the presence of the big brown bear.

The next day, at 9 P.M., the big brown bear started to leave the area. It was in no hurry. It took two baths in a small pool, shaking the water off like a dog, and several times rubbed its back against some rocks. Once it hit the snow, it walked for an hour, disappearing over a snowy pass near midnight. I followed its every step with my binoculars and was very impressed. Even when they are not in a hurry, these bears travel with incredible speed and agility. But I did not enjoy only the bear. The sunset over the mountains was beautiful, too, and made faraway Illiamna Lake look like pure gold.

It was a fine boar measuring well over eight feet.

During the morning of the fourteenth, we concentrated on relocating the mating couple, but we were unsuccessful. At noon we decided to move camp to a spot from which we could work the boar and sow in case they showed up again. It had taken us about eight hours to climb the mountain, and it took two hours to come down. We spent another day in the valley, seeing fresh tracks and dung. On 16 May at noon, Fred wrote to me in the blue notebook: "Let's resupply before striking out again into new territory. If we break camp now, we can have a steak dinner tonight!"

We were welcomed in base camp that night by Dennis and Harold. Hunting from base camp, they had seen nine bears, including two sows with cubs—one with three one-year-old cubs, and a smaller chocolate-brown sow with two last-year cubs, one of which was almost white. They had also seen the boar and sow.

We stayed in base camp on 17 May, using the opportunity to have a shower and resupply. Throughout the afternoon and during the night we had some rain, and it was overcast when we set out on the morning of 18 May on our second backpacking-hunting trip. It was the first of four days with extremely low tides, allowing us to walk the beach to the next valley. In four hours we covered about seven miles easily, and we saw many ground squirrels, marmots, seals, a sea otter, and all kinds of birds. I took a nice picture of a bald eagle landing on its nest.

At noon we found fresh tracks on the beach of a big bear. I sat down to glass, and Fred scouted for a campsite from which we could watch the beach without being seen. All of a sudden I saw a brown bear. It walked around a little knoll on top of the hill and disappeared. I made eye contact with Fred, who was a hundred yards away, to indicate the spot where I had seen the bear. At that moment the bear showed up again, and Fred saw it immediately. He wanted to go for it at once. I was more inclined to wait. Fred's note to me in the blue notebook was, "If in doubt, attack!"

We attacked, heading for a second knoll about 125 yards to the left of the knoll where we had seen the bear. By the time we reached the steep bank, the sun popped out. For the first twenty yards, we had to pull ourselves up the bank by grabbing roots and branches. We reached a steep slope covered with dense alders. We could not see where we were going and made a lot of noise. The higher we climbed, the stronger the wind was. And then I saw the bear.

As I pushed myself backward while sitting on my rear, I was tense but felt no fear. Running into a bear at close quarters is something you should avoid—even more so if it is two full-grown bears. I decided to go for the brown boar. At once it leapt up on all fours and looked straight at me. With a horrid expression on its face, it stood up and was broadside, the upper half of its body well clear of the brush. I went for the shoulder. At the shot, the bear turned 180 degrees. I saw blood pour out of its off shoulder, where the 400-grain Swift A-frame softpoint had left the body. I thought it was mortally wounded.

It ran for a few yards and showed itself broadside again. My second shot hit in almost the same spot. The bear ran out of sight. I reloaded full, and Fred and I started to follow the blood trail. Thirty yards away we found the boar dead. It was a fine boar, measuring well over eight feet. Both bullets had passed through the body just behind the shoulders. The bullets had not broken the shoulder, as I had intended. My insufficient knowledge of bear anatomy could have had serious consequences if the bear had chosen to charge rather than run. Fred told me that the blond bear had turned and vanished the moment the brown jumped to its feet. We never saw the blond bear again.

It took me the better part of an hour to get a pack frame, as well as parkas and cameras, from the beach to the kill. Fred did not need much help with the skinning, and I went back to measure the distance between the bear and me when I had first fired. Though the broken ground prevented exact measurement, the distance between us could not have been more than sixty feet!

Fred managed to get the entire hide into his backpack, which I could not believe. His carrying it down to the beach proved to be an even more impressive achievement. We pitched the tent near a bear trail at the beach and had a good night's sleep. The next morning, I packed the bear skull and all I could carry in my backpack, but it was clear that we had to leave behind the tent and a lot of our gear. I eagerly volunteered to go and retrieve camp over the following days.

We made maximum use of the extremely low tide, taking a shortcut over part of the bay. Near base camp, I almost fell when fording a narrow but fast-flowing stream. As we walked into camp late that afternoon, we were surprised to be welcomed by Dennis and Harold. They had made an exhausting stalk the day before and had come close to taking a bear. Harold had sprained a knee during that stalk, and they had decided to take a day off.

The next morning I went alone to retrieve camp. I found the small tent in good order, visited the kill site (the carcass had not been touched), stayed there overnight, and managed to get everything into my pack the next morning. I was not looking forward to fording the narrow stream with my heavy load, but all went well. And I had bagged a nice bear in a way I had previously only dreamed about.

CHARGED BY A BROWN, A GRIZZLY, AND A POLAR BEAR

BY
JEFF DAVIS

Editor's note: With the passage of the Marine Mammal Act in 1974, polar bear hunting in Alaska became closed to nonindigenous peoples.

KEEP OUT. TRESPASSERS WILL BE MAULED ON SIGHT. If a bear could post signs like this around what it considers its private domain, it would be a lot of help. People often venture unknowingly into a bruin's territory, and the bear's territorial instinct can cause the animal to charge an unsuspecting intruder. But, of course, not all charges stem from territorial defense. Master guide John Swiss has been licensed in Alaska as a hunting guide since 1951, and he has observed countless examples of bear aggression, some that were territorial defenses and many that were not. Despite having endured more bear charges than he can remember, John has had to kill only three bears in defense of life: a brown, a grizzly, and a polar bear.

* * * * * *

The first bear John had to shoot was a brown bear. This was back in 1951, when he was still a young, green guide. Leon

John Swiss's Polly Creek Camp on the west shore of Cook Inlet.

Shellabarger, John's bear-hunting partner at the time, met two hunters at the airport in Anchorage. After making sure the hunters had purchased the required hunting licenses, Leon flew them to John's Polly Creek cabin on the west shore of Cook Inlet. The Polly Creek cabin has been John's brown bear hunting headquarters for half a century.

One of the hunters was older and more experienced than John. This man suggested that his newly minted guide borrow one of his unscoped rifles for hunting in the heavy brush. Brush is too dense for scope use, and the hunter wanted his guide to be able to react quickly if they got into a pinch. John complied, taking the hunter's Model 70 .300 H&H Magnum on the hunt.

The next day, the two hunters and John got up early and started up Polly Creek looking for bear sign. The first two miles were rough. Swampy, uneven terrain slowed their progress and sapped their energy. But after two miles, they were on drier and more open terrain, enabling them to proceed at a much faster pace. After a day of walking and glassing, they returned to the cabin for a night of well-deserved rest, and after a few days, despite the arduous daily trek to and from the hunting area, the older hunter managed to shoot a respectable brown bear.

The hunting party's wanderings up and down Polly Creek had spooked most of the bears out of that area. To locate the younger hunter's trophy, John decided to try the Crescent River drainage, a few miles south of Polly Creek, since he had seen ample bear sign during recent scouting trips to the Crescent Valley. Crescent River was still full of spawning salmon, a yearly event that drew brown bears from miles around. Leaving the older hunter at the Polly Creek cabin, John and the younger hunter took off in a floatplane and landed about six miles from the mouth of the Crescent River near an old trapping cabin that they intended to use as base camp.

They didn't sleep much that first night. At 11 P.M. an unhappy bear let out a terrific roar. It was obvious that the bear was close by and that it cared little about sharing its river with humans. The two interlopers were bombarded with periodic

John Swiss with a brown bear taken on the Alaska Peninsula.

roaring throughout the night. Up early the next day, John and the client hunted in the area near base camp, but they could not locate the noisy bear. The second night was a repeat of the first night—more bear bellowing and little sleep.

On the third day, John and the hunter followed bear trails along the banks of the Crescent River. Soon after venturing up a side stream, they encountered a large brown bear, and the hunter shot the bear. After taking photos, they began skinning. The hide squared over nine feet, a nice trophy even in those early days of John's guiding career. Strapping the hide and skull to packboards, they headed back downstream, happy with their accomplishment.

About a quarter-mile from base camp, John heard a twig snap in the brush ahead. Always alert along a salmon stream, John signaled his hunter to stop. As the late-afternoon light faded, they silently watched the brush where the noise had come from. On a small knoll a short distance away, a large brown bear materialized. The wind had not been in their favor, blowing on their backs and toward the bear, and, to make things worse, the hunter had been smoking. There was no doubt that the bear knew exactly where they were. John and the hunter grabbed spruce logs and waved them, while John shouted, "Get the hell out of here, you noggin head!"

The bear did the unexpected. It immediately charged. The bear came at them full tilt through the brush and uneven terrain, making it difficult for John and the hunter to follow its path. John yelled, "Shoot when you can see him!" John and the hunter both shot at the same instant and missed, the foot-long flame from the gun muzzles almost blinding them. Meanwhile, the bear was still coming, and when it dropped into a depression, John and the hunter jacked fresh rounds into their rifles' chambers. As soon as the bear came into sight, they both shot again, and the bear dropped dead seven paces from them. After examining the depth of the grooves on the bullet recovered from the bear's neck and comparing the grooves to the lands in both rifles, it was determined that John had fired the death-dealing shot.

The fact that the hunters did not have scopes on their guns probably saved them from a good mauling. It is difficult enough to see through a scope in thick brush in broad daylight. In evening twilight, it is nearly impossible.

That night, John and the hunter got a full night of deep sleep without any interruption from the bear that had tried so hard to drive them out of its territory.

* * * * * *

The second time John had to kill a bear on a guided hunt was around 1960. The incident occurred near the headwaters of the Noatak River in Arctic Alaska, north of Kotzebue. John and his hunter had spotted a nice grizzly in a stream. The hunter shot, wounding the bear, but the bear made it over the far bank and disappeared into the brush beyond the stream. John told his hunter to wait while he circled around the brush. John's intent was to flush the bear out of the brush and toward the hunter, figuring that as soon as the bear winded him, the animal would come out of the brush and head straight into the hunter's rifle sights.

Well, it almost worked. The bear came out, but two hundred yards below the hunter, and then it plunged into the creek. John was worried about a confrontation between the hunter and the obviously angry bear, should the bear get its feet on dry land. He hurried to the bank so that he could back the hunter up if the hunter got in trouble. But the bear changed its mind and at midstream began paddling back toward John's side of the creek. By that time, John was waiting on the four-foot bank for the bear.

"Go back across the river, bear. I don't want to shoot you," John warned the snarling animal. But the bear kept coming, and now John had it in his sights.

As soon as the angry bruin got its feet on the bank, John shot it, knocking it backward into the water. The dead bear floated down to a sandbar, where the hunters managed to drag it out of the water and muscle it into position for photographs.

* * * * * *

During the 1950s and early 1960s, John ran his polar bear operation out of Kotzebue. He would fly his Super Cub from Cook Inlet to Kotzebue, a trip that normally took six and a half hours. His hunters would fly from Anchorage to Kotzebue on Alaska Airlines, a three-hour trip.

On that fateful day in April 1963, the weather forecast in Kotzebue called for clear skies. His hunter had arrived the previous day. John had made sure the hunter had a license, and John outfitted him with a set of blue arctic flight pants to wear over his long johns. Then the hunter was issued a thick parka with a fur ruff, GI mukluks (knee-high boots), and thick elbow-length mittens. A certain amount of time was devoted to the hunter's walking around a nearby Inuit village so that he could become accustomed to wearing the unfamiliar garb. The hunter's rifle bolt was dipped in gasoline to remove any trace of oil, which would freeze and render the rifle useless in subzero temperatures. Once reassembled, the rifle was zeroed in by firing at a cardboard box placed on a piece of offshore sea ice. After the rifle had been tested, and after a thousand questions had been asked and answered, the hunter climbed into bed for an anxious night.

Long before first light the next day, John was up and rustling breakfast and working on keeping the Super Cub's engine warm so that it would start at daybreak. When using a bush plane in Arctic Alaska, the plane's engine oil had to be drained into a pan each night. The oil was then kept warm overnight by being stored in a heated building. Next, an electric heater-cover was draped over the engine. The heater-cover was equipped with timers so that it turned on at a specific time. On nights when the temperature plunged below minus 35, the heaters were left on all night. Once the plane's engine had been warmed sufficiently, the heater-cover was removed and the warm oil added. John did all this, and at daybreak the engine blasted to life. The hunt was on.

Flying west, John kept a close eye on the ice pack a few hundred feet below. He soon located an area where numerous bear tracks had stamped out a large flat area. The snow in that area was speckled with bright-red blood. What could this be? John guessed that a couple of boars had been fighting over a sow in heat. Tilting the plane's wings in the direction of a set of tracks that led away from the bloody site, he followed the tracks

The world-record polar bear taken by Shelby Longoria (left) in 1963. Since the largest polar bears in the world live in Arctic Alaska, this record will probably stand as long as polar bear hunting in the state remains open only to indigenous people.

about four miles, until he sighted the bear. After determining that the bear was large enough to satisfy his hunter's wants, John landed on a wide, flat span of ice behind a pressure ridge two hundred yards from the bear.

After John landed, the two men quickly gathered their equipment, which included a 16mm movie camera and tripod, and crept up the pressure ridge that shielded them from the bear's view. When they reached the top, they discovered the bear standing on another pressure ridge one hundred yards away. The bear must have heard the plane, for it knew they were there, and didn't like it. As soon as it saw their silhouettes atop the pressure ridge, it started toward them.

John was busy setting up the tripod when he noticed the bear descending the far pressure ridge. John told his hunter to hold under the bear's chin and shoot. The bullet struck the bear's left front leg, but it did not slow the animal's progress. A second shot, taken when the bear reached the bottom of the pressure ridge, missed. While John filmed the hunt, he also coached the hunter, and by now, the bear had reached the base of the pressure ridge they were on. "Shoot that damn bear," John yelled.

"I can't. My gun is jammed," screamed the hunter.

"Then get the hell out of the way. That bear's a-comin'!" John pushed the tripod aside and bent over to grab his rifle. Meanwhile, the hunter sprinted toward the plane. John remembers seeing yellow belly hair fly above him when he bent over to grab his rifle. The bear's chase instinct caused it to pass up John and go after the running hunter. "Kill the son of a bitch!" yelled the hunter over his shoulder.

John grabbed his pre-'64 Model 70 .300 Weatherby Magnum and launched himself down the pressure ridge in pursuit of the bear. He couldn't shoot from the ridge because the bear was between the hunter and him. As John started down the ridge, the wounded bear reached the hunter, and grabbed his upper right thigh in its mouth, pulling the thoroughly frightened man down to the ice. As John raced across the ice toward the angry bear, he thought, *Here I go again. I'm going to have to kill this bear, and all because it was too stubborn to leave when it had the chance.*

John ran up to the 1,400-pound white mountain of fur and placed the rifle's muzzle to the bear's neck and pulled the trigger. The bear relaxed instantly. John racked another round into the chamber and fired again. The hunter scampered forward, and then ran behind the plane as John reloaded his Winchester.

"I think the bear is dead," John said, gazing at the claw marks the hunter had made in the ice in his desperate attempt to pull himself out of the bear's maw.

"Drop your pants," he ordered the hunter, adding, as he caught his breath, "I want to see how badly you're hurt."

The hunter wore long cotton underwear, Eddie Bauer thermal underwear, wool pants, and heavy military flight pants. The cotton in the flight pants was puffing out where the bear had chewed, but the hunter's buttocks and thigh were only slightly bruised. The bear's teeth had been unable to penetrate to the skin. With so many layers of clothing protecting him from the weakened bear, the lucky hunter walked away from a polar bear mauling literally without a scratch.

Soon John's partner, Nelson Walker, landed and helped the shaky guide and hunter skin the bear. Eight hours later, John's pulse was still running 105 beats per minute, as the adrenaline continued to course through his system. They discovered that the movie camera had been running up until the time John had inadvertently pushed the tripod over as the bear ran by him.

After so many years and literally hundreds of encounters with wild bears, John Swiss has had to shoot only three, a testimony to his caution as a hunter and his regard for the bears of Alaska.